Arturo Islas

The Uncollected Works

Arturo Islas
The Uncollected Works

Arturo Islas

Edited, with a Critical Introduction, by Frederick Luis Aldama

Arte Público Press
Houston, Texas

This volume is made possible through grants from the City of Houston through The Cultural Arts Council of Houston, Harris County.

Recovering the past, creating the future

Arte Público Press
University of Houston
452 Cullen Performance Hall
Houston, Texas 77204-2004

Cover design by James F. Brisson
Photo by Cynthia Farah Haines and Courtesy of the
Department of Special Collections, Stanford University Libraries

Islas, Arturo, 1938–.
    [Selections. 2003]
    Arturo Islas: The Uncollected Works / edited, with a critical
introduction, by Frederick Luis Aldama.
    p.   cm.
    ISBN 1-55885-368-5 (alk. paper)
    1. Mexican Americans—Literary collections.   I. Aldama,
Frederick Luis, 1969–   II. Title.
PS3559.S44A6 2003
818'.5409—dc21   2003044432
                                                          CIP

♾ The paper used in this publication meets the requirements of the
American National Standard for Information Sciences—Permanence
of Paper for Printed Library Materials, ANSI Z39.48-1984.

3 4 5 6 7 8 9 0 1 2   10 9 8 7 6 5 4 3 2 1

For Jovita and Arturo Islas Sr.

Table of Contents

Poetry

Essays & Lectures on Chicano Literature

Acknowledgments

As I began to sift through the Arturo Islas Papers at Stanford's Special Collections library to write *Dancing with Ghosts: A Critical Biography of Arturo Islas* (University of California Press), I discovereds, within the fifty-two boxes, a trove of unpublished scholarly monographs, poems, and short stories. With the Islas family and Diane Middlebrook's blessing (Islas's dear friend, colleague, and literary executor), I began to select the material that would form this book. I wish to thank Maggie, Roberto, and Steven at Stanford's Special Collections for helping with the excavating and copying. I wish also to thank Arte Público's Nicolás Kanellos for recognizing the importance of this project. Lastly, I would like to thank all those Chicano/a scholars, writers, and teachers past and present who, like Arturo Islas, serve as role models and inspiration to us all.

Introduction

Since the hard-won publication of his novel *The Rain God* in 1984, Arturo Islas has secured a significant place in the field of Chicano/a letters. Today, *The Rain God* peppers the American literary landscape in colleges across the nation—even appearing on high-school English syllabi. Of course, there is much more to Islas than *The Rain God*. There are his other novels: the boldly poetic, darkly complex sequel, *Migrant Souls,* and his rapid-fire, caló-narrated, city-set *La Mollie and the King of Tears.* Indeed, the wrapping of time/space and language around characters as they move through and experience the world in these novels draws from a lifelong commitment to exploring other artistic forms of expression: short narrative fiction and poetry. As far back as his first creative writing class with Hortense Callisher in 1957 at Stanford, Islas began to sculpt a multiplicity of Chicano/a voices, experiences, and visions. In this collection, I recover Islas's short fictions, poetry, and essays on Chicano letters that have remained, with few exceptions, unpublished. With this collection of Islas's many different writing styles, storytelling modes, and poetic sensibilities—some written in journals and handwritten on paper and others more formally typed—I seek to stretch and broaden our vision of Arturo Islas as writer and thinker.

Long before Islas finally gained the ear of New York's William Morrow and Avon that picked up the small-press publication of *The Rain God* and published its sequel, *Migrant Souls,* he had begun crafting complex imaginary worlds that defied simple binaries such as Chicano versus Anglo, Mexican versus North American or that reflected his own experiences growing up along the U.S./Mexico border. Early short fictions such as "Poor Little Lamb," "Boy with the Eyes of a Fawn," "The Submarine," and "Clara Mendoza," to name a few, are creative explorations of life on the border and a panoply of characters' experiences that complicate what it means to be Chicano/a: both urban and rural, Mexican and American, straight and queer. And in a story such as "An Existential Documentation," young Islas deftly shows how the border is not simply a geopolitical construct, but something that Chicanos must face wherever they travel and live in the United States. Islas continued to explore and refine his vision of characters inhabiting different borderlands—cultural, racial, familial, and political—with the fictions he wrote in the early 1960s and in the 1970s. In "Tía Chucha," for example, Islas sidesteps a romanticizing of Chicano culture and family by creating characters that have internalized a Euro-Spanish, *pureza* colonialist ideology to a self-destructive end. And in "The Dead," Islas uses his autobiographically informed character/narrator to explore the complicated cultural and social boundaries that prevent men from being able to love and desire one another without feeling dis-eased. This was also the period when Islas developed more fully a variety of poetic voices that crisscross boundaries of form and content: some metaphoric and traditional in form and others wildly experimental visual-verbal sketches.

All of the works collected here creatively reflect and revision Islas's crossing many borders and learning to inhabit many borderlands: from straight to gay and from El Paso to San Francisco, for example. The works also reflect a central motif in Arturo Islas's work: recovery. Many of his fiction, poetry, and essays recover bodies and voices much as the wind-whipped sands sweep across and reveal new borderland topographies. Such worlds identify those Chicano/a subjects that inhabit a constant state of "recovery" and desire for health and life as they feel dis-ease in a xenophobic, heterosexist Euramerican mainstream and macho Chicano world. The uncovering of his works make visible other bodies and voices that make up his literary imagination in toto and also recontour our sense of a formation of contemporary Chicano/a letters and add strength and

health to the struggle against the dis-ease felt by Chicanas/os (queer
and straight) in a homophobic and racist world.

Of course, "recovery" is an especially loaded term biographical-
ly. In September of 1946, when Islas was eight years old and about
to begin an eagerly anticipated school year at Houston Elementary
in El Paso, he contracted the polio virus. As a result, he not only had
to spend a long stint in a local sanitarium recovering, but he had to
spend a lifetime feeling physically inadequate: his left leg was left
shorter and, even after a surgery on his right leg in high school to
help even the lengths, he had a discernible limp for the rest of his
life. Though he learned to dance up a storm—often dazzling his
peers at high school hops—he never fully recovered psychologically. And, when Islas was thirty-one years old, he had to return to Stanford to finish his dissertation, months of suffering from a mis-treat-
ed ulcerated intestine that led to a three-part surgery—an ileostomy
and colostomy—that left him in a hospital recovery ward with a
plastic appendage attached to his stomach. With his so-called "shit-
bag" at his side that would fill up with feces of its own accord and a
sutured anus, his sense of himself as a monster—already ostracized
as a result of his sexual preference and racial identity—was magni-
fied ten-fold.

Islas's attempts at recovery were physical and psychological.
His writing often proved to be the venue for him to work out and
recover—at least momentarily—from such traumatic events. During
his breakup with his great love, Jay Spears, in the mid- 1970s, his
creative prose and poetry became necessary outlets. (One of the central conflicts in this relationship was that Jay wanted to be the pene-
trator in bed, but couldn't because of Islas's post-op. body.) We see
this vividly in the chapters reproduced from Islas's manuscript,
American Dreams and Fantasies. From "Kokkomaa" to "La familia
feliz," from "María" to "Compadres y Comadres," the vignettes all
gravitate around an autobiographically informed narrator/protago-
nist's failed love with the character Sam Godwin. And though Islas
curtailed his poetry and short fiction writing after he discovered he
was HIV positive on January 14, 1988, he threw himself into his
novel writing—*Migrant Souls* and the revising of *La Mollie and the*

King of Tears—an act of recovering from the trauma of knowing that his body was unraveling at the molecular level. (For more details on Islas's life and his various stages of recovery, see my book *Dancing with Ghosts: A Critical Biography*.)

Islas's life was not only about various acts of physical and psychological recovery. He spent a lifetime inhabiting and uncovering multilayered temporalities and geographical spaces. Islas was born on May 25, 1938 during the period when then president of Mexico, Lázaro Cárdenas, established a relationship with the United States economic relations. As a result, as Islas grew up, El Paso became increasingly a binational metropolitan economy. However, as young Islas experienced living in *el segundo barrio*, this binationalism did not work in his favor—nor for other Mexicans and Mexican-Americans in the larger community. As goods were manufactured by cheaper labor in Ciudad Juárez and moved across the border for consumption, El Paso became increasingly a racial apartheid: Recent Mexican émigrés and older families were confined to the area where Islas grew up in the southern part of the city nearest the border and the wealthy Anglo elites lived in the northern suburbs. And, of course, brown bodies that once moved with relative ease and freedom back and forth across the Stanton Street and/or Santa Fe bridges between Mexico and the United States became more and more regulated. The *migra* was fast becoming the panoptic surveillance force we see today, *maquiladoras* mushroomed overnight, and natural resources like the Rio Grande River were dammed up—with Mexican laboring arms—and controlled for energy resale at high prices to the Islas's and others eking out a living in El Paso.

Islas grew up in a border town bursting at the seams of contradiction. More and more goods were being brought across the border in this deregulated trade zone while brown bodies were more and more regulated: the ebb and flow of *braceros* was controlled by the needs of Anglo corporate development on the U.S. side while all commodities consumed by those like Islas and his family at a high price continued to pass over the border freely.

The dust-swept El Paso border town was far from a Mexican-American utopia. The prejudice against Mexicans was like the constant heat waves that rippled in the El Paso air. So while Islas's strong grand-matriarchal figure, Crecenciana Sandoval, and her "very intelligent" sisters used education to transgress racially inscribed occupational divisions (Mexicano as only laborer vs. Anglo as only professional), they reproduced their own hierarchies of difference. We see this creatively reflected in the chapters that make up Islas's manuscript *American Dreams and Fantasies*. In "María," "Nina," "Reason's Mirror or The Education of Miguel Angel," "Tía Chucha," and "La familia feliz," the reader encounters a number of fictionalized family members that include "Mamá Chona" based on his grandmother Crecenciana. Mamá Chona, like her sisters, have internalized an assortment of racial prejudices based on a pure (Spanish)/impure (*indio*) duality. To fortify against an everyday dominated by Anglo racism, those like Crecenciana snapped into the age-old, pure/impure racist dichotomy circulated by the Mexican elite. Crecenciana derived her sense of self-worth by staying out of the sun to keep her skin *güera*, a light-olive complexion allowing her to lay claim to a pure Spanish blood line (in fact, she was a shade of chocolate brown). She told young Islas that the Spanish she was making sure he spoke without a hint of an accent was pure Castillian and not the impure Mexican dialect. Islas was taught that only the Spanish side of his heritage was to be preserved. Later Islas would refine this in *The Rain God* wherein his narrator reflects how "the indian in them was pagan, servile, instinctive rather than intellectual, and was to be suppressed, its existence denied" (142). Ironically, to fight Anglo prejudice against Chicanos, Crecenciana internalized myths of whiteness and purity identified as Euro-Spanish, and opposing them to the darkness and dirtiness she ascribed to the *indio*, she performed an exclusion similar to the one she herself had been the victim of all her life. This internalized racism comes to a dramatic crescendo in his short story "Tía Chucha" when the dark, Amerindian-featured Tía Chucha's desperate attempt to live by a Mexican *casta* system without the monetary means leads to her tragic demise. She dies poor and is discovered by Miguel Chico in a house filled with an overwhelming stench, with cats and *cucarachas* everywhere, and her body lying in filthy sheets.

Of course, this internalizing of an Euro-Spanish/*indio* duality caused rifts between the darker and the lighter family members. Crecenciana, for example, loved Islas deeply. He was *güero*, male, and her first grandchild to be fluent in her pure Castillian tongue. (Had she lived long enough to discover that Islas was gay, he would have been cast aside as a *desgraciado* and an *indio*—no matter his skin tone or "accentless" Spanish.) And when Crecenciana's sister Jesusita gave birth "out of wedlock" to her son Alberto, she became a family outcast—an impurity (interview with Jovita Islas). In protest, Jesusita crossed back over the Rio Grande with her man that was as far as her sister was concerned, akin to becoming a tramp. The other sister, Virginia, discarded this pure/impure myth, living her life unwed with her partner in a house filled with hundreds of cats. Finally, Crecenciana had internalized a worldview that she could not enact on an everyday level. As Islas described in his fictionalized epistle "Dear Arturo," that he wrote for Wallace Stegner's creative writing class in 1962, "the only moments my grandmother became real to me were those times when she, the well-educated Mexican aristocratic lady, would weep because she had to wash the dishes because it was the maid's day off. She taught me to be polite and courteous, which I learned quickly because those qualities endeared me to everyone, except my father." She could not afford to hire an *india*, for example, to wash dishes and clean house. Often, because she refused to dirty her hands, she would let the filth pile up around her. Working hard to don the Spanish *señora* look, she'd wear black clothes and gloves that stifled in the hot desert sun. Crecenciana died an unhappy woman filled with unlivable contradictions.

Islas spent a great deal of his early childhood with Crecenciana, inheriting both an appreciation for education and a sense of value placed on white purity (the family's mythologized European descent). As demonstrated in his narrative fiction and poetry, Islas also inherited an oppressive patrilineal sense of the pure/impure that resulted from his Catholic upbringing; Crecenciana—and his mother—translated the pure/impure into the Catholic saint/sinner duality that hummed at a heightened frequency in Islas's childhood as he participated more and more in the church. However, just as Islas rejected the Church and its heavy baggage—especially after coming into his own as a gay Chicano in the late 1960s and early 1970s—he also rejected his family's internalizing of a Spanish *pureza*, racist ideology. In his fictionalized autobiographical essay "An Existential Documentation," he writes: "This summer I will see if poverty breeds sanctity. I will spend as much time in the Mexican [Juárez] border town as possible. My relatives will not like that. They cannot see why I bother with 'those people'." Islas's interest in reaching out across borders to "those people" to understand better his indigenous Amerindian roots also stems from the fact that he spent most of his childhood with nursemaids like María, fictionalized in the chapters "María" and "The Dead" in his manuscript *American Dreams and Fantasies*. Here, he describes the character María—"part of the family from the time I was born"—as having beautiful, dark-brown skin and long black hair; she was a huge influence in terms of his appreciation of a world view in contrast to his grandmother's racist *pureza*, and the person who allowed him to more freely explore his male gender. He fictionalizes the moment when María would help him dress as a girl and dance as well as those afternoons when they would make dresses for paper-doll cutouts. So, while both parents worked so that Islas could grow up with all the opportunities of "making it," this ironically exposed him to a *mestizaje* and gender-bending consciousness contrary to the family's values. In his poem "Aztec Angel," he conflates his identification as a queer outlawed subject with his *mestizo* sense of self, writing: "Drunk / Lonely / bespectacled / the sky / opens my veins / like rain / clouds go berserk / around me / my Mexican ancestors / chew my fingernails / I am an Aztec angel / offspring / of a tubercular woman / who was beautiful."

The Islas family's economic shift into the lower-middle class allowed them to purchase help from *el otro lado*. Ironically, as just mentioned, this engendered a complex racial and gender consciousness in a young Islas that he explored directly in his various fictions. However, this did not redirect completely Islas's gaze from white bodies. In his narratives and poetry we see him struggling with an internalizing of a white-targeted desire. In Islas's lifetime, he never fell in love with Chicano men, always falling for Anglo athletic

types. When Islas first formed crushes on men as a young man, they
were his exact opposite; somehow, he thought they would fulfill all
that he lacked. In his short story "The Submarine," his fictionalized
character "Art" is in love with an unattainable, distant, Anglo J.D.
And in his fictionalized epistle "Dear Arturo," he explores this prob-
lematic desiring of the "self-protective" and "elusive monster" type
in the Anglo character Gary. And in "An Existential Documentation," Islas identifies the object of his desire as the white, adventur-
ing-athlete male who "wanders about alone in his sportscar, swims
in the sea, and climbs the cliffs along the shore" and whose "emptiness in him [. . .] begs to be filled." These characters among many
others—like the fictionalized Jay Spears as the character Sam Godwin who appears in his manuscript *American Dreams and Fantasies*—are the type of men that represented everything that Islas
was not: Islas grew up a Chicano who inhabited racial and social
margins. He grew up physically disabled. He grew up identifying
with an overcaring, sentimental, emotionally expressive mother.

Narrative Fictions

While Islas read and wrote feverishly as a teenager, it was not
until his second year as an undergraduate at Stanford that he dropped
a career in science and turned formally to creative fiction. He saw in
writing a way to untangle and understand better the racial, sexual,
cultural, and political borderland of his childhood and adolescence.
As an English major he enrolled in many expository and creative
writing classes. He also became an editor of the undergraduate literary journal, *Sequoia*. While many of his peers could not understand
his fascination with the racial and economic contradictions that he
would often write about, many were dazzled by his skill as a writer.
Islas worked steadily and unconditionally on his prose, thus gaining
him admission in Hortense Callisher's graduate creative writing
seminar when he was a junior. The genre traditionally used by
authors to texture those at society's margins, the short story form,
particularly appealed to Islas as a venue to explore the complex and
contradictory racial, sexual, and gender relations that make up a
rural and urban U.S./Mexico borderland.

During this period, Islas experimented with voice and point of view to write short stories set mostly along the U.S./Mexico border. For example, in the short story titled "Poor Little Lamb," Islas invented a third-person narrator to tell the story of Miguel Chávez—a character less concerned with upward mobility than with a need to ground his own body sexually and racially within a *mestizo* sensibility. (Miguel was a name that Islas adored and a name that would reappear throughout his writing career.) Here Islas experimented with how the personal—Miguel's need to connect with his estranged father, for example—reaches into larger social contexts: how racism and elitism are internalized by those who are themselves the victims of racism. To rid himself of an oppressive past, Islas allows Miguel the possibility of finding meaning in a present that is free of the father and that is still anchored in his ancestral heritage. In "Clara Mendoza," Islas paints in detail the lives of three border-inhabiting sisters: Clara, Luisa, and Arabella Mendoza. Here Islas set these Mexicana characters at the story's center to demonstrate how they are forced to use their gender-inscribed roles as women within a patriarchy to either fall victim to or escape a violent macho world. In this story, Islas chose to disrupt readerly expectations by infusing into this U.S./Mexico borderland a strong sense of the metropolis and modernity. His character Arabella, depicted as very cosmopolitan, smokes American brand cigarettes, carries a "glossy black purse," and wears "white-framed sunglasses" and "orange-colored lipstick." Interestingly, Islas is also critical of those characters, like Arabella, who do not use their cosmopolitan identity to self-emancipate, but rather to oppress their fellow sisters. The modern exists in Islas's borderland, but less as a form of white feminist liberalism and more as a function of how characters internalize American imperialist oppression. In the story "A Boy with the Eyes of a Fawn," Islas chose to explore the figurative possibilities of a narrative that follows the life of a Juárez prostitute character, Theresa. Here Islas uses leitmotif and symbol (veils, vision, and eyes) to critique how Mexican and American patriarchy similarly use religion to oppress a racialized and gendered underclass. And in "The Submarine," Islas uses the third-person point of view to fictionalize himself as the character "Art", who crosses to the Mexican side of the El Paso/Ciudad Juárez border to meet up with the character's love-interest, J.D. Here, Islas boldly tells the story of the unrequited love between two young men—the Chicano Art and the Anglo J.D.—that can only surface when both are on the Mexican side of the border, free of familial surveillance and where illicit behavior is allowed. Islas turns away from a preoccupation with race and class to introduce the tragic tale of these characters' frustration with and ultimate suffocating of their love and desire for one another. After a night of drunken debauchery, the two wake up in J.D.'s yard wrapped up together, and the narrative shifts into Art's point of view: "We cried. We sat down on his mother's geraniums and cried. We stayed there for about two hours until everything started to clear up and the sky got all pink and the goddamn birds started making a racket. I told J.D. to go to bed before his mother woke up and saw us. Now, I wish she had seen us. [. . .] But J.D. got up and ruined everything by shaking my hand". Finally, in his story "Orejas de papalote" ("Dumbo Ears"), Islas transforms autobiography—his child protagonist's ears stick out (like Islas's) and he grows up in a patriarchal, dysfunctional family—into an exploration of childhood. Islas delves deeply into his protagonist Faustino García's pain as he is shunned by other children on the playground. After the children mercilessly tease Faustino, Islas describes him as he "gasped for air and tried to swallow," with "anger and shame [. . .] radiating from inside his chest." Islas then turns the everyday into a powerful probing of this character's anger toward an absent father and a hatred that is directed toward himself. The seemingly banal reaches beyond itself once we learn that Faustino's pain grows not from being teased for having big ears, but from the fact that he shares this physical trait with his father, who abandoned him for "la Gringa". At home, Faustino's pain crescendos when he reaches for his father's razor blade and cuts himself. The story is a venue for Islas to critique a patriarchal social structure wherein fathers (whether present or absent and Mexican or Anglo) pass on a self-hatred from one generation to the next—a self-hatred that either translates into direct acts of physical self-mutilation or in the victimizing of loved ones.

After his undergraduate days at Stanford, Islas continued to hone his craft at fiction writing in the same university as an English Ph.D. student in the 1960s, then as a professor in the 1970s and 1980s. Narrative fiction would prove to be that arena whereby Islas could explore personal conflicts and relive biographical experiences within the expansive realm of the imagination; his earlier interest in writing short stories that touched on issues of race, class, gender, and sexuality continued to grow; so too did his skill as a storyteller continue to sharpen. In the various chapters that make up the book *American Dreams and Fantasies*, Islas explores issues of racism within and outside the Chicano community as well as queer love and sexuality. In "Tía Chucha" (the seed of which later bloomed Islas's novel, *The Rain God*), Islas untangles the love and hate that binds together the eponymous character with her grandson and narrator, Miguel Chico. He also adds to the plot Miguel's meditation on his love affair with an unnamed narratee and the character Sam. This intertwining of family saga with gay love story takes place in each of the chapters—"Nina," "La familia feliz," "Reason's Mirror," "The Dead," and "Kokkomaa"—that make up *American Dreams and Fantasies*. Here, Islas deftly weaves together stories of generational antagonism, infidelities, and inherited familial behavioral dysfunction with an exploration of the illusions and delusions of queer love; his narrator/protagonist even delves into meditations on S&M. In "Reason's Mirror," Islas's Miguel Chico learns to control a self-mutilatory impulse that originated from feeling like a sexual outlaw—a queer Chicano shunned by family and society. To take charge of and control his acts of self-destruction, Miguel Chico wrestles with a monster whose carnivorous appetite leaves its breath smelling "of fresh blood and feces." Moreover, as the narrative shifts back and forth between the past of Miguel's childhood in the southwest desert and the present in a "city of light and fog," the reader begins to see how dysfunctional familial patterns—a father who role-plays the silent macho and a mother who role-plays the martyr—superimpose themselves onto Miguel's identity. Just as Islas did in the 1970s, Miguel turns to experimental sexual encounters in an S&M scene as therapy to deal with destructive behavioral patterns. Miguel reflects on one occasion: "What interests me is the collaboration of the tor-turer, his or her sense of what is expected in those turbulent sessions, the matching of wits and flesh in a fantasy, as if one were able to choose to be a dream figure in another's dream and still remain a dream to oneself. The sex of either does not matter, for each assumes ancient, sexless guilts and hoists them onto the scaffolds of Mother and Father." In "María," Islas turns from the S&M scene as therapy for deep racial and sexual trauma to chart the experiences of Miguel as a child whose first role model is a Seventh Day Adventist Mexi-can nursemaid, María. From an early age, Miguel indulges in a rosy world of dresses and dolls—a pre-hetero-eroticized world of imagi-native abandon. His father's machismo together with María's new-found faith, however, send him escaping to his mother's closet to hug her "clothes in terror." Over time, as Miguel internalizes a world reg-ulated by religious morals and heteronormative values—good versus bad and male versus female—polymorphous play turns to fear and self-destruction. However, as past and present become one and the queer subplot unfolds, Miguel comes to reject the S&M play of his Anglo love-interest in search of something that can stand outside of the religious macho baggage of his childhood. Islas situates his read-ers in a dramatic present in "Nina" to meditate on the impossibility of interracial queer love as caught up within Catholic and Protestant religious doctrine. Here, Islas's Miguel explores S&M as a model for understanding not just his memories of childhood trauma, but as a way to come to terms with his lover Sam's (whose father had aban-doned him) sadistic impulses and constant rejection. For Miguel, then, family and romantic relationships are made of elaborate imbal-ances of power. To live a more harmonious life means to actively acknowledge and break free from patterns of self-destruction inher-ited from the older generation. In "La familia feliz" and "Kokko-maa," Islas continues to explore issues of desire, the body, and spir-ituality that feed into relationships. To indulge in the pleasures of the body means to be identified as a sinner, the character Miguel strug-gles to overcome. Here, Islas more forcefully foregrounds how Euro-Spanish myths of purity tangle with Catholic doctrine to deny the body as well as delimit imaginative, relational possibilities.

Islas revised *American Dreams and Fantasies* into the manuscript he titled *Día de los muertos / day of the dead* and sent it out to East Coast publishers for review for publication in the mid-1970s. While Islas revised the storytelling form—showing more than telling—he did not alter the explicit queer Chicano content. This more than ruffled East Coast editors' feathers. For example, editor John E. Woods at Harcourt Brace wrote to Islas's agent: "There's something strangely bloodless and abstracted about it. I assume in a certain sense Mr. Islas intended this as a device to hold in check some of the rage, craziness, and sexuality of his material." After Islas sent a draft of the manuscript to Farrar Strauss, he received Roger Strauss's reply: "I don't think it is right for us on the basis of this 'taste'." And Macmillan's editor, Henry William Griffin, responded: "Interesting, very interesting indeed, but I'm afraid our sales force would be very hard put to sell a thousand copies." After receiving dozens of rejection letters, Islas revised and revised the manuscript until the queer content only whispered—albeit—powerfully in the background of a story that focused on the family.

Steady rewriting and revision finally transformed *Día de los muertos / day of the dead* into the beautifully lyrical and subtle novel that Islas titled *The Rain God;* he finally saw it published in October, 1984. Soon after *The Rain God* appeared on bookstore shelves, it began to receive local critical and popular acclaim. The first print run of 500 hardbacks sold well enough for its publisher, Alexandrian Press, to print a larger run: 1,500 paperbacks. The paperbacks sold out almost immediately. Word of mouth—friends and colleagues—along with Islas's ruthless self-promotion helped ensure continued sales. By June 1985, *The Rain God* had sold over 3,000 copies. Its success helped the novel travel overseas, and a Dutch press translated and published the novel as *De regen god* early in 1987. Its continued popularity helped Islas negotiate its copyright release from Alexandrian Press—a press too small to handle what became a huge demand. With the help of agent Sandra Dijkstra, Islas hooked a contract with Avon to publish *The Rain God* as a paperback in 1990—swiftly turning *The Rain God* into one of the best-selling and widely acclaimed novels in Chicano/a letters.

Poetic Forms

Islas's short stories and novels fictionalize biographical fact and complicate characterizations of old and young Chicanos and Chicanas inhabiting cultural, linguistic, national, and ideological borderland spaces. Islas used a variety of narrative techniques to achieve this effect, including the unraveling of narrative voice—especially in *The Rain God* and *Migrant Souls*—that often used a densely compact style of poetry to open readers' eyes to an expansively imagined story world. Such a mythopoetic contains Islas's mentor's sensibility: critic and poet, Yvor Winters. In 1960, Islas took a course titled "Chief American Poets" with Yvor Winters. This was the beginning of what would become an insatiable appetite to learn how to craft poetic verse. So, alongside his more theoretical studies as a Ph.D. in English and honing his craft as a short story writer, Islas began to train as a poet under Winters's aegis, formally studying and mastering the use of enjambment, apostrophe, synesthesia, and the lyrical iamb, for example.

Under Winters's strong and steady guidance, Islas came into a poetic sensibility wherein he learned to use a suggestive and richly imagined poetic language to transform personal experience into something beyond itself. He learned, according to the Wintersean "poetics of rationality," to balance vivid and emotional poetic language with a more cerebral-driven symbolism. He learned to balance a crafted use of syntax and words with the philosophical to effect a balanced emotional response in the reader. That is, he learned not to disorient the reader with too much symbolism (Winters disliked the French Symbolists as well as Yeats and Frost and other poets that, in his opinion, relied too much on destabilizing techniques) or sublime emotion, but to write in a poetic voice informed by ordinary language, speaking equally to the intellect and to the body of the reader. He also learned to use poetic language not as a mask to hide behind, but as a way to connect with and understand better his world. Under Winters, Islas learned to explore the dense textures of words themselves as they poured from the mouth, vibrated in air, and were registered by the ear and brain. Islas applied Winters's theory of "unity of form and content," using meter and syntax as a unified grammar that reflects a worldview. Islas apprenticed dutifully, writing poetry exercises, keeping notebooks brimming with detailed analyses of other poet's use of meter, rhythm, and tone; he also wrote detailed analyses of a given poem's connotations and how it spoke to the broader context of human consciousness. Islas learned to become a poet with vision and imagination, but not outlandishly so; he learned to write poetry that was intense but not overwrought.

Yvor Winters's "poetics of rationality" helped form Islas's poetic and critical sensibility. However, this was prefaced by Islas's earlier readings of Spanish philosopher-poet George Santayana. As an undergraduate in the late 1950s, Islas often sought solace in Santayana's poems—especially when feeling blue after discovering that men he had formed crushes on failed to reciprocate his love. And Santayana's turn away from the divine to the body as a site of sensory expression to understand our place in the world was particularly attractive to Islas, who had turned from the Church and who wanted to understand his same-sex desiring body with more clarity. Islas was also drawn to poets and novelists that were keenly aware of the human body, such as Walt Whitman, Federico García Lorca, Ralph Waldo Emerson, Emily Dickinson (even writing a poem in her honor, "In the Manner of E. Dickinson"), and Elizabeth Bishop; and to novelists like Marcel Proust, Colette, D.H. Lawrence, Mishima, and E.M. Forster. As Islas moved from his undergraduate to graduate studies, and from his interest in Santayana to Winters, he experimented with writing, for example, poems that balanced the powerfully forward-thrusting style of a Hart Crane poetic line with that of a slow meditative line of Emerson. He would invent queer, Chicano poet-narrators who balanced philosophical meditation and psychological investigation within traditional sonnet verse structures. In Islas's poem "Light," for example, he balanced the self with a Jungian notion of the "God-image" by inventing a fully constituted poet-narrating Self that fails to apprehend its Other: that "golden one who was not ours, / who was not mine."

Islas thought that the poet should invent poems that would reach beyond itself. One such poet that Islas championed for her word-in-the-world sensibility was Denise Levertov. He considered that she had successfully managed to open up the poetic line in such a way as to combine the pleasure of verse and image with a painful sense of violence present in her everyday world. This was a goal that Islas sought for his own poems. And to this end he did not hesitate to mix low- and high-brow, canonic and popular cultural expressive forms. Consider, for example, his sexy four-part video song titled "Anna, Albertine, Isabel, and Emma" (first names to Western-canonic female characters). And, Islas playfully announced in parentheticals alongside these video poems that they were to be recited by twentieth-century gender-bending figures like Boy George and Annie Lennox. So not only did Islas intend to use the video poem as a glamorous multi-mediatized aesthetic to reinvent the lyric form and reach out into his contemporary world, but, in dramatizing a poetics of transvestism, he challenged and complicated the familiar notion of lyric voice.

Islas experimented with a wide variety of poetic strategies. In his poems "Aztec Angel," "Cuauhtémoc's Grave," and "Resident Fellow I," Islas used the *corrido*/ballad form, European-identified lyric modes, and a prose-poetic style to take his readers into the hybrid world of Chicano/a subjectivity as shaped by an ever-evolving mix of contemporary and pre-Columbian knowledge systems. In "Resident Fellow I," Islas invented a Chicano poet-narrator with a global reach. The poet-narrator is a border subject looking to turn a profit by transforming pre-Colombian heritage into a commodity to be consumed in the capitalist marketplace. Islas wrote: "An Aztec face, red clay, two-fifty / At the Juárez market." In "Aztec Angel," Islas played with visuals of form—mixing a horizontal reading of the lines with a cascading verticality—that both mimic the angel's fall and allow the poem to dance vertiginously on the page. Islas also used the technique of linguistic code-switching to suspend the reader somewhere between English and Spanish, between a Mexican-identified culture and a mainstream United States. The poetic line and subject enter into the fluid space of Chicano identity that connects but is not shackled to a collective past. These more Chicano-identified poems address issues of memory, identity, history, and

heritage in order to validate and reclaim a lost Chicano, mestizo history—but not in any sense to delimit Chicano/a subjectivities imag-
inatively or psychically. Here Islas formed a Chicano poetics that
fused Aztec/Nahualt archetypes with queer Chicano subjectivity—
on a personal and interpersonal level—to turn the Chicano object
back into multilingual/sexual inhabiting subjects.

Islas's mid-1970s poetry made room for an aesthetics of resistance, but not as an essentializing poetics. Certainly, Islas experimented with a raza rhetoric that was present in José Montoya's "El
Louie"—a poet-narrator who similarly speaks through linguistic and
racial in-between spaces to wedge in and break up the hegemonic
language systems—but not to a racially exclusive degree. Islas also
experimented with a poetic voice much like Gloria Anzaldúa's that
plays with hetero-normative behavioral codes. By crafting an overt
same-sex poetics, Islas further stretched the limits of a traditionally
macho Chicano poetics seen in, for example, Rodolfo Gonzáles's *Yo
Soy Joaquín / I am Joaquín*.

After years of writing poems informed by a Wintersean "poetics
of rationality," Islas came into what one might identify as his
"major" poems between 1973 and 1978. Not entirely coincidentally,
this was the period when Islas attained a politicized identity as queer
and Chicano. In a poem written toward the end of that period enti-
tled "Faggots," Islas invents a poet-narrator who powerfully collapses the homophobic present with the equally homophobic but more
barbaric past. The poet-narrator takes the reader as far back as the
Middle Ages: to the time of the Inquisition and to Dante, who
depicts Satan cannibalizing bodies at the end of the Inferno. For
Islas, there has been little progress or enlightenment in the struggle
against homophobia.

The period of Islas's "major" poems also coincided with his deep
self-loathing and suicidal self-doubt that grew from a tumultuous
romance with Jay Spears—his so-identified "muse". After living
together for three years in the early 1970s, Jay Spears decided that the
monogamous domestic life was not for him; he actively sought out a
lifestyle that, at least at first, went counter to Islas's more domestic
inclination: Spears wanted to indulge in a post-Stonewall, queer-

emancipated S&M sex and drug scene; Islas wanted to build his nest. The poems that Islas wrote, inspired by and reflective of this period, are among his best. In them, concision of poetic form combine with a culturally significant iconographic imagery that expresses an erotic of pain and pleasure experienced in a relationship between the poet-narrator and a Jay Spears-like figure.

Islas also invented poet-narrators who speak in many different voices not only to convey the complexity of desire as caught up in a white/brown erotic dialectic, but, in the Wintersean tradition, to energize the poem by yoking together the emotive and rational at the level of the content and form. In the poem "Desire," for example, Islas used enjambment to dramatize the power behind the emotions carried by each line. Islas constructed the poem so that visually the lines would spill over the edge of the stanzas, or what Islas identified as boxed rooms. Here, Islas invents a poet-narrator who cruises from room to room where different lines and voices represent lineups of possibilities that are ultimately mutually exclusive. (Islas's allusion in "Desire" to lesbian poet Elizabeth Bishop's *Geography III* seems unavoidable. Bishop, too, was interested in how a series of poetic lines can form boxes/rooms that suggest only partial views into contained worlds. Perhaps as a consequence of her closeted lesbian identity, she used the poem as a medium of half-knowledge and secrecy.) Poet and colleague, Diane Middlebrook remarked of this poem to Islas, "You *subsume* a significant history; yet that history can't be known except syllable by syllable," further describing how his poetry walks a liminal line between the "waking life" and "dreaming" where the poet captures "the glower of things to come forward into time." This is one of the many forms Islas used to explore the seen/unseen, conscious/unconscious, absence/presence dialectics of same-sex desire.

Islas often used the trope of the transvestite to complicate otherwise reductive ontologies and epistemologies. He shared this device not only with Bishop's cross-dressed poetics, but also with the Chicano *rasquache* sensibility. Unlike Wintersean poetics of rationality that aimed to balance reason and emotion, here Islas's *rasquache* poetic actively juxtaposed traditionally divided spaces (Spanish versus English, Western canonical versus Chicano non-canonical, straight versus queer) to make apparent how such divisions work to segregate bodies and subjectivities. For example, in his poem "Blueboy," blueberries, yellow rose, hand prints on buttocks and Hieronymus Bosch and D.H. Lawrence make for a textured *rasquache* aesthetics that emplaces a queer Chicano sensibility. In his poem "Ambush," he invented a poet-narrator who cruises S&M clubs only to discover the Greek god of fertility, Priapus. And in the already mentioned poem "Motherfucker or the Exile," Islas's poet-narrator alludes to the snake-tailed, many-headed dog of Greek mythology, Cerberus. Islas's Cerberus, however, does not guard the gates to Hades, but is a bouncer at an S&M club. In "Bondage & Discipline," Islas invested his queer-identified poet-narrator with the power to cause pain, but this time as a process of self-healing: on a literal rack, the poet-narrator wrenches from deep cavities within his psyche those destructive patterns of inherited dysfunctional familial behavior.

Islas's writing of "major" playful poems also coincided with his heavy bout with alcohol and drugs. Often, Islas used these as themes for his poetry. In the poem "Moonshine," Islas created a soaked-in-a-scotch-haze poet-narrator who does not pen a Hallmark ode to love on Valentine's Day, but plays instead with *spirited* double entendres: "moonshine" (alcohol and night) and "lunatic" (moon and crazy). The poet morphs into the moon, the *luna,* then the *luna*tic, multiplying himself as he stares drunk at his own reflection. Poetry became a space in which Islas could exercise self-control in public by externalizing the chaos of the private.

Much of Islas's poetry was unpublished in his day, for he was plagued by feelings of insecurity concerning his talent in this domain. He only sent a few poems out to be reviewed by literary journals. And in spite of the massive corpus that he produced, he never published collections.

Essays and Lectures

As a Chicano teaching the first Chicanas/os at Stanford University in the late 1960s and early 1970s, Islas knew that there must be a move to recover Chicano/a textual productions. Given the publishing climate of the day—mainstream publishers deemed a few of the Mexicano migrant or ethnic ghetto novels worthy and the small, Chicano-based houses were only just beginning to appear on the horizon—there was much to be recovered and discovered. Islas looked to his Chicano/a students' creative writing as the site of literary recovery. During the early 1970s when Chicanas/os were becoming a more visible presence at Stanford—this, after much student protest and Chicano faculty demand—Islas directed his students to write narratives about the Chicano/a experience. (By the time Islas taught his first Chicano/a literature and writing class, the number of Chicanos had markedly risen. In 1970, for example, there were nearly two hundred Chicanos enrolled at Stanford: seventy freshman, twenty transfer students, and nearly forty graduate students.) As time passed, he began to amass a sizable collection of short stories, prose-poems, and literary essays written by his Chicano/a students and about Chicanas/os characters.

He called these first generation Stanford undergraduates his "pioneers," applauding them not only for their dedication to making visible Chicano/a creative expression, but also for their brave struggle against institutional and individual racist acts at a long distance from home. On one occasion, Islas describes his course as giving "Chicano upper classmen the opportunity to read and write about the literature that derives from their own background. It will also provide students the opportunity to write fiction and poetry which draws from their Chicano heritage and experience. There is a dearth of literature from the Spanish-speaking culture in this country. Its particular language is rich in possibilities and has been explored only recently by contemporary poets Alurista and Omar Salinas." In response to the growing numbers of Chicanos/as on campus and to the early 1970s burgeoning field of Chicano letters, Islas looked to his proximate own to collect, teach, and effectively institutionalize the Chicano/a voice.

His acts of recovery were by necessity in the present. The 1974 publication of a journal Islas pushed hard to establish, *Miquiztli: A Journal of Arte, Poesía, Cuento, y Canto*, marked a moment at Stanford when people were ready to pay attention to Chicano/a creative expression. The journal sought to explore all facets of Chicano/a identity, especially within the U.S./Mexican borderland space where culture, history, and racial identification (Mexican, Amerindian, and Anglo) and experience would intersect. In the inaugural issue, Islas identified this as the journal that would give voice to, he writes, "the fact of our double heritage" and that would provide the venue for Chicano/a literary expression for an "audience interested enough to understand and appreciate it" (vol. 1, no. 1). The multiple heritage of language (Spanish/English), culture (Mexican/Indian and American), and race (Chicano and Anglo) became the site for Islas's articulation and celebration of difference that would complicate simplistic brown versus white and marginal versus mainstream paradigms of racial opposition. Rather, it became a site of multiple junctures—not unlike Islas's multiracial El Paso—where one could acknowledge difference within a frame that allowed for a less parochial (Mexican versus Anglo, for example) understanding of the world. Islas's involvement with and writing for *Miquiztli* marked a significant moment in the rise of Chicano/a literary studies at Stanford, for it allowed Islas and his students to articulate the vast spectrum of Chicano/a experiences—many students were a first generation away from working in the fields—through a variety of expressive forms, such as poetry and prose, short story and autobiography. Also, to read Chicano/a literature for Islas was also to evaluate it. He didn't believe, for example, that all texts written by Chicanos—or any writer for that matter—merited treatment as literature if it didn't hold up to an evaluation based on form and content. In the second volume of *Miquiztli*, for example, Islas writes, "more often than not, much of the fiction we do have is document, and sometimes not very well written document. Much of what is passed off as literature is a compendium of folklore, religious superstition, and recipes for tortillas. All well and good, but it is not literature" (vol. 2, no. 1). Islas used his classroom and journal as a forum to recover and build a complicated array of Chicano/a textual voices and experiences.

    Islas pushed to "legitimate" our multidimensional cultural and racial heritage in teaming up with freshly minted Chicano professors, such as historian Al Camarillo, anthropologist Renato Rosaldo, and cultural critic Tomás Ybarra-Frausto. Together, they organized and team-taught courses (for example, an "Interdisciplinary Research Seminar on Chicano Culture"), including on the syllabus titles like Ron Arias's *The Road to Tamanzuchale*, Charles Tatum's *Chicano Literature* and Francisco Jiménez's *The Identification and Analysis of Chicano Literature*. However, Islas's lectures, whether as part of a team or alone, were both laudatory and critical of Chicano/a literature. He had been trained to judge literary texts according to their formal qualities and to analyze how effectively they reflected and commented on the "real" social landscape *hors texte*. For example, in a lecture on Ernesto Galarza's *Education of a Barrio Boy*, he discussed the book's importance as a retelling of Galarza's migrant farmworker life as well as how the book lacked narrative subtlety and stylistic polish. Islas would tell his students to develop a discerning, readerly taste that would both appreciate a book's content—Galarza's trials and tribulations—and also its form—in this case, Galarza's lack of nuance and storytelling craft. Furthermore, Islas was also careful to distinguish between Chicano writers who were able to tell complex stories of the Chicano self in society and those who, like Galarza, represented a one-dimensional portrait of the Chicano struggling to survive in the United States. Later, with the popularity of minority studies on the rise, he not only continued to team-teach, but also to teach his own courses, choosing for them subjects that went beyond the Chicano authors. Thus, he taught courses like "Hispanic American Novels," where, according to his own description, students "will read and discuss works by some of the major contemporary Hispanic American writers," and he expanded the Chicano/a literary canon to include Latino writers such as Gabriel García Márquez (*One Hundred Years of Solitude*), Mario Vargas Llosa (*Aunt Julia and the Scriptwriter*), Carlos Fuentes (*The Good Conscience*), and Juan Rulfo (*Pedro Páramo* and *The Burning Plain*).

By 1975, with *Miquiztli*, Chicano/a literature courses peppering the curriculum, and the Chicano Fellows Program well underway, Islas turned his focus to writing the seventy-page scholarly monograph titled, "Saints, Artists, and Vile Politics: An Introduction to

Chicano Fiction and Autobiography." The project as a whole both engaged and critiqued the "uneasy relationship" (his words) between Latin American and Anglo literatures. While many of his colleagues at Stanford praised the project, Islas never found any interest among the academic presses. And although Islas was encouraged to turn sections of the monograph into articles and send them out for publication, after several rejections from more politicized Chicano/a journals such as *Grito del Sol*, he decided that perhaps those outside Stanford's walls were not quite ready for such Chicano/a scholarship. In "Saints, Artists, and Vile Politics," Islas combined an Yvor Wintersean analysis (close reading combined with a candid, subjective judgment) with a racialized edge to read a variety of Chicano writers, among them Oscar "Zeta" Acosta, Rudolfo A. Anaya, Ernesto Galarza, and Rolando Hinojosa, along with some Latin American authors, such as Gabriel García Márquez. In a study far ahead of its time, Islas not only constructed a North and South American literary frame of analysis, but also articulated an intricate method for reading Chicano literature that paid attention both to its poetics and its themes. As such, "Saints, Artists, and Vile Politics" critiqued traditional studies of American literature that followed an East-to-West critical gaze (with the "real" writers largely inhabiting the East) by analyzing how Chicano/a literature existed along a North-South continuum of genre influence and exchange. Islas also dared to use the autobiographical voice to shed a different light on his primary texts—this during a time before the multicultural confessional voice had become a legitimate mode of scholarly critique in the academy. For example, in his discussion of *Barrio Boy*, Islas concludes, "I consider myself, still, a child of the Border, a Border some believe extends all the way to Seattle and includes the northern provinces of Mexico. [. . .] Like some of my characters, I often find myself on the bridge between cultures, between languages, between sexes, between nations, between religions, between my profession as teacher and my vocation as writer, between two different and equally compelling ways of looking agape at the world." Islas sought to construct theoretical bridges that were anchored strongly in the autobiographical. As such, he attempted in his scholarly work on Chicano/a literature to clear a space where he could develop a comparative analytical approach that was also grounded in the personal. He sought to think and write across disciplines (scholarly and personal) as if walking, as he wrote in "Saints, Artists, and Vile Politics," "from one side of the border to another without any immigration officers to tell me where I should or should not be."

Islas came of age as a Chicano writer and scholar during a splitting in the way literature was to be studied in the U.S. academy: between a traditional belletristic literary appreciation of literature and the new wave of French theory that sought to question universal truths and structures and deconstruct the text. Islas found himself stuck between the two: pulled by his training under the guidance of Stanford's belletrists Wallace Stegner (principal advisor), Ian Watt, David Levin, Thomas Moser, and Yvor Winters and also pulled by the new French approaches to scholarship that spoke to issues of Otherness and that sought to destablize traditional paradigms that read Europe as the literary center and the Americas as peripheral. Islas's border-savvyness—as an undergraduate, graduate, and professor at Stanford, he could enter and be political in a community of mostly straight male, Ivy-league trained academics, and then return to his writing and life at the canonic and social margins—led to his strategic mixture of a belletristic analysis with a deconstructive zeal for the political and marginal. In this manner, Islas cleared a space that was informed by both methods of approaching the Chicano/a literary text.

Closing Remarks

Islas spent a lifetime shaping and sculpting narrative and poetic form to texture a manifold and oft-contradictory Chicano/a self. His narrative fictions, poems, and essays crisscross borders of genre, form, and theme. His ability to move across textual borders springs from a lifetime of learning to negotiate society as a gay Chicano. Border crossing in language, poetic form, and narrative technique were his tools for understanding a society that swept those considered diseased to its invisible margins. For example, in his fictionalized memoir sketch, "The Loneliest Man in the World," the narrator comes to terms with his own outlawed sexuality, his relationship with a self-destructive father, and a student's death from an AIDS-related disease. Islas bends genre and uses language to understand better a world governed by heteromasculine-identified insecurities that lead to destructively patterned relationships that systematically and violently force hierarchies of difference: straight versus queer, sinner versus saint, and whore versus virgin.

This introduction to *Arturo Islas: The Uncollected Works* is presented as a moveable frame that highlights only a few of the rich textures that the works themselves offer. It aims to begin to enliven and enrich our understanding of Islas vis-à-vis the works collected here and his already published *The Rain God*, *Migrant Souls*, and *La Mollie and the King of Tears*. Finally, it seeks to recover a complex gay Chicano author who spent a lifetime engaged in physical and textual acts of recovering and discovering in order to clear a space for the articulation of a complex Chicano/a identity and literature and thereby make healthy a contemporary American literary and social corpus.

Bibliography

Aguilar Melantzon, Ricardo. "Torica with Arturo Islas : An Interview." *Nova Quarterly* 22.4 (1987): 2–4.

Aldama, Frederick Luis. *Dancing with Ghosts: A Critical Biography of Arturo Islas.* Berkeley: U of California Press, 2004.

_____. *Critical Mappings of Arturo Islas's Narrative Fictions.* Editor. Tempe: Bilingual Review Press, 2004.

_____. "Fictional Recoveries in the Early Life of Arturo Islas." *Recovering the U.S. Hispanic Literary Heritage Vol. IV* (forthcoming, 2005).

_____. "Ethnoqueer Re-Architexturing of Metropolitan Space." *Nepantla* 1.3 (2000): 581–604.

Bruce-Novoa, Juan. "Homosexuality and the Chicano Novel." In *European Perspectives on Hispanic Literature of the United States.* Ed. Genvieve Fabre. Houston: Arte Público Press, 1986: 98–106.

Burciaga, José Antonio. "A Conversation With Arturo Islas." *Stanford Humanities Review* (1992): 158–66.

Burgess, Clarissa. "Tlaloc-Rain God." University of Texas, Ramirez Home Page. 30 Oct. 2001 <http://www.cwrl.utexas.edu/~ramirez/clarissa/tlaloc.html>.

Calderón, Hector. Rev. of *The Rain God. Revista Chicano-Riqueña* 8.2 (1985): 68–70.

Cantú, Roberto. "Arturo Islas." *Dictionary of Literary Biography.* Vol. 122: Chicano Writers, Second Series. Eds. Francisco A. Lomelí and Carl R. Shirley. Detroit: Gale Research, 1992:

146–154.

de Jesús Vega, Manuel. "Chicano, Gay, and Doomed: AIDS in Arturo Islas' *The Rain God.*" *Confluencia: Revista Hispanica de Cultura y Literatura* 11.2 (1996): 112–18.

Fowler, Carol. "Death and Family Dominate Novel." Rev. of *The Rain God. Contra Costa Times* 26 Jan. 1985.

Galindo, Luis Alberto. "El dios de la lluvia-RAIN GOD." *La Communidad* 241(1985): 12–13.

Gillenkirk, Jeff. "Migrant Souls." Rev. of *Migrant Souls. Nation* 250.9 (1990): 313–314.

Gladstein, Mimi. Rev. of *Migrant Souls. The El Paso Times.* 11Mar. 1990: 2D.

Gonzales-Berry, Erlinda. "Sensuality, Repression, and Death in Arturo Islas's *The Rain God.*" *Bilingual Review* 12 (1985): 258–61.

Gonzalez, Ray. "One great haiku in a lifetime: An Interview with Arturo Islas." *Guadalupe Review* 1 (1991): 124–134.

_____. "The migrant soul of Arturo Islas." *Guadalupe Review* 1 (1991): 116–123.

Goode, Stephen. Rev. of *The Rain God: A Desert Tale. Nuestro* 8.7 (1984): 48.

Gutiérez Castillo, Dina. "La imagen de la mujer en la novela fronteriza." In *Mujer y Literatura Mexicana y Chicana: Culturas en Contacto.* Ed. Aralia López-González. Mexico: Colegio de la Frontera Norte, 1988: 55–63.

Halper, Leah. "Ofrenda for Arturo Islas." *San Jose Studies* 19.1 (1993): 62–72.

Islas, Arturo. *La Mollie and the King of Tears.* Albuquerque: University of New Mexico Press, 1996.

_____. "Interview." *Bay Area Reporter* 10.13 (1990): 3, 29.

_____. *Migrant Souls.* New York: William Morrow, 1990.

_____. "Chakespeare Louie." *Zyzzyva* 4.1 (1988): 79–84.

_____. *The Rain God: A Desert Tale.* Palo Alto: Alexandrian Press, 1984.

_____. "The Politics of Imaginative Writing." In *Critical Fictions.* Ed. Philmena Mariani. Seattle: Bay Press, 1991: 72–74.

Márquez, Antonio C. "The Historical Imagination in Arturo Islas's *The Rain God* and *Migrant Souls.*" *MELUS* 19.2 (1994): 3–16.

Mayer, Henry. "An Immigrant Family's Diminished Dreams." *The San Francisco Chronicle Sunday Review.* 18 Feb. 1990: 3.

McKenna, Teresa. *Migrant Song: Politics and Process in Contemporary Chicano Literature.* Austin: U of Texas Press, 1997.

Mungo, Raymond. "Strange Murder in the Desert." Rev. of *The Rain God. San Francisco Chronicle.* 4 Nov. 1984: 5.

Neate, William. "Repression and the Abject Body: Writing the Family History in Arturo Islas's *The Rain God.*" *Revista Canario de Estudios Ingleses* 35 (1997): 211–232.

Ortiz, Ricardo L. "Sexuality Degree Zero: Pleasure and Power in the Novels of John Rechy, Arturo Islas, and Michael Nava." *Journal of Homosexuality* 26.2/3 (1993): 111–126.

Portillo, Febe. "Syncretism in counter-hegemonic literature by Latinos in the United States." Diss. Stanford U, 1988.

Rice, David. "Sinners Among Angels, or Family History and the Ethnic Narrator in Arturo Islas's *The Rain God* and *Migrant Souls.*" *LIT: Literature, Interpretation, Theory* 11.2 (2000): 169–97.

Rieff, David. Review of *Migrant Souls. Los Angeles Times* 28 Jan. (1990): 3.

Román, David. "Arturo Islas (1938-1991)." In *Contemporary Gay American Novelists: A Bio-Bibliographical Criticial Sourcebook.* Ed. Emmanuel S. Nelson. Westport: Greenwood, 1993.

Rosaldo, Renato. "Fables of the Fallen Guy." In *Criticism in the Borderland: Studies in Chicano Literature, Culture, and Ideology.* Eds. Héctor Calderón and José Saldívar. Durham: Duke U Press, 1991: 84–93.

Ruiz, Vicki. Rev. of *The Rain God. El Paso Herald-Post.* 12 Oct. 1984.

Saenz, Benjamin A. "Incarnations of the Border." *Ambiente* 1990: 13.

Saldívar, José David. *Border Matters: Remapping American Cultural Studies.* Berkeley: U of California Press, 1997.

_____. *The Dialectics of Our America: Genealogy, Cultural Critique and Literary History.* Durham: Duke U Press, 1991.

_____. "The Hybridity of Culture in Arturo Islas's *The Rain God*." *Disposito: Revista Americana de Estudios Comparados y Culturales* 41 (1991): 109–19.

Sánchez, Marta E. "Arturo Islas' *The Rain God*: An Alternative Tradition." *American Literature* 62.2 (1990): 284–304.

Sánchez, Rosaura. "Ideological Discourses in Arturo Islas' *The Rain God*." In *Criticism in the Borderlands: Studies in Chicano Literature, Culture, and Ideology*. Eds. Héctor Calderón and José David Saldívar. Durham: Duke U Press, 1991: 114–126.

Shorris, Earl. *Latinos: A Biography of the People*. New York: WW Norton & Co, 1992.

Skenazy, Paul. "Afterword." *La Mollie and the King of Tears*. Albuquerque: U of New Mexico Press, 1996: 167–198.

_____. "Borders and Bridges, Doors and Drugstores: Toward a Geography of Time." In *San Francisco in Fiction: Essays in a Regional Literature*. Eds. David Fine and Paul Skenazy. Albuquerque: U of New Mexico Press, 1995: 198–216.

Tatum, Charles. *Chicano Literature*. Boston: Twayne, 1982: 135.

Unger, David. Rev. of *Migrant Souls*. *The New York Time*s Book Review 20 May 1990: 30.

Velásquez-Treviño, Gloria. "Arturo." *Bilingual Review* 17.2 (1992): 168.

Vilescas, José Jr. "Opinion." *El Paso Times*. 14 Oct. 2000: 13A.

EARLY FICTIONS

Orejas de papalote
(Fall 1957)

Faustino García clenched his hands, set his bare feet in the fine, brown sands and waited for silence to fall upon the children around him. Then he lowered his head and charged full speed toward the wall. He hit it hard and fast, feeling the impact tremble through his neck down his back and muscles of his legs and out of his feet into the earth which felt it too because it moved. He focused his eyes.

"Órale!" yelled his cousin Memo and all the children who lived on their block. They stood around Tino in awe and waited for him to raise his eyes, straighten his neck, and grin in triumph.

"How do you do it, Tino? You sure are a *cabezón.*" Tino shrugged and leaned against the adobe wall. They were all looking at him, and it was the moment he loved most of all: that look that exists only in the eyes of a child who respects another. The pain in his head made it even better because it intensified the pride. But he did not do it for the pain, but because it made him proud to be able to do it the hardest of all.

"Let us feel your head, Tino." He did not answer. While he still felt the pain he kept his jaws clenched; he grinned knowing this was the best he could do.

"It sure is hard," said his cousin Memo, as he patted Tino on the head and rubbed his ears. The others lined up, each wiping the dirt from their hands on their clothes before feeling Tino's head.

"Doesn't it hurt?" Margarita, Memo's little sister, asked.

"Sure it does. But it goes away after awhile and then it really

3

feels good."

Tino and Memo were older than Margarita, but she went with them almost everywhere. During the summer they would sell popcorn at the stock car races on the weekends. He and Memo would go through the crowd while she stayed behind to help Mrs. Washington with the machines. The old lady would give Margarita fifty cents for an evening's work but Memo and Tino would get ten cents for every dollar's worth of popcorn they sold. Once, between them they made four dollars and twenty cents. Memo had taken three of the dollars because he was older, but Tino had not liked the way his cousin had done it. Each had to give half to their mothers. Now that school was starting again, they would only be selling popcorn at the Friday night high school football games. They did not make as much money, but they had more fun.

Memo felt Tino's head again. He looked down at his eight-year-old cousin. "I'm going to ask Mamá why your head is so hard."

Tino shook Memo's hands off. "Don't, Memo. She'll tell and they won't let us do it anymore. It's the best game we have."

"I don't like it. You always win." He had his hands on Tino's shoulders now and was holding him against the wall.

"Come on, Memo. Don't tell. Don't be a *chismoso*." Memo pressed him harder against the wall. He grabbed at Tino's ears and started to laugh.

"I know why you can do it now. Your ears are bigger than anybody's. *Orejas de papalote, orejas de papalote!*"

Tino struggled vainly. "Let me go, *cacoso!*"

Memo kept laughing and shouting. "Tino has Dumbo ears." He let go of one of his ears and flicked the other.

Tino bit him in the stomach and started running across the backyard.

"*Orejas de papalote!*" They were all screaming at him now. His face was white. His mouth was dry and his ears were burning.

"You take that back," he yelled, trying to catch the figures as they darted about him, grabbing for his ears.

"Why don't you fly away? Haven't you learned to wiggle your ears yet?" Their chanting reached full pitch.

Tino chased them all and caught none. "I hate you! I hate you!" They were jumping in a kind of dance, laughing, jesting cruelly. He gasped for air and tried to swallow. Anger and shame were radiating from inside his chest, and the early autumn sun was burning his face. Tino gnashed his teeth and glared at them. He wanted to call them bad names, but he felt that if he opened his mouth he would crack open like a clay jar.

He ran home and into his house without stopping, quickly slamming doors on his way into the bathroom where he locked himself inside, climbed up on the washbowl, and looked in the mirror. He saw them sticking out of the side of his face. Sticking out, big and ugly, like things apart from himself. His father's razor still lay on top of the rack above the toilet, unused for six months because he had gone on a long trip and forgotten to take it with him. Tino reached for it and held it hard and clumsily. He could still hear the children screaming. Their taunts mingled with his own sobbing and the dripping of the water from the faucet and his mother's voice, far away through some mysterious door, asking, "Tino, *¿qué pasa? ¿Qué estás haciendo?*" and his own voice answering before he could stop it. "I'm cutting my ears off!"

She pleaded for him to open the door. Tino dropped the razor into the bowl, fell to the floor, unhooked the latch, and gave himself to her.

"*Pobrecito, pobrecito*," she said again and again. He heard her through the pounding in his head which hurt with a different, deeper pain, and his ears were burning more than before because they were still there and he knew it.

"*¿Por qué*, Tino? *¿Por qué?*"

He did not answer and he never told her.

The next day, Tino got up before the sparrows began making their usual racket. His eyes were puffy like the *sopapillas* his mother was frying. He picked one up from the table, bit off one of its corners, poured honey into it, and ate it silently. He wiped his hands and got up from the table.

"*¿A dónde vas?*"

"To Memo's."

"*No vayas.*"

"I have to go, Mamá. Leave me alone."

Tino ran out of the house before she could answer. He knew she was crying. Ever since his father had gone away, she cried about anything, happy or not.

He walked slowly, stepping on all the cracks in the sidewalk. He went into Memo's backyard and walked to the wall, yellow as the morning sun caught fire. He put his hand on its still cool surface and stroked it. He felt its coolness come together with the coolness of the sand under his feet somewhere inside his stomach. It was fresh and smooth, and his heart remembered yesterday's triumph.

"What are you doing, Tino?"

Tino turned and saw Margarita standing behind the screen door of his *tía*'s porch. Her hair was stuck to her neck and her nose was all stopped up because she was allergic to grass. She opened the door and talked to him.

"Are you going to play with us today, Tino?" She took a ribbon out of her dirty blue dress.

"No."

"What are you doing here then? Why don't you go home?" She smiled with curiosity and something else that Tino did not like behind her eyes.

"I don't know."

"Are you going to hit your head against the wall?"

"Maybe."

"Why, Tino?" She leaned over and scratched her knee.

"Because I feel like it. And I don't care what you or anybody calls me."

"I think *orejas de papalote* is a cute name," she said. She was tying the ribbon in her hair. "We're going to play kick-the-can today."

"Games with rules! They're boring."

"But doesn't your head hurt at all?"

"I don't care if it does."

"*¡Órale, Orejas!*" Memo was walking toward them. He grinned, exposing his yellow, uneven teeth. His face was dirty and there was a pimple on his chin. Tino walked toward him.

"I don't want you to call me that any more, Memo."

"All right, *Orejas*, I won't call you *Orejas* any more." He picked up the hoses, turned on the water, and started watering the patch of grass near the wall.

"You'd better stop, Memo, or I'll . . ."

"You'll what, *Orejas*?"

"I'll tell my father when he comes back."

"Uncle Nacho?" asked Margarita.

"You'll see, Memo, he'll fix you."

"He's not coming back, baby." Memo started sprinkling water near Tino's feet. Margarita put her hand on Tino's shoulder. He stood silent and afraid. "Mamá told us that he went with La Gringa." She touched his ear and giggled.

"You're lying. He's coming back. He is. He is."

Memo wet Tino's feet. Tino lowered his head and charged right into his stomach, and then used his legs to kick Memo wherever he could. "You're lying, you're lying," he shouted. Memo was doubled up on the ground. Margarita ran toward the house shouting, "Mamá! Mamá!"

Dazed, Tino watched Memo rock on the ground. He heard the porch door slam and saw his aunt crossing the yard.

"¡Faustino! ¡Faustino! *¡Ven aquí, malcriado!*"

"You go to hell," Tino yelled at her. He climbed over the fence and ran down the alley. He picked up a rock and threw it at a cat behind the trash can. The cat jumped onto the fence and then up to the roof of an abandoned adobe shack. He followed it with his eyes. Behind it, a kite was fluttering in an early breeze. He is coming back, Tino said to himself. I know he is, and I'll tell him about the wall and how I won every time. When he got home, he took his father's razor and buried it.

A Boy with the Eyes of a Fawn
(Fall 1957)

Teresa first noticed him in the church after she had gone out of the confessional and was walking toward the altar railing to say her penance. "He has the eyes of a fawn," she thought, and began to say her rosary. It was the first time Padre García had made her say an entire rosary for penance.

"*Santa María, madre de Dios . . .*" She smiled as she said the words now growing old on her lips from repetition. When she had first begun going to confession, everything had seemed hypocritical to her. Now, it was just her way of life. Go to confession on Saturdays and make a living the rest of the week. Her thoughts wandered as the beads passed under her middle-aged hands. She was thinking of the boy with the eyes of a fawn.

She turned her head slightly, pretending to smooth her black veil, straining her eyes to see if he was looking at her. He was gone.

Suddenly she stopped abruptly in the middle of the "Padre Nuestro," arose quickly from her knees, and almost ran to the vestibule, pausing only to light a candle before the statue of the Virgin de Guadalupe and murmur, "Mother of purity, protect me."

The sunlight startled her and caused her to stand against the bronze door of the church so that her eyes might adjust to the glare. There was no one on the white marble stairs. It was the first time she had ever seen them empty. She did not look at them very long, for the reflection hurt her eyes. Slowly she unpinned the veil from her hair. He was gone. She walked across the street to the square.

Juan was sitting on the brown bench by the candy van. He was leafing through a paperback book he had bought. Teresa always saw him with a paperback book in his hand, ever since the day they had taken Pepito away. He never read them, he only carried them with him wherever he went. It gave him something to do with his hands, he said. Juan was always the same.

"Hey, Teresa, Teresa!" He always shouted. No matter how near you were to him, he always shouted. "Teresa, you think I got all day? Goddamn women! They think all you got to do all day is wait for them. Hurry up, I got to talk to you."

She felt like going back into the confessional again. She wanted to feel the warmth of having someone care for her, even if it was only Padre García behind the screen. She wanted to feel the security of the altar railing hurting her arms when she pressed down on it.

"Good afternoon, Juan."

"Good afternoon! In five minutes it will be good evening! What's the matter with you? You know it's Saturday night. O'Brien is mad as hell. He's been bitching at me all afternoon."

"Why didn't you come into the church for me?"

"Too many people. Have you eaten?"

"No."

"Come on, we'll get something on the way. Come on, what's the matter?"

Teresa did not hear him. In the middle of the square, standing by the fountain with one foot raised on its ledge, she saw the boy. She knew she was staring, but she could not turn her eyes away from him. The bells of the church sounded the Angelus and the sun was still high enough to make the dirty waters splashing from the fountain glimmer dully in front of him.

"Teresa, for God's sake, if you want something to eat, let's get the hell out of here."

The boy turned, hearing Juan's voice, embarrassed for Teresa. She pretended to be looking diagonally across the square, but she met the boy's gaze for a few moments. His face flushed. Turning quickly, he expertly dodged an old woman who was carrying a baby in one arm and a pail of tamales in the other. Only his eyes stopped the old woman from swearing at him. Teresa almost called to him, but Juan grabbed her arm as she was raising it in a gesture of "Wait!" The boy with the eyes of a fawn disappeared.

"What's the matter with you? You crazy? He's just a kid. Come on, hurry up!"

The sun was behind the church, its lower rim already behind the mountain. Teresa and Juan walked down the main street growing colorless with the oncoming twilight. There was not enough darkness for the neon signs to show any contrast of color with their surroundings. Everything seemed gray to Teresa, even the people. They passed by an old streetcar which had been converted into a diner. "Let's go in here," Juan said.

"I'm not hungry."

"Come on. You got to eat something. O'Brien has big plans for you tonight. You're entertaining the best customers tonight, Teresita."

She hated it when he called her that. "Don't tell me. I don't want to know. Let's go in, huh?"

"Well, that's what I've been trying to do, for Christ's sake."

They walked into the diner and sat at one of the tables near the street so they could watch the people go by.

"Juan?"

"Yeah?"

"Juan, do me a favor, huh?"

"What? Get to the point."

"Fix it so I won't have to go tonight."

"You crazy? What's the matter with you? You just don't 'fix it up' when you goddamn please. Besides, we need the money."

The waiter came. Juan ordered for both of them.

"Just as a favor for me? Just this once, huh?"

"Hell no! You want O'Brien to knock us off the list. You want to run around by yourself working for peanuts? I'm doing you a favor. I'm seeing that you get there on time. Jesus Christ, fix it up, she says."

"Quit swearing. People are looking at us."

"Let 'em. Sometimes I think God used shit instead of clay when he made people, anyway."

"Forget it, huh?"

"Damn right, I'm gonna forget it. Just let one start asking you to fix it up, and pretty soon they all are."

"Please shut up."

They sat in silence, listening to the footsteps of the people passing by. Across the street, a girl standing between two soldiers laughed. The food came. It was hot and greasy and heavy. Teresa pushed the plate away from under her.

"What's the matter?"

"Nothing. I've got a headache, that's all."

"Better eat," Juan said, his mouth full of green chile.

"Just order me something to drink, all right?"

"What's the matter with you?" he said with his mouth still full. "Come on. Tell Juan what's bothering you. I always take care of my girls, don't I? Tell Juan what's wrong."

"Nothing. Just eat, will you?"

He started to pick up a taco, then dropped it back on the plate. He wiped his hands on his faded brown coat. "Haven't I always been there when you needed me?"

Teresa didn't answer.

"Haven't I always seen that you were fed and clothed and taken care of?"

She still didn't answer.

"Haven't I always gotten the best customers for you?"

She looked away.

"So I can't fix it up for you every time you see a goddamn boy on the street who might be him."

Teresa didn't want to cry, instead she told him angrily to shut up. He took the paperback book out of his pocket and started fingering it.

She looked at him. He lowered his eyes. He did not like looking at her when she was like that. She smiled and looked out into the neon-lit street to see if the boy with the eyes of a fawn was looking for her.

"Juan," she said, in a casual way.

"What?" He was still hurt and responded in that injured tone which defeated her.

"You should go to confession sometime," she said after awhile.

The Submarine
(Fall 1957)

By the time I got to the Submarine, that's the nightclub we hang out at during the summer when everyone is home from school, J.D., Ronnie, and all the other guys of the old high-school crowd were pretty well plastered. I walked up to the bar and ordered a shot of tequila without any lime or anything before any of them saw me. Tequila is the best, the cheapest, and the quickest way to get stoned.

Everyone had been at it since eight o'clock that night, and by now, the silent pall before the hysterics begin had settled around the bar. J.D. was on the end stool telling a dirty joke. When he saw me, he kind of slid over to my end of the bar and said out loud, as if he hadn't seen me all summer, "Hi, Fart, how the hell's my buddy?" All the guys call me Fart because it rhymes with Art—my name. Pretty damn clever. J.D. put his arm around my shoulder and just held it there while he finished his drink, whatever it was, with a noisy gulp. He'd never put his arm around any of the guys, unless he was drunk. He thought it was kind of queer, like wearing Bermuda shorts. But ever since he'd been back from college, he'd worn Bermuda shorts to all the parties as if it were an individualistic thing to do.

I swung around on the stool, ordered another tequila, which he insisted on paying for, and laughed when he kept his arm in mid-air still holding on to something. His face was all lighted up, but the usual sparkle in his eyes was gone. We started talking about having to go back to school. We'd already talked about it, but it was the only thing either of us could think of to say. After awhile we stopped talk-

13

ing and just drank.

Ronnie was in the far corner of the room arguing with the waiter about some type of drink. That Ronnie! You could tell he was drunk on his ass by the way he was yelling and trying to sing the words of a song he had learned in Spanish from a prostitute he had slept with all summer. All the guys called him Ronalga, which means "Ron-butt" in English, and he loved it. He was always telling me he was a Mexican at heart. One time when we were watching a strip, the old hag on the stage with a St. Christopher medal around her neck came up to him practically naked and asked him to dance with her. Everyone howled, he was in such a panic. He kept doing little steps by himself and the old whore kept trying to get close to him and finally left him there by himself. But he was having too much fun and kept saying, "*Ay, qué sultra, qué sultra.*" He didn't believe it when I told him there was no such word in Spanish. "*Sultra* means sultry, Art." He was the only one that ever called me by my right name. "Sure it does, Art." And he bitched about it all that night.

The rest of the guys stood around, drinking and talking about their girls. When they were with them, they never talked as intimately to them as they talked about them when they were drunk. It was really very funny. I liked these guys. But ever since everyone had come back from college, being with them wasn't the same as before. For awhile, I thought it was just my asinine self, but after a few reunions I felt like nobody could talk to anybody anymore. It scared me because at school I hadn't been able to get across to anyone, and it sure was a lonely feeling.

Out of all of them, I liked J.D. and Ron the best. We'd gone through high school together and always did everything together, except when I was vice president of the student body and J.D. and Ronnie ran against each other for president and Ron lost; I'd voted for Ron because J.D. was kind of an insensitive bastard and I didn't think it meant as much to him to get it as it did to Ron. He must have been drinking gin fizzes all night, because he had a special joke about them and I could hear him telling it. He almost cried from pure joy when he saw me.

"Art, why in the hell did it take you so long to get here?" He said it while trying to focus his already nearsighted eyes, and it was pretty damn funny. He always looked like a bad little boy with egg on his face when he didn't think I approved of what he did.

"Just got off work," I told him, trying to imitate him, but he was too far gone to catch on. He bought me another tequila. After five shots, I was feeling pretty damn good. I enjoy drinking now. I acquired a taste for it my first year away from home after I'd decided not to be a Catholic any more.

After awhile, the noise started and people were coming in and out; the bartender was in hysterics trying to throw us out because we were getting too loud with everybody singing and cussing and laughing and drinking. Everyone except J.D., although he was trying hard to let himself go like everyone else. Ronnie went to the head to throw up. That's what I liked about him. He was always very considerate, even when he was drunk.

J.D. asked me to go over and sit at one of the tables with him. I'd seen him drunk before, but never like this. I think he was about to cry. "Geeze, Fart," he finally said, "what in the hell am I going to do?"

It was always the same with J.D. He never really loved anybody, not even himself, I don't think. But there was always some girl he thought he was in love with, but couldn't do anything about it because his mother always got in the act. Talking to J.D. when he was sober was like talking to his mother and father. He had some fantastic sense of responsibility toward them. Ever since he was a freshman in high school and they made him quit running around with a gang called the Street Angels and had him operated on to remove the tattoo on his leg that had initiated him into the group. He has never been the same since. Always afraid that his parents might not approve of him. Someday he'll inherit their chemical corporation, just as long as he does what they say. They never really tell him anything. They just suggest it, and being J.D., he does it.

"Geeze," he kept saying, "I think I'm in love this time, Fart."

I took another sip of tequila. I could see that this time he was going to talk a lot longer than usual. I enjoyed it, because ever since his operation, these were the only times I knew what he was really

like. He was about to cry, and I didn't know what I was going to do
if he did. I hate it when guys cry. I hate it when girls cry, come to
think of it. But there's just something about a guy crying that I can't
stand. It makes me sick. I'd only seen him cry once before, when we
were in the eighth grade and he asked me over to his house for an
after-school snack. He and his older sister got into a fight about not
having put the car into one of the garages, and J.D. shouted, "Bev-
erly, you bitch!" And she screamed, "J.D., you bastard!" And they
both looked at each other and started crying just like that. God, I was
embarrassed. I didn't know what to do. So I went out and sat on the
stairs. After awhile he came out and it took me a long time to convince him that his sister didn't hate him. It was always my job to talk
him out of something. I think he expected it. That's why he always
told me about his unacceptable love affairs.

It was really very simple. All you had to tell him was that he
didn't *really* love her, that he didn't *really* want to take her out any
more, and all that shit until he decided, as if it were his own idea, that
he had his head up his ass. He washed down three more drinks,
whatever they were, and bought me another tequila. I sat there half
listening to his puny rationalizing, agreeing at the right times and
trying to look interested and understanding and buddy-like. But
mostly, I looked at the urine-colored liquid I was drinking and
thought about Harriet.

Harriet was in love with J.D., which was all very wonderful,
except she was Jewish and sensitive. She's not beautiful at all when
you first look at her, but after awhile she becomes beautiful. Like
looking at a painting you don't like at first and then all of a sudden
you like it. I'd taken her out quite a lot during the summer and we
had talked about everything. She was the only one that ever made me
feel like myself. She was always saying, "Poor baby, nobody loves
him," meaning J.D. She had a favorite theory that there was a difference between loving someone and being in love. We could tell each
other anything and she was always saying how grateful she was to
have someone like me that she could express her innermost thoughts
to. What a girl! Everywhere we went, she impressed someone. At
bullfights, one of the matadors would always dedicate a kill to her,

not even knowing her or anything. She was just that kind of a girl.

We always pretended we were married when we went anywhere that nobody knew us. Waiters and bartenders always believed us. Sometimes we'd argue about the "children" and she would talk in a Jewish accent and I would talk in a Mexican accent, and people would turn around and stare at us. It was really great just to be with her and not even have to say anything. It was like being two deaf-mutes and still we could talk to each other.

I could tell a lot about her, but I think the thing I like most about her is that she is never anybody but herself. She says and does what she feels, and if she doesn't, she tells me how awful she is. I even asked her to marry me one night. She looked at me a long time and then said, "Not now, but I'll be your mistress." I sure ruined that night. After that, everything I did and said hurt her. I didn't mean to hurt her, but I couldn't help myself. I didn't want her to feel sorry for me or anything, so I guess that's why I did it. The night of our last date she told me she thought she was in love with J.D. I didn't say anything because I wanted to sound very impartial about the whole thing, but I felt like hell about it. I didn't take her out anymore, and she started going out with J.D. Last night at one of the country club parties, she told me everything. J.D. hadn't been paying any attention to her all night and everybody but J.D. could see how much it hurt her.

"Oh, please, Art," she begged in that tone of voice that automatically made me her goddamn brother, "take care of him for me tomorrow night. I know about the drunk. Don't let him get put in jail or anything. I couldn't stand it if anything happened to him. What am I going to do, Art? You're the only one who knows what he's like. I can't even talk to him. He always seems to be a thousand miles away, as if no one's there. You know what he said? He said he was only going to tell me once that he loved me. He said it as if he were talking to a can of sardines. I think it hurts him to say that he loves me. I need to be loved, Art. He has to tell me all the time."

Poor Harriet.

J.D. was still blubbering about having his head up his ass, when Ronnie kind of poured himself into the chair next to me. "What's this son of a bitch doing? Telling you his troubles?"

I smiled when he said "son of a bitch."

Then he turned toward the bar and yelled at the top of his lungs, "C'mon, let's go to pig alley. Art, c'mon, let's get the hell out of this dump." He kept yelling like a bastard, and the bartender came over to me and asked me to lead the group out of there or else. I must have a knack for attracting people.

The stairs at the Submarine are pretty damn steep, and Ronnie missed every one of them. J.D. kept singing, "Oh, we're a bunch of bastards, scum of the earth. . ." and I kept pushing and pulling and coaxing and finally got them all outside. Ronnie passed out, and I told two of the most sober guys to take him across the river and put him into my car and stay with him. J.D. was barfing right out in the middle of the street. I don't know why, but I felt like hitting him. I grabbed his arm and guided him toward the alley and kept saying, "Wait, J.D., wait." But he didn't wait and he got barf all over himself and me. I took off my shirt because I was getting sick and I knew I couldn't get sick, not yet. We sat in the alley for about fifteen minutes, and I kept telling him that everything was going to be all right and all that shit that doesn't mean a thing. He stood up once and looked at me. I asked him if he thought he could make it across the bridge. He said he thought he could. It was really pretty damn funny: J.D. and I walking across the bridge arm in arm. If I had been someone else, I'd've taken a picture of us. I almost went into hysterics when he told the border patrolman that he wasn't an American citizen but a Mexican bastard who had just fucked every whore in the whole goddamn place.

When we finally got to my car, Ronnie was in the backseat asleep. The other two guys had left. Goddamn, that made me mad. I told them to stay with him. Some people never want to take care of anybody else, not even when they're drunk.

I took Ronnie home first, because I knew that no matter what happened, his parents had sense enough not to ask any questions. His little brother opened his bedroom window, and I pushed Ronnie through it. He sure made a hell of a noise. Just before I left, he shouted clear across the backyard, "Thanks, Art. And you're not a Fart!"

I drove away fast because I was laughing hard enough to wake up the whole neighborhood.

J.D. barfed out of my front window all the way to his house. It sure pissed the hell out of me because I'd washed the car that morning. But I knew I was going to end up driving everybody home that night, so I should have thought twice about washing the car.

When we got to J.D.'s house, he insisted on sitting on the front steps and singing as loud as he could. I tried to quiet him down because I wasn't in any mood to talk to his mother or answer any of her goddamn questions. Then all of a sudden, I got sick. I couldn't help it. I just had to throw up. I could barely see the outline of his mother's geraniums across the lawn. I walked over to them and let go. Everything turned loose.

J.D. came over to me and said, "You bastard, why didja heave there?"

I said, "Shut your goddamn mouth, you son of a bitch."

I'm ashamed of what happened next. We cried. We sat down on his mother's geraniums and cried. We stayed there for about two hours until everything started to clear up and the sky got all pink and the goddamn birds started making a racket. I told J.D. to go to bed before his mother woke up and saw us. Now, I wish she had seen us. I would have laughed right in her prudish face and told her that I personally had clobbered her geraniums. I think I might have even pissed on them right in front of her.

But J.D. got up and everything by shaking my hand and saying, "If I don't see you before you leave, take care of yourself, Fart."

All I could say was, "Thanks." Then I told him to hurry up and go to bed. I must have a way with people. They always do what I say, because I take care of them.

Poor Little Lamb
(Fall 1957)

Miguel Chávez had wanted to be a doctor for as long as he could remember. But it was when he stood two feet from the woman in labor, that he wished he were a doctor more than ever before in the eighteen years of his life.

She lay moaning quietly, her legs spread apart and propped up at an angle of sixty degrees. Miguel had watched surgery often during that hot Texan summer of 1956, but this was his first encounter with natural childbirth. Lost in the sterilized world of ether and surgical dressings, he watched as a blue little body emerged silently and with steady determination, ignorantly pushing its way into a life of troubles. Blood from the mother's womb flowed in a stream from the table to the floor, staining the sheets with a dull tomato-red color. It took only fifteen minutes for the ugly Mexican baby to become a member of the human race. The last connection with life in his mother's womb was cut and tied. It was done.

The doctor turned to the woman and began cleansing the inside of her belly as the crying of the newcomer mingled with the clanging of surgical instruments. Miguel watched, astonished at the indifference of the doctor as he moved his hand in and around the woman's viscera. Finally, he struck her on the exposed part of her stomach with his open palm and brought out a blood clot nine inches long and four inches wide. It dropped to the floor with a sharp smack. Miguel's intestines groaned, and the doctor laughingly remarked, "Now you know how you came into the world, Mike."

Yes, he knew. Whether he had wanted to enter the world or not was another matter. Had he been given the choice, he would have remained wherever he had existed, if at all, before entering his mother's womb. As it happened, he was born into a Spanish-American middle-class family in the state of Texas. From his race he inherited two traditional characteristics: sentimentality and pride.

The first years of his education were spent in loneliness and fear. An intelligent student, he would nevertheless sneak into the closet of the first grade classroom and cry, overwhelmed with a longing for his mother and a terrible fear of whether he would be able to do his lessons correctly on the following day. Even as a child, he strove for perfection. The crying spells became evident to his parents during Miguel's second year of grammar school, but when they asked why he cried, he could not answer. His father was ashamed of him, complaining that his first born—and a Chávez at that—was a spoiled brat. His mother, preoccupied with nursing Miguel's little brother, defended him when she could. The climax of those three years of nervous strain came on September 30, 1946.

It began with a simple headache and developed into a pain in his back accompanied by chills and fever. His father called his illness a pretense in order to gain attention and refused to call the doctor. Miguel matched his father's accusation with the determination to attend school regardless of the numbness in his left leg. Later, he triumphantly watched his father's face as the pediatrician diagnosed the paralysis in his leg as polio. Miguel was like his father: they both had the stubbornness of the Chávez lineage in their blood.

Miguel's illness, although he did not realize it until much later, transformed his former fear into confidence, and during the year of hospitalization that followed, it strengthened his desire to become a doctor. His education became all-important in attaining his goal. He was popular with his fellow students and successful in his studies. He graduated from high school with high scholastic honors and gained admission into a renowned university with the added bonus of a fourteen-hundred-dollar scholarship.

But his reason for living was torn apart in the first two months of his college education. Gradually, the talent he thought he possessed was cut to pieces. The delight he had once held for studies became a frustrated effort to enjoy what was being taught. Grades became more important than knowledge, perfection more important than actual learning. The most crushing blow of all was the realization that perhaps he did not have the ability to become a doctor. The return of his childhood fear was inevitable. It was a different fear—not only a fear of not remaining the best, but of not doing well enough to remain at the university. The sentimentality of his nature created self-pity within him, but his inherent pride would not let him admit it.

It was during a Saturday night stag party that he wondered what the climax of those few months of college would be. It was too early to tell, but something had to happen. He felt very lost and sorry for himself as he looked at his hands and wondered if they would ever deliver a baby, or hold a scalpel, or stitch an incision. In the background, a group of his college friends sang,

"Oh, we're poor little lambs who have lost our way . . .

Baaa, baaa, baaa . . .

Oh, we're little lost sheep who have gone astray . . .

Baaa, baaa, baaa . . ."

That night he got gloriously drunk for the first time in his life.

Clara Mendoza
(1957)

Clara Mendoza stroked the roof of her mouth with her tongue. She tasted the dust that diffused invisibly particle by particle. She was washing water glasses of assorted sizes in the fountain that was across the highway from the bull ring parking lot.

The water in the fountain was brown and the soapsuds looked like the cream-froth of a *café cappuccino*. Her elbows on the gritty ledge, she knelt in the sand and turned a glass in her hand, watching the reflections of the refracted bits of sunlight that bent away from it onto the water. Humming nervously, she accompanied the proud melody of "La Virgen de la Macarena" that burst from the ring in cutting tones through the heat and dust of the Sunday afternoon.

Across the highway, Luisa Mendoza leaned against the counter of the lemonade stand, closed her eyes, and massaged the bridge of her nose. She heard the trumpet and the buzzing of the flies that hovered around the three clay jars covered with overturned pots.

Seeing that the taco vendor was not watching her, she unbuttoned the collar of her Sunday blouse and began fanning herself with the flyswatter. She saw her younger sister crossing the highway, awkwardly balancing the tray of newly washed glasses. Luisa buttoned her blouse deftly and assumed a respectable and indifferent attitude.

The music announced the entrance of the bullfighters. Luisa raised her head and remembered that Miguel was last on the card.

The crowd hailed the first bull as Clara slid around Luisa, holding the tray against her waist with one hand and sliding open the yellowish panel door with the other. A strand of her black hair brushed against one of the overturned glasses as she stooped and saw that there was a spider trapped in one of them. She looked at it with disgust and fear.

There was a tumult of applause from the arena. Clara looked up and squinted to read the sign on the telephone pole, reassuring herself for the twelfth time that Miguel was fighting last. She licked her finger and held it up over her head.

"There's a slight breeze," she said softly.

Luisa scowled. She picked up one of the glasses and rubbed out a soap stain with her apron. As she set it down, she saw the spider spinning its web.

"Sometimes, Clara, I wonder if you ever stop dreaming." She lifted the glass, but the spider continued spinning and did not escape from its transparent prison.

Clara poured herself some lemonade. It was lukewarm and it made her sick to her stomach, but her throat felt dry and her lips were parched. "Shall I go get some more ice?" she asked.

Luisa was interrupted by the trumpet as it reported the judges' demand for the first kill of the afternoon. The mob in the ring was silent, there was a stifled shout, and then a triumphant "¡Olé!" The music was happy.

Clara sat on an empty mango crate and tried to remember how many times Miguel had fought. She was awakened from her unproductive reminiscence by Luisa's nudge on her shoulder. Her older sister nodded toward the parking lot where a girl was expertly making her way through the labyrinth of parked cars. She stopped in front of a side rearview mirror, straightened her dyed-red hair, and moistened her orange-colored lipstick. She opened a glossy black purse and brought out a white glove. She was putting it on as she walked toward Luisa and Clara.

"Good afternoon, dear Clarita. And you too, Sour-face." She took off her white-framed sunglasses and moistened them with two short puffs of breath.

"You're late, Arabella," Clara said to her older sister. "They've started."

"I only came to see Miguel. He's last today," she added as non-chalantly as possible.

Luisa swatted a fly with a loud whack and flicked it off the front of the counter toward Arabella.

"Hey, be careful, it's new." She jumped back, smoothing the front of her dress.

Jeers and boos arose from the ring.

"Maybe it's the last new one you'll get, eh?" Luisa said through her teeth.

Arabella walked toward Clara. "Did you pray for me at mass, my little one?" she asked, placing her hands lightly on the stooped shoulders of her youngest sister.

"I love the color of your dress," said Clara. It's green, she thought, green like that sofa we used to climb on when we were children and Mamá was alive.

"Stupid! Clumsy!" cried the mob in the arena.

"You're stupid!" Luisa had screamed at Miguel when he first moved into the neighborhood of big white houses. "You're stupid!" Arabella had imitated. Clara screamed also. . . .

They were standing barefooted on the soft green couch, leaning out of the window like three screeching monkeys curiously watching the passersby. "You're stupid!" they screamed all together and gig-gled because it was a new word they had learned from Mamá. Beau-tiful Mamá, with the olive-colored eyes and thin, straight nose, which she wiped ceremoniously while she told Mrs. Romero about their papá's shortcomings. Secretly, they had listened behind the scarlet drape separating the dining room from the parlor and heard her call their papá a stupid, irresponsible man who did not realize he had a wife and children.

"Stupid! Stupid!" Luisa cackled. They giggled until Clara dropped her doll. Such a beautiful doll, wrapped up tight like a tamale in the costume of a matador, with large staring eyes. They saw its head break into three clean pieces on the sidewalk and began to cry. They all loved it, but it was Clara who went to pick it up.

Down on the sidewalk, Miguel had stood near the Chinese elm

while Clara intermittently rubbed her nose with the back of her hand as she picked up the headless body and looked at the three neatly spaced pieces as if someone had decided just exactly how it should break.

"Why are you crying?" Miguel asked.

Clara pointed her soiled finger at the three pieces of wood.

"That's all right," he said, "I have some glue. We can glue it back together."

"Oh, no," she had stopped crying, "it won't help. His responsibility has gone out of him." She remembered having mispronounced the word, but neither she nor Miguel questioned her statement. All men have lost their sense of responsibility, her Mamá had said, and so it was . . .

All men, except Miguel, Clara thought, if she and her sisters could help it. Even as children, before they left the big white house, they had taken care of him indirectly. Once, they had even divided the parts of his body among them and prayed for that particular section at every mass.[1] Since then, they had cared for him, as those mothers care for the children they bear and are unable to raise properly, seeing him only occasionally, following his successful career in the only consistent and binding thread of their lives, the morning newspaper. They were proud of him, and because they loved him, he was their responsibility. They could be happy selling tortillas in the market during the week, and lemonade to the mob on Sunday, as long as they were a part of Miguel's life, even if, as Clara thought as she looked at Arabella, one of her sisters did things you did not mention to anyone.

The trumpet announced the entrance of Miguel's first bull.

"What's the bull's name?" asked Luisa.

"Saturnino," answered Clara, gazing momentarily at the marquee on the telephone pole again.

There were screams from the crowd as Arabella started lighting a cigarette. She took it out of her mouth and waited. Clara clutched

---

[1] Islas added a note regarding the symbolic reading of this event: "Legs and arms for Arabella. The trunk and head for Luisa. And the eyes for Clara."

at the medal around her neck and Luisa jangled one of the pots on a jar in her attempt to swat a fly.

"*¡Olé!*"

Arabella sighed and lit her cigarette. "Clara," she said, "here's some money. I'll need more cigarettes for later. Please, little one."

Clara took the money, picked up a newspaper to shield her face from the sun, and began walking across the lot toward the ring.

"Luisa . . . Miguel's asked me to marry him."

Luisa turned toward her sister. "Are you pregnant?"

"Yes. I thought you might like to know."

There were cheers and loud applause from the ring.

"I wish you and your bastard child well." Luisa began slicing lemons.

"You don't understand, Miguel doesn't know yet. He didn't know when he asked me."

The *olés!* from the mob were gaining momentum.

"Even Miguel knows how to count the months," Luisa said.

Arabella dropped her cigarette in the sand and stepped on it. "Hail, my respectable sister." She reached into the stand, brought out a glass, and reached for the lemonade.[2]

"At least I could have offered him purity," Luisa said.

"I gave him love." Arabella poured lemonade into the glass.

Luisa's laughter stifled in her throat and she began to choke. The mob screamed and there was a silence louder than Luisa's coughing. Arabella began running toward the ring.

Clara was already inside. "Mother of Mercy!" she whispered, her eyes blinded by the sun's reflection on the sand and widening with fear.

---

[2]While in the story, Islas only intimates that Arabella is a prostitute, in a hand-written addendum that appears at the end of the story, he makes sure this is a known fact, adding:
Luisa tells Arabella: "I wish you wouldn't talk like that in front of Clara."
Arabella responds: "Why not?"
Luisa: "Actions speak louder than words."
Arabella: "Well, my pious one, you can sell lemonade and tortillas, but that doesn't mean I have to."
Luisa: "It's better than selling myself."

Everyone was standing. In a corner of the arena, men in white were preoccupied with an invisible problem. A *picador* was frantically waving a light-blue cape at the bull in a kind of ridiculous and grotesque dance. The bull snorted and pawed the sand, its left horn red and dripping slowly.

Arabella ran toward Clara and looked at her, then at the white forms in the corner of the ring. Her cry seemed incongruous with the hot and silent reflections of the afternoon.

At the lemonade stand, Luisa continued to choke loudly, tears flowing swiftly down her cheeks and onto her blouse. She reached for the glass of lemonade on the counter and raised it toward her. She saw the final wrigglings of the drowning spider and the thin strands of its web floating haphazardly in the yellow liquid. She watched it drown, and squatting down like an old woman receiving communion in order to attain a youthful bliss in paradise, she poured the contents slowly onto the sand, seeing the droplets separate and role together as mercury, while a wavelet of steam rose like incense near the dead spider.

An Existential Documentation[1]

. . . because I know that what I will say has been said before by others, and probably more effectively; it will be said again in the future; it will be experienced by all who are suffering to realize their existence.

I will not color my thoughts and feelings with the words of "authorities." It is a lie to use their words in expressing myself, for if I have not realized what they are saying, then their words are only words and have no meaning for me. Students are usually confined to studying the weavings of others; perhaps that is why so few become weavers.

I was confined last year, fascinated by the weavings. Laboriously, I followed the threads of the philosophers. Their abstract conceptualizing wove alluring patterns. I cast off the garments of the Church and upbringing, and surrendered myself, naked, to the cloth of freedom.

Now, I am as a child who has had a nightmare, screaming with anguish. Everyone is growing alike and I am frightened. They are doing the same things, saying the same things, acting the same way, wearing the same clothes. They are sick with sameness and do not realize it. And I am alone, because even if I, too, live as they do, I want to break away. I know that I must be alone in order to do so. Only in loneliness will I assert my individuality.

Loneliness hurts.

---

[1]The first chapter of what Islas intended to be a theological novel, June 2, 1958.

I suppose I am looking for God. But I am a human being. I want to use my reason to its fullest capacity, and, in this way, prove to myself the dignity and depravity of man. How will I know that the God I say I am looking for exists? Does He exist because I think He does?

I understand neither my good nor my evil. I want to believe in Him. But it must be either one way or another. I refuse to fertilize the weeds of mediocre complacency.

Yet, I do not even know why I must do this. The sociologist and psychologist offer tempting answers for my motivations, but I detest their motivations. The logical conclusion of their "scientific method" is the reduction of man to a simple mathematical formula. It is easy to say that no one is responsible for his actions or those of others. It is easy to say that there is nothing wrong or nothing right.

Today, I am not sure whether God exists. There are times when I do not question with my mind or my heart; there are times when my entire being is a question mark. Sometimes I even feel that the existence of God is irrelevant; that it does not matter whether Christ was God or not; that all that matters is to live for the present, deeply and humbly. I have no reasons for these feelings. I wonder if they would embarrass anyone who read them. I do not care. A child gives no reasons for what he says; a child accepts. But children can be cruel.

I have had three interesting experiences with Bernanos' *The Diary of a Country Priest*. I loaned it to a Catholic friend of mine who goes to communion every Sunday and who looks upon me with uncertain pity and suppressed apprehension. He is going to be an engineer. After two days, I asked him how he liked it, and he replied that it was dull. I agreed that perhaps it was difficult at first, but that it was worth the effort. He said nothing for a few minutes; then in an apologetic tone of voice which embarrassed me, he said he did not think he was going to have the time to read it and for me to go for it when I wished. I do not understand him. I want to receive communion again, as he does, and believe as I did once that Christ is in the host. I feel sorry for him. But who am I to feel sorry for anyone?

Recently I met someone who believes that ideas are all that matter. He derides what he calls my need for people. He says that people, in their imperfection, only use me. He says I am a crutch and a tool. I tried to tell him that something greater transcends my need, but I faltered. I think it is true that thoughts that have stirred our hearts too deeply are always in some way troubled and confused. They are incommunicable; I think that is why they stir our hearts and insult our intelligence. It is a kind of suffering not to be able to express them. Ideas become corrupt when they are made realities in human beings, but they can be expressed. That is the attraction of the realm of ideas: it is refuge.

I digress.

I do not know why I speak to this person. He has a way of laughing at what I say. But it is a false kind of laughter, and it does not hurt me very much. Because he has not spoken to anyone in so long, he says he considers me a novelty. I think he is rationalizing. I gave him the *Diary* for his birthday. It was the only thing I could think of that would fairly give a reason for my "need" of people. He asked me if it was a gift. He does not believe anyone wants to give him anything. Perhaps it is because he has everything he wants materially. He wanders about alone in his sports car, swims in the sea, and climbs the cliffs along the shore. He claims that he has never known love or loved anyone. It is an emptiness in him that begs to be fixed. I want him to realize that he, too, is running after his soul. But you do not tell anyone such things in our society. That is why I gave him the *Diary*. Maybe he will realize . . .

It was through him that I met a girl from his hometown. She is graduating and will become a teacher. She is a Catholic convert. It is almost uncanny the manner in which I meet people at the right time; it is as if I asked for them specifically. I talk to her about the Church and I ask her why she goes to Mass. She cannot explain; she only knows that for her, it is necessary to go to church. I mentioned that I had read the *Diary*, and her Oriental eyes became translucent. You must read it again and again, she said, and you must stop thinking of the Church as a whore—she is a mother. But why do I need Her?

There is no time for the things that matter. No time. I hate time. I think that God is timelessness.

I received a letter from A today. She, also, has broken the umbilical cords of the church and occasionally even curses the idea of God. She is still in love with a married man. He has a little girl whom I have seen only several times. I know his wife; no one likes her. A says he needs her, even if they both know that what they are doing is wrong. She asks for advice.

What can I say to her? They are asleep in their own lust. They know they are committing adultery, but they refuse to realize it. I love A for what she is. She is the only human being that knows and loves me for what I am. I cannot tell her that human love is imperfect, that she and her lover will tire of each other's bodies. I cannot tell her that she is in love with God. She is a woman of infinite understanding and irrepressible love. I think she could be a saint. I love her.

Besides, it is not my problem. Or is it?

I cannot speak to anyone anymore. I cannot talk about the weather, or automobiles, or politics, or even religion without becoming uneasy. It seems that everyone in the world prefers hitting his head against a wall rather than love his brother.

I am a farce, and I hate it. I am afraid to do the things I think and feel are right because I am afraid of not being accepted. People hate the transparency of others. They prefer the respectable facade to the true core of a person. I cannot blame them. The core is so rotten.

People ask me for advice—why, I do not know—and I encourage them to do things that I cannot do. If they only knew what I am, they would laugh. If they laughed heartily, I would be glad; but they would only be amused for awhile. I laugh sometimes, but, most of the time, I revel in self-pity. If there is a devil, he exists as self-pity. I am so insignificant, a nothing, a transparent form full of air, with no pupils in my eyes. Perhaps that is why I drink in order to fill myself up and not be so transparent.

What a lot of ridiculous sentiment all this is! I am happy now, and I am unable to share it with anyone. It is much easier to share misery.

This summer I will see if poverty breeds sanctity. I will spend as much time in the Mexican bordertown as possible. My relatives will not like that. They cannot see why I bother with "those people."

I do not think it is poverty as such that is essential for the attainment of sanctity. I think it is poverty as a denial of the false god of materialism that matters. There are many other false gods to deny on the road to sanctity. I remember our Mexican maid asking us which road we would choose—the one of roses that led to Hell, or the one of thorns that led to Heaven. She would take particular joy in describing the horrors of the thorny road. Of course, it was our choice, but we were children then and had not experienced the pain of bleeding feet.

Poverty is overrated in the lives of the saints. It is not because they are poor that they are saints. It is because they know that God sees their needs and they believe, in their hunger and nakedness, that they will be fed and clothed. Some say that men will not listen to the words of Christ on an empty stomach. It is not the empty stomach of the body that matters; it is the empty stomach of the soul.

Christ did not mind being poor. But then, He said, he was God; why should He mind being poor? Perhaps if men considered themselves gods, then they would not mind being poor. But when people think of gods, they think of rich gods. There is a danger there, and people still starve—needlessly and helplessly.

I have just returned from sitting in church. I have been going lately and I do not know why. I go in the middle of the night when I am certain that no one is there. And I sit. It seems that everything I have to say has been said before I even open the door to the vestibule. I just sit. I do not even think or feel. It is absurd.

I am tired. I have not been tired for a long time. Mentally and physically tired. It is worse than being bored. My being feels like a clay statue deteriorating into mud after a few moments of observing a seasonless world. I envy those who are able to laugh at themselves and at others; those who know what they want and risk all, even happiness, in their attempt to gain it; those who sleep ceaselessly; those who believe in something as indisputable truth. I envy them, but I do not wish to be like them. I want to find myself and forget myself once and for all. But I am so tired . . .

The Face of Our Soul
(Fall 1959)

Some of us spend our lives looking for our souls which, if the truth be known, are nowhere to be found in this world. Not in one place nor in another, nor even in ourselves in these weak, corrupt, and beautiful forms we assume for no reason whatsoever. If they exist, our souls live elsewhere, waiting patiently, unable to guide or influence us except through imperfect and utterly incomprehensible means which frustrate more than serve us. Like dogs whining while listening to a Beethoven quartet, unable to grasp its purpose and only knowing that its sound drives them mad. For here, we are soul-less. What perishes is only a form, an accidental shape that, no matter how deformed or lovely, how bent toward ill or good, how comical or tragic, means nothing whatsoever, for everything tends to its own destruction and that of others. As we grow, we reduce. But there, on the other side of the earth, the soul some of us sought, thought we possessed, vainly strived for within ourselves or in the touch of the beloved other, lives its own unconnected life, imperishable, indifferent to our desires, laughter, grief, suffering, and joy. For those of my race, unable to transcend its fleshy form, perhaps there is a moment, a kind of test, when if we recognize the face of our soul, which in this life we thought we saw in another toward whom our desire impelled us, or heard in a recurring piece of music, or read in a splendid poem. Perhaps there is a moment of recognition and union that then saves us from yet another journey into one more imperfect form.

That I conceive of this, does not make it exist. These words may be the rantings of a terrified animal, smelling itself, unable to accept its extinction. I suppose it is the myth by which I live day to day because I have accepted, have had to accept, that I will not be united with the person I have loved for so long. I do believe that I will be united with my soul and that my task (very simple and not as conscious as I am stating it) in this life and in any other I may live is to come to that moment of reunion when my body and its soul will find each other at last. Else these partings and the subsequent grievings as well as the idea of coming together again, which fills me with joy to bear the grief, have no meaning, and this life, then, is truly lost.

Dear Arturo
(Fictionalized epistle, 1962)

You say to play the game with taste, but finally I've never been able to do it. Despite my background, I find good manners (or in my case, "courtesy," since that word Gary chose to describe me to you before we first met) the most refined way to lie. The only moments my grandmother became real to me were those times when she—the well-educated Mexican aristocratic lady—would weep because she had to wash the dishes because it was the maid's day off. She taught me to be polite and courteous, which I learned quickly because those qualities endeared me to everyone, except my father, her youngest son, who knew better but could not bring himself to rescue me from all those women.

But I don't want to tell you about my background; I am not interested in "ethnic" details like that. Whatever there is of the Mexican left in me will emerge in subtle ways and explain better than I will in words the differences between me and those I have loved. The heart is a labyrinth and unknowable.

I gave him an *abrazo* as I was leaving, a warm formality I don't mind exercising. I almost wept again, but the tears did not come; only my voice broke, a strange hollow sound, the sound of dry leaves.

"I love you!" I told him. He said nothing and only looked at me closely.

"I'll miss you." He nodded, still silent.

"I just need some time."

"We've got a lot of that," he said.

"You've got a lot of it," I said to myself.

Gary is so self-protective. You've taught him to cover his ass well. He'll give it to you in bed, but keep the real part of it to himself. That is why I refuse to believe that all this turns on an asshole, or lack thereof as in my case. I once asked him if he slept with me because he felt sorry for me. "You're sick," he replied in that cold-hearted way of his. It's my perverse notion that he loves me more than Eric or Tim or Paulette because he has been most cruel to me. "Between Eric and me, I know which one of us you're going to hurt." He is a master in the art of refined punishments, flashing that perfect smile, and giving you that endearing child's look (how well I know the art!) as he whips you with rejection. He'll show you just enough in order to keep you running back for more, making excuses for him all the while. He's young, you think, and inexperienced about other people's feelings. Other people, in fact, do not exist for him except to keep him comfortable and give him pleasure as he lords it over them with his superior intellect and love of opera.

He fascinates me and I cannot stop watching him. The last night we were together, as he was drinking my tears, I told him that he didn't understand all those operas he loves so well. Passion is something he avoids in himself and provokes so cleverly in others, for his amusement. "I have an embarrassment of riches," he told me in reference to all the attention he has been paid lately. Is it, as Eric says, he himself caught in the net, "the attraction of rejection?" Help me find out, Art, because I want to choose life once and for all or end it. Yes, I have more character than Eric, but that's because the past has inflicted it on me and always against my will. In those days three years ago when I was holding on to walls in this house learning to walk again, feeling my guts fall out with every step, I would curse survivals. At any rate, one develops character when one doesn't have the goods in hand, and that's the way of my life. My mistake was in asking for more food; it frightened your nephew out of his wits. It galls me to think that I prepared him up to the point where he could offer more food to someone else. "Do you hate me?" I asked Eric early last Saturday morning. "No. Do you hate me?" "No," I told him, but since Gary has chosen him, it's a great deal easier for him

to feel magnanimous. Will I have to hate Eric in order to win Gary?
I feel indifferent toward Eric. He becomes real to me only in association with Gary. I see his car parked where mine stood so many more
times before, and walk in on Gary sleeping after spending the night
with Eric who has left for work, trick towel and tube of lubricant
lying on the floor with his underwear, records that he used to play
for me on the record player. That's when Eric becomes real to me
and I detest him for helping Gary hurt me.

How casually Gary plays the game, teaching me such casual
gestures, the slight upward turn of his top lip in order to express disdain, or asking in that scoffing tone, "What are you dying of now?"
Ah, Art, what exquisite refinements you have bred in him, and for
what reasons?

Have you and I become friends, you wanted to know, during our
last elegant lunch together. To me, everyone is a friend until they
prove themselves otherwise. We simply travel in different directions,
but now it occurs to me that you are just as hidden as Gary, just as
charming, just as perceptive. I tell you everything and you counsel
me, but say nothing about yourself in return. Once when I asked you
about your life, you told me it would bore me to know. Gary's soul,
like yours, scuttles hastily out of sight whenever another confronts.
Maybe Eric's clumsy pouncing will work for him after all; Gary has
been praising him for it these last two months. Our mutual friend
wants to be captured after all, or at least he wants us to think so. Elusive monsters.

LATE FICTIONS

Tía Chucha
(January 1970)

As a child, I resented having to visit Tía Chucha. I felt that she was nothing to me, a feeling reinforced by my father, who always spoke of her (when he had to) with contempt. She was his mother's (my grandmother's) sister. That's all I knew, and because I was in my grandmother's care during the week when both my parents worked full-time to support all of us, I had to accompany her on the weekly visit to Tía Chucha's apartment.

She lived with Mr. Davis. She had lived with him for some time, and they lived together until they both died two years ago. At the time, I didn't know or care that they were "living in sin," and that my father's sisters—particularly Tía Virginia and Tía Josefina—used that as an excuse for not visiting her. Tía Chucha never seemed to care what anyone thought of her arrangement with Mr. Davis. I suppose that's what endears her to me now. When she died, she left modest sums (hardly more than a total of six thousand dollars) to those members of the family who had always gone to see her. My middle brother Mario received a hundred dollars.

I remember most the way she smiled. *Muy rancio como todos los viejos.* A little like my grandmother, whom we were instructed to call Mamá Grande and never, never *abuela* or *abuelita*. Only lower-class people called their grandmothers that: *muchachitos malcriados y sin respeto.* She would have been appalled by the term Chicano, but she would have thought César Chávez a saint.

They were the oldest human beings I knew, except for my Tío

Celso, who was really my mother's uncle and who cut my hair for free every two weeks. He smelled of shaving lotion and Vitalis. *Mi abuelita* (I can call her that now, since she's dead, and smile now at how we used to call her that behind her back and later when she was growing deaf, right to her face) and Tía Chucha must have been at least sixty when I was born, but no one has ever said how old they were for sure at any given time, not even after their deaths. Rumors from my mother's side of the family say that my grandmother lived to be ninety-two. Perhaps. As far as I was concerned, and in the callousness of my late adolescence, she ceased to be alive when she could no longer remember her own children, much less *their* children. Tía Chucha survived her some seven years, retained her wits, and smelled the same to me: of dry sticks and cats and the way hair smells when it hasn't been washed for awhile.

She was lame for all the time I knew her, and she used her cane and crutches with grandeur as if they were extensions of herself. During those visits, she and my grandmother would sit and talk for hours. I don't recall about what. They were ladies, and their conversation was for its own sake, so I never bothered to listen. Not at all like the arguments about religion between Tía Virginia and her *cuñado,* Eduardo, when we would all be ordered out of the house so that we might not hear our uncle take the name of God in vain. We heard him anyway and trembled, knowing that he would burn in Hell for all eternity. "*¡Condenado!*" Tía Virginia would scream in her rage for the Lord. And my uncle would laugh and scream back that he hoped so because he didn't want to be in heaven with anybody, especially her.

Tía Chucha and my grandmother had both been teachers in Chihuahua before the *villistas* forced them to travel north to Juárez and then, by osmosis, into El Paso. Tía Chucha remained a citizen of Mexico in order to draw some sort of pension from the government. Both certainly remained aristocrats and ladies. Their hands were never in dishwater, cleaning house was something for the *criadas* to do. The only time I saw my grandmother lose her composure was when my father scolded her for letting the dishes pile up in the sink. I remember how she held the dishes one by one underneath the hot water in such a way that her fingers would not get wet, and cried before, during, and after the whole loathsome task was done. Until the day she died, Tía Chucha refused to do menial work with her hands. And with great pride she would say, *"No tenemos qué comer, pero cuando salgo, me pongo mis guantes y mi sombrero."* God forbid that the sun should touch her skin.

I didn't like touching her or my grandmother. When I had to give her an *abrazo* at our arrival and departure, I would close my eyes and hold my breath. She would hold me just long enough for me to have to breathe again and inhale her sour acacia mustiness. Then she would give me a quarter and tell me to hide it somewhere. That way when I needed it, I would find it and be surprised. I never hid it; what good would a quarter do me years from now? Such a gift was a great sacrifice for her, but I didn't think of that. I bought my *chicles* and chewed them.

Whether or not she married remains a dark mystery of the past. I'm certain that she and Mr. Davis were lovers but in all of their life together, no one ever heard her speak to him or of him except as "Mr. Davis." He was less polite; he called her "Dolly." I don't remember ever hearing him say more than that. Their apartment, and later the house out in the desert in which they died, was filled with cats. She fed them all—there might have been twenty to thirty at a time—and made certain that a small entrance door that would swing both ways was built into their front and back doors. My mother, who is terrified of cats, always sat at the edge of the chair offered to her during her occasional visits. Tía Chucha would murmur apologies, but the cats stayed, and my mother would be sick to her stomach when she got home. But she felt sorry for Tía Chucha and went to see her as often as she felt she could bear it.

I forget when I last saw her. My cousin Chita and Aunt Emma saw her last. They had been there to clean up the house and change the linen. Both Tía Chucha and Mr. Davis had been very ill and unable to get up from their respective beds. The stench was overwhelming; cats and *cucarachas* were everywhere; the sheets were filthy. Somehow, Mr. Davis had managed to feed them both during those days when no one had been able to visit them. He was breath-

ing heavily but was quite conscious and lucid. Tía Chucha was barely alive and in a coma. Emma—who has never married, bore a child
out of wedlock, and is the most loving of my *tías*—insisted that she
be taken to a hospital where she might die more comfortably. She
asked Mr. Davis if he wanted to go also.

"No, Emma," he had answered.

"You come too, Mr. Davis. I'll fix it so that you can be together.
You are not well."

"No, Emma," he said. "I know Dolly is going to die. I don't want
to see her dead."

No one knows if he said goodbye to her before she lost consciousness or if she was ever aware that she died in a cold, antiseptic place away from her cats and her lover. I like to think that Mr.
Davis was able to touch her hands and that she knew it was he who
was touching her before they took her away in the ambulance. He
died several weeks later of pneumonia. Emma says that the house is
still out there in the desert, not yet sold, full of cats, *cucarachas,* and
the wind.

The Dead
(Circa 1974)

When Sam Godwin left him, Miguel Chico flew back to San Francisco without telling anyone anything. Over the years, he had grown so used to swallowing his real thoughts and feelings that all he needed was two long sips of a scotch and soda in order to resume the life he had made for himself in California and away from the desert. He could only think of his family in El Paso as oppressive and had decided long before that if they knew him as he truly was, they might not reject him, but worse. They would fall into that monumental silence that denied the existence of anything unpleasant in the world—especially in the Angel family's corner.

In that silence and conspiracy of denial, the Angel family reflected the attitudes and customs of the town that prided itself in having the sun shine down upon it almost every day of the year, including those days when freakish blizzards transformed the desert into a moony landscape. In Miguel Chico's eyes, what lurked underneath that sunny disposition toward everything was anything but hospitable or even friendly. Fear and hatred of anything alien or foreign to that bright and cheery facade would be dealt with summarily and with impunity.

In their common stance toward life, the town and his family reminded him of a smoker Miguel Chico had encountered once while changing trains between London and Oxford on his first visit to England. The young man sat in the middle of the small station next to the chimney fireplace and lit one cigarette after another during the hour long wait. What made Miguel recall the atmosphere of his hometown was the way the young smoker inhaled the poison deeply into his lungs and then expelled whatever remained quickly; with four or five short breaths he blew it away from him and toward the other occupants of the waiting room. In that way, although he was killing himself in an addictive and obvious manner, Miguel reasoned, the young man could retain the illusion that, in fact, he was not in danger because he himself would remain untainted outwardly by the smell of smoke on his clothes.

Miguel watched him first with some surprise, for he was filled with the stereotypical notions of how much more civilized the British were to Americans, and then with fascination when he began to see some connection to the way the Angel family always blew its smoke away from itself and in the direction of others who were—it was taken on family faith—less civilized, less worthy.

When he walked back into the house where he and Sam Godwin had lived for three years, he was still thinking about what it was in him that kept others at a distance, even when they said they loved him and admired his gifts as a human being. He walked straight to the liquor shelf in the kitchen cabinet. He had said goodbye to Sam in that kitchen and had told him that the house would be lonely without him. "The house, for Christ's sake," Miguel said aloud. He was unbearably lonely. He would live without Sam or anyone. He had been through worse, as the ileostomy bag at his side reminded him at least six times a day, although on several occasions since Sam's departure, Miguel was tempted to agree with Oscar Wilde that physical pain was infinitely preferable to psychological pain.

He opened the cabinet and there on the bottom shelf, neatly arranged and spaced, were his new friends, his allies in the fight against Anglo ennui and Latin, emotionality. Scotch for anger, vodka for grief, at least three half gallons of each for future battles and skirmishes. And in the fridge, beer to bolster his self-confidence in the company of the real men and wine to put him to sleep, his eyes wide open, during the endless and monotonous university dinner parties.

The following day, he was scheduled to give a lecture on select-
ed poems by Emily Dickinson. He himself had chosen them months
before when Sam was still living in the house. That old choker was
gone now and in his place, Miguel Chico felt nothing and no one. He
glanced at the poems as if he had never seen them, as if he could not
see them. Sam would have chided him for selecting only those that
were spoken by voices from the other side of the grave. "You are in
love with death," Sam told him on more than one occasion.

"No, Sam, I am in love with you, and it makes me feel like I'm
dying. I can't help it." With Sam, he could tell the truth without
slanting it.

"Oh, come on, Miguel, lighten up. You knew I was leaving after
three years. That's about as much as any two men can have and still
not hate each other."

He had accepted all that Sam said as the real and all that he felt
as the unreal. He had collaborated in a lie that would almost destroy
him, but that time he had responded to Sam's notion of love between
men with a force that astonished even him. "I don't believe that. You
can leave because you are not in love. If you were, you'd feel as shit-
ty as I do."

Sam held him close. "I love you, beaner. I always have," he said,
meaning it his way. Then, disengaging himself, he added, "But now,
it's time for me to go and grow up." He was packed and ready to take
the late afternoon flight to Washington D.C. Miguel drove him to the
airport, smiled goodbye, and drove back to the house, which in only
a few hours had been gutted and destroyed, although all the plants
and furniture remained in place.

Miguel poured himself a scotch. It was angry time, he could
feel it rising from his chest and into his throat like a gas flame over
which he had no control. Sam left because Miguel was somehow
not enough for him. In what ways he was not enough, Miguel would
just begin to fathom in that first year of the void. The scotch was a
balm on the flame and almost extinguished it. The poem he was
rereading rose to the surface of the page and he saw it. Captured for
a moment, he said, "'The little tippler!' Oh, my God, Sam, our lit-

tle Emily was a drunk!" The silence overwhelmed him and a new terror began creeping into his heart. God, you're going to end up an old queer. And from that moment on and many to come, he would believe that.

Reason's Mirror or The Education of Miguel Angel[1]

Modern man likes to pretend that his thinking is wide awake. But this wide-awake thinking has led us into the mazes of a nightmare in which the torture chambers are endlessly repeated in the mirrors of reason. When we emerge, perhaps we will realize that we have been dreaming with our eyes open, and that the dreams of reason are intolerable. And then, perhaps, we will begin to dream once more with our eyes closed.

—Octavio Paz

The monster in Mamá Chona's womb was now in Miguel Chico's presence. "I am a nice monster," it said to him softly, "come into my cave."

The two of them were standing on a bridge, facing the incoming fog. The monster held him closely from behind and whispered into his ear in a relentless, singsong manner. "I am the manipulator and the manipulated." It put its velvet paw in Miguel's hand and forced him to hold it tightly against his gut. "I am the victim and the slayer," it continued. "I am what you believe and what you don't believe. I am the loved and the unloved. I approve and turn away. I am the judge and the advocate." Miguel wanted to escape but could not. The

---

[1]Beginning of manuscript *American Dreams and Fantasies* written summer/fall, 1975; later appeared dramatically revised and part of the chapter titled "The Rain God" in his novel *The Rain God*.

monster's breath smelled of fresh blood and feces. "You are in my
caves, and you will do whatever I tell you to do." It moved away
from him. Miguel Chico continued to feel its form pressed tightly
against him, and the odor of its breath lingered, forcing Miguel to
gasp and struggle for air. The fog, he thought, would revive him. He
kept his back to the monster and looked down and out at the sea, no
longer visible.

"Jump!" the monster said in a tone of exhilaration. "Jump!"

Miguel felt loathing and disgust for the beast. He turned to face
it. Its eyes were swollen with tenderness. "All right," he said, looking directly into them, "but I'm taking you with me."

Miguel clasped the monster to him—it did not struggle or com-
plain—and threw both of them backwards over the railing and into
the fog. As he fell, the awful creature in his arms, Miguel felt the
pleasure of the avenged and an overwhelming sense of relief.

He awoke. The sense of release was still very much with him. He
put on his bathing shorts and, notebook and pen in hand walked out
of the cabin. The light on the smooth granite stones of the island dazzled him. He sat in his place by the water's edge. It was a sofa-like
indentation in the rocks and suited him perfectly. His feet were
washed gently by a sea that froze over in the winter and was warmed
by the gulf stream in the summer. Bending over his notebook, the hot
Finnish sun on his shoulders, he started writing. He began with the
dream.

Nina[1]

Like most Mexican-American children brought up in the forties, my cousins and I were Catholics. In that period in the southwestern part of the country, the Church taught its children to be afraid. The priests and nuns were predominantly Irish, although some were of German and French ancestry. In the poor peoples' parish on the south side of El Paso, there were two Portuguese priests who gave sermons in an incomprehensible Spanish filled with lisping and flowery language that made the children giggle and their parents wonder silently in what country these servants of the Lord thought they lived. Very few of these Christian disciples understood or cared to find out about the culture of their Mexican charges. In their eyes, we were loathsome, deprived sinners in the desert, who, before we were seven years old, had to learn that suffering, remorse, and self-sacrifice were the only true paths to God the Father. The few popular priests that had been assigned to the parish were transferred quickly to another part of the country or they suffered from nervous exhaustion.

Joy was allowed to surface at Christmas and Easter; the greater part of the year was devoted to penance and expiation. In the same town and in another religious tradition, you were to be born four years after my First Communion.

Before I attained the "age of reason," I had already received all my training in masochism without being aware of it. It would lie

---

[1] Chapter from Islas's manuscript titled *American Dreams and Fantasies*—an early draft of *The Rain God* that was written, then revised summer/fall 1975 after Islas stayed on Kokkomaa Island, Finland.

within me unnoticed for a long time until that moment when our friend in Manhattan (I will call him Sam) revealed to me his preference for S&M in sex, his voice cracking with fear that he might lose my friendship. He wanted to tell you about himself also, and I encouraged him to do so. He struck the sinner's pose in that revelation scene, and I responded to his pain by holding his hand and reassuring him of my devotion, like a parent consoling a troubled child.

In a similar scene, when you revealed your passion for another and told me that the liaison had existed throughout the time we lived together, I listened much less dispassionately.

"I still have some things to work out with him," you said, as I held your hand and placed my arm around your shoulders, shaking with fear and remorse.

"Fine," I replied in my ignorance about my own feelings, in my romantic illusions about "our" relationship.

Later, in that same confessional moment you said, "I feel as if I am on stage all the time. I'm tired of being judged."

I did not understand then that it was *my* stage you meant, my judgment you thought you feared. In my spiritual pride, for I had forced the revelation by reading the letter you had written your dream figure, I resolved to be your comfort as any true Christian martyr might be. You became my god on earth and I became your servant; so long as you kept me near your suffering heart, I felt alive. Nothing, no one else mattered; we were special to each other and apart from all others. At last, I could say with Job that my redeemer lived. For through you, in your company, beyond the particular circumstances of your wounds, which you had revealed to me alone, I saw clearly the outlines of the cross I had been told existed for me. With a joyful heart, I would shoulder it and enter the kingdom of heaven. In your perfect, healthy body, your touch, the color of your hair and eyes so like the sentimental Jesus picture cards the nuns gave to us—honey-blonde hair, icy-blue eyes glazed with sweetness—in the suffering and contrite self you exposed to me, I saw the Lord of my childhood. Good Friday was real; Easter, a ghostly afterthought with no substance whatsoever.

It has taken me many journeys across continents to learn that in the separate realms of the sadist and masochist, for S&M is the game you and I played out psychologically, the "reality" of the props—be they real or imagined, all those binding devices—is akin to the "reality" of the props in the passion of Jesus that we as children at first found terrifying and then ignored after countless prayers along the Stations of the Cross. The lesson we learned (again unconsciously, and which my experience with you has forced me to exhume) was: if a man can suffer like that, he must be God if one is God, no matter how many props are binding one's body and soul, how tight the straps around the wrist or balls or ankles or brain or heart, one need not fear, for the Daddy who is present has no reality of his own. If there is pain, so much the better, during and after, for it assuages the guilt born of the pleasure. Behold the Savior.

The dominant emotion of my childhood, then, was fear. Hell was as far away as the local movie house, where for nine cents, before and after the main feature (usually glamour girl musicals and westerns), my cousins and I sat in awe as we watched World War II in the newsreels. We sensed *that* was real and feared that the bombs were only a few miles away. The voice of the commentator became the voice of God for me. The double and separate constellations of the sadist and masochist were at work outside the Church in the military camps. If Sam and those like him are still in Hell, it is because they have preferred to remain there.

When the nuns spoke to us in Catechism about Heaven, they did so with such sweetness that immediately we knew there was no such place. Many years later at the university, reading Dante, Aquinas, and fellow Latins, I still found the idea of Heaven totally incomprehensible, as it should be. The nearest I have come to it on Earth is in the correspondences I am moved to perceive on this island far from the place of my birth. Of course, finally, such matters have nothing to do with geography, and these connections are possible even south of Market or in the Bowery, in the desert or in the fog. But here, on this island, I am aware that joy is possible in the persistent lapping of the water against the rocks a few steps away, through the grove of pine and birch and alders, and in the air that brings these sounds and smells to me through the open window. (There is a word in this language that captures the sound the water makes when it meets the rocks or the hulls of ships: *liplatus*. The accent is on the first syllable, the "i" is pronounced like a long "e" and the "a" as in "father." The "u" is said like "oo" in "moon." Said over and over, the word becomes what it describes.)

I am not speaking about the romantic impulse to identify with nature. Nature, as such, has always frightened me, and instead of surrendering to the forest or the sea, I never feel more *self*-conscious than when confronted by them. If there is a paradise for me, however, it exists in the coming together of the forces within the trees, the rocks, the water, and my still doubting, vulnerable sense of a similar and vibrant movement within myself. Sometimes, when I look up quickly from the page and out of the window at them, the motion of the leaves and of the waves beyond, fixed in a two-dimensional view for a moment, is one and the same. Gradually, as my eyes adjust, I can distinguish their differences, their absolute and arbitrary distance from each other (so like the gap between parent and child, between you and me), which only my perception can bridge. And as quickly as the second dimension falls into the third, the sense of my difference and my power apart from the landscape is felt and vanishes. One of my tasks in these pages is to describe that sense of loss, more vast than the loss of a lover or a child or a friend. I feel deeply the frustration of a dog listening to a Beethoven quartet.

Purgatory, because it seemed so much like daily life, terrified me most of all. I could see all those dreary, lifeless, undistinguished souls climbing slowly up a mountain and thought of commuters on an especially bad day making their way home on crowded, polluted freeways. In Hell, at least, one had the distinction of having attracted divine notice, even if wrathful. The Heaven of the nuns and priests and my aunts on my father's side did not appeal to me because I hated the sound of harps and the taste of milk and always, always have preferred sugar to honey. Purgatory filled me with the horror of sameness. It was forever Sunday there and somber with twilight. There was no rest from that joyless climb and each pace, consistently and imperceptibly the same, fist pounding the heart in endless mea culpas, until the longed-for shore was reached at last, and the angels stood waiting to row one across to paradise, everyone cheerful as winners in a beauty contest. What tedium. My image of you and of us kept me from seeing the horror of day-to-day life alone.

Grief, the kind occasioned by the premature and always unexpected loss of someone or something—a child, a lover or friend, an organ of the body—is like drowning. In my godmother's instance, the loss of her only son Antony has made her turn her mourning into an already profound fear of dying. Tears do not come easily to her and, because she is so stubborn in her fears as well as her loves, she refuses to drink at all any more. Thus, she has no help in swallowing her grief. With what care she sees me pour out my scotch or bourbon and then watches me sip it. When I was a child, she would sit across the breakfast table from me and make sure that I ate every spoonful of cereal and drank every drop of the glass of milk I detested. In defense, I placed the milk and cornflakes cartons between us. Her stare made it impossible for me to enjoy my food, and if she was called out of the kitchen, I would rush to the sink and throw away the milk. Poor Nina. Her intense, well-meaning yet maimed sense of loving have cost her dearly. And she, like you, like Sam, denies her pain. For her, the consequences are evident in her hysteria and feeling of suffocation when she thinks of cemeteries in the desert, of sand sliding into the folds of her burial garments. For you, the consequences remain to be seen.

Once, in a summer visit from Manhattan to this city, a year after you and I no longer lived together, Sam undressed in my presence. As I gaped at the bruises given him by one of the masters he allows access to his body (and could not keep myself from saying out loud, "Who was the son of a bitch who did that to you?"), he told me that he was not aware of his pain. He did not mean physical pain, for he became angry with that man and had walked away. I did not want to think that he was tied down or strung up at the time, since the black-and-blue marks were on both sides of his body. I wanted to understand the impulse that leads him to those men. He, like you, would have nothing of my notions that in your respective ways, you were seeking the father who had abandoned you.

"What excites you about those guys?" I asked him.

"Their anger," he said casually, and then added, "Stop trying to figure it out. You don't know anything about it."

Nevertheless, on that same journey, he wept and said that he wanted to change his life as I drove him to the airport. He was on his way to another master in Manhattan, who would take him to Fire Island for their sessions. I, misguided lover of illusions, believed him. That belief kept me from feeling what in fact was true: that he was lost to me, that my desire for his well-being could only be expressed at a distance, for in close-up, I saw him throwing himself at the masters. Toward him and toward you, like my godmother, I committed the sin of thinking that I possessed another. Only, unlike her, I allowed myself to mourn over his condition and your going away from me.

In the first weeks of that first year you were gone, I awakened to unbearable feelings of loss, self-recrimination, emptiness, nothingness. There was no sense of time moving in that house where you and I had lived together for three years. In the darkness and intolerable silence of that empty space (empty? I was there, wasn't I? I didn't think so, I felt annihilated) I was even afraid of the light slowly creeping into my bedroom. I did feel like a resentful parent whose ungrateful child has left him behind, only this time, the parent himself had become a blind, helpless child frantically scurrying about to avoid being cornered by its pain. I dreamed that in my next operation, they would cut off my legs at the knees. And in my waking hours, I actually could not walk through the streets of the city you and I had shared.

I became a child thrown into the deep water by his father before the child can swim. Did my cousin Antony strain as I did to surface and breathe an air free and clear of another's obsession and misguided affection? Did he feel any pleasure in the movement of the water down his throat and through his lungs once he had given himself up to the acrid waters of that man-made lake in the desert?

Your leaving me behind released the vapors of the numerous and separate griefs I have stifled all my life. It was a visitation of grief without escape. Has everyone been as afraid to be born as I? Is the separation from our previous life, certainly not just from the source of our immediate nourishment, so awful that we must resist it with all our might, even as we know it to be inevitable, inexorable, and completely out of our control? Did I, in these moments before leaving those other realms I have denied (at least in the flimsy concepts of the heaven, purgatory, and hell in which they have been presented to me) respond by saying, "No! I won't go!" Did I know in that other dimension and by some mechanism of a cosmic flash-forward, the life I was to lead here? Most of it seems wasteful and stupid for at the end, each of us destroys himself.

I feared failure as much as my cousin Antony embraced it in order to declare his independence from his mother's love. Your separation from me became a symbol of my separation from the womb, of having to enter into daily life on my own. For a time, I had to be fed and nourished by others, just as in the months after my operation, when they removed all of my large intestines including the rectum and anus, and I had to learn to walk and talk and eat and sleep all over again. I have balked at each birth in my life, at each shedding of an old, relentlessly clinging skin that refuses to break. When you walked out, leaving the door open to the grief that was to ransack my heart, I sounded my godmother's pain over losing her only son. For a long time after your late night plane had left the airport, I sat in the waiting room watching a young woman weep on her lover's shoulder. I felt an eerie, cruel sense of exhilaration, for my eyes were dry. I could hold onto, contain, control my grief; I was not going to be an embarrassment to myself or others, especially you. My jaw tightened as I gazed at the tearful girl across from me. Women in this country can display their hurt and cry without shame. Men must hide their injuries, and so their version of hurting becomes even more painful, for they must pretend not to hurt.

When you phoned, waking me at four in the morning West Coast time to say that you had arrived, I said, "I feel all right. You're not gone as long as I hold you in my heart." I wanted you in my arms; my body was not fooled by my mind. And my heart, oafish blind muscle, was in shock. I put down the receiver after wishing you well in finding an apartment, a new life far from me. I got up and went into the bathroom to change my bag. As I wrapped the rubber band around the bag and attached it to the appliance at my side, I imagined the rest of my life as a series of changing bags of shit and partings at airports. There was no room in my imagination for another life—a new self. Irrevocable as my gut, you were gone. The rubber band snapped into place. I went back to bed and surrendered to my grief.

Nina and Antony, I have felt both sides of your feelings for each other: those of the dutiful parent and those of the child who is gone just as we begin to know him. Only later, on this island, was I to come to question myself. Why do I need to suffer, apart from all my cultural and familial training to do just that? Why do I have to keep giving birth to these new selves? Is it so that as I pass through the canal, as I float through the jelly of loss and grief, I will be able to say what Antony could not as he floated away from us "Year! Yes! I want to be born I want to live in this world!"

María[1]

The American myth denies the tragic and erotic imagination. To look on death as an inextricable part of life or on old age, its prelude, as something to be revered, even longed for, is alien to what we are taught is the American spirit. In this society, youthfulness (not to be confused with the young) is prized above all things; old age is an embarrassment, and death is ignored altogether.

In this city, south of Market in one of those hideous hotels where the displaced and elderly find themselves, an eighty-four-year-old woman, Mary Baldwin, was found raped and beaten in her room. On Mother's Day of the previous year, she had been interviewed for a television program depicting the conditions of old people on social security. Her bright, white face betrayed no self-pity. She was asked if any of her children or grandchildren had sent her greetings of the day. "Oh, no," she replied, "I haven't heard from any of them for years. They have lives of their own and they don't need this old woman around their necks." The rapist had tied her down and gagged her; she was sent to the geriatrics ward of the city hospital in a catatonic condition. Both her hips were broken.

Denial of the erotic takes many forms: a conspiracy of silence about the erotic lives of its most respected, most often taught writers, as if their sexual conflicts had nothing to do with the styles they

---

[1]Chapter from Islas's manuscript titled *American Dreams and Fantasies*—an early draft of *The Rain God* that was written, then revised summer/fall 1975 after Islas stayed on Kokkomaa Island, Finland.

adopt to guide us to their visions of humanity; pornography and its preoccupation with the dirty joke, which denies the erotic altogether, since "getting off" requires a complete separation of mind from body and no emotional connection with the object pumping or being pumped; and in males, a training that short-circuits the emotions and suppresses them in its obsession with the power relation between the erotic and the sexual, but not in the more complex relation between the erotic and the emotional.

In your presence now, I find myself having to be on guard. Willing to touch and be touched by you, I sleep in the same bed, see and smell the tracks left on your body by others, disciplining myself away from my own sexual desire for you toward an emotional connection not dependent upon whether or not you "feel" like fucking with me. It's not easy; my instincts rebel. You retreat. The story of our respective and mutually exclusive romantic and sexual compulsions (although in the abstract, they are similar) is a tale to be told in another context. In this one, I am concerned with those myths in our respective cultures that have kept us apart, that make it so difficult (if not impossible) for one man to love or lust after another. There is nothing intrinsically dirty about the penis or the asshole.

It is a stereotypical notion among "masculine" writers that the homosexual male hates women. I have always felt emotionally closer to and more comfortable with women, except when the sexual entered into the connection, for I felt then that I was being asked to give my body without desire. A mutual friend, who shares my feelings toward women, has revealed to me that he would not be sexually drawn to other males if it weren't for his compulsion toward sadomasochism. He feels no sexual desire for those men he loves and respects, who feel the same toward him. In the sexual realm, these affectionate friends cannot fulfill his needs. How would it be different with women, I asked him; the compulsion would not disappear. He did not answer. When I last visited him in Manhattan, I arrived as agreed late on a Sunday morning in winter and woke him. Before he could stop me, I went into his bathroom. There was blood in the sink, the shower stall, the toilet, the towels scattered about. I thought of all the blood I had left behind in hospital toilets and pans. When

I returned to the bedroom, he apologized.

"Shut up," I said. "Have you seen a doctor?"

He thinks I disapprove of him because of his sexual habits. Projecting disapproval onto others, I have learned, is a way of keeping one's own feelings of guilt at bay. I was sick and frightened for him.

"The doctors all tell me the same thing," he said.

"What do they say?"

"To stop doing what I enjoy doing."

"Look, I don't care what you do with your ass, I care what happens to you. Maybe you ought to stop for awhile. Give it a rest."

"You sound like the doctors."

"I don't mean to sound that way. Has the bleeding stopped?"

"Almost."

"Are you in pain?"

"No. I took some downers."

"You'd better watch out or you're going to end up hauling a bag around like me for the rest of your life."

"Well at least I'll have more fun than you getting it."

"Right. Want me to help you clean up the fun in the bathroom?"

"Give me a break," he said.

I left. The sex of his tormentor did not matter. A fist is a fist.

In my case, too, I cannot get emotionally close to another man, but I can fuck him. I can get close to women, bask in intimacy, feel a deep connection, and not want their bodies. Many of us have been taught that self-possession is the highest masculine virtue and therefore incapable of intimacy. And so we pay homage to renunciation, fleeing from intimacy: you and our mutual friend in pursuit of independence, I through my fear of solitude.

The answer to those who believe the condition of the homosexual male to be an illness and therefore remedial is simple: who would *choose* to be a homosexual person in this or any society? Even now, the states and cities of the union are voting on whether or not to grant us the right and privilege of teaching their children (as if Socrates, who they quote out of the other side of their mouths, had never existed); whether or not to deny us a place to live; in short, whether or not we are to be considered a part of the human race. No one in his or her "right mind" would choose such a state of existence. Homosexual human beings are not freaks of nature; the history of the race attests to their existence from the beginning of time. Why doesn't anybody say, plainly and simply, that those who take the Bible literally on this or any other issue are idiots? Will a single passage in Leviticus determine the lives of millions? The message of the New Testament seems lost to most in American society: "Love thy neighbor as thyself." *No exceptions.* It is the greatest, most difficult, imaginative concept in all of Western literature.

The following portrait of my nursemaid María is a partial answer to the Bible readers; mostly, it is an examination of the way in which love and death came into my life. In no way is it an attempt to explain my sexual preferences. I refuse to deny my erotic imagination any longer, my preference for your touch above all others, my supreme delight in being inside of you, committing, the Bible readers tell us, an "abomination." María! Are you listening to the words of the child you cared for, the child you instructed out of Christian foolery every day for six years that every pleasure was a vice, especially any pleasure below the waist? I have much against you.

The American male learns to value his privacy and isolation, his individuality above all things, even family and friends. The Mexican learns from the cradle that he is part of a family and that he is only as good as his family. Like it or not, we are taught to recognize the existence of the other, to share ourselves, and this lesson spills over into our relations with those outside the family and culture; hence our reputation among Anglos as hospitable, warm, and generous. Privacy, individuality, isolation are alien, even terrifying, states for most of us. No matter how far we may stray from the family fold to universities or cities and countries where there are few or no Mexican people, the hold this idea of family has on us cannot be destroyed except at great cost.

How many times I imagined you to look on me with disdain for not wanting to close the door to my room; how many times were my gestures of affection seen as invasions of your privacy or as tokens of that illusion of us you found so stifling? "You give too much," you said in one of our many stations of the cross-country calls that first year apart; you said it after I had already given and you had already taken. Even as you let me hold you in my arms in sleep, I knew you were going to let me go in order to protect and guard your distance, your sense of self as singular and independent, needing others only on your terms. For me, freedom has always meant having no more to lose.

To be denied the sounds and smells of your pleasure is a great sadness to me. "Tell me your fantasy," I was asked by another very like you at the moment of penetration. "You are," I said, with a conviction meant for you. That other person could not have known the sense of reality he gave me, even as I was pretending to play his game, having understood that the release for him was in the fantasy, for the sensual is disavowed by these fugitives except when contained within the limits of the appurtenances they keep around their beds: chains, straps, dildos, anything to enhance what they consider the "boring" and tediously natural act of sex. I've not been able to assume that attitude.

Death and eros, then, are the subjects of the section that follows. María was part of the family from the time I was born. Like countless other Mexican women from across the river, she spent time caring for the children of others in order to make enough money to feed her own. My mother, who earned thirty dollars a week at her job for an optical company, paid María twelve dollars a week including a room and meals, so that I would not come home from school to an empty house; and before elementary school, so that I would not be alone or in my grandmother's way. Mamá Chona disliked these women, but she relied on them.

María was a smart woman with a strong back and an energy that pervaded the household. She renounced Catholicism when I was six years old and embraced the Seventh Day Adventists with a frenzy that changed her life and her behavior toward me. I have no idea from her past why she both hated the functions of and meticulously cared for the body. A letter from my mother, who had not seen her for many years, will serve as an apt introduction:

Dear Mickie,

I've been wanting to write you about María's visit because I know you have been curious about what has happened to her. She had written me during the holidays to tell me that she was coming to visit, but I didn't think she would. One Tuesday January morning, I heard someone knocking at my door around 6:30. I was afraid to open the door and when I did, there she was. A taxi driver was helping her with her suitcases, three of them, and sundry paper bags containing her vitamins, medicinal herbs, etc. I was very surprised, but both of us reacted at the same time by giving each other a strong hug. She had arrived from Phoenix at 2:30 in the morning and had waited at the bus station until morning because she did not want to wake us. She had traveled from L.A. to Arizona to visit a sick friend, then here to be with another sick friend—me.

As you know, the Seventh Day Adventists stress clean living, and judging from her, she is quite an example. She is now 78 years old and she walks and stands straight as a rod. The only noticeable difference in her after all these years is her hair, which is now all white, white. Her face is not lined for someone her age and she remembers almost everything, though once in awhile there are lapses in her conversation when she loses her train of thought. She reads the Bible constantly and of course, if someone will listen, she reads it aloud. She is a fanatic about her vitamins, herbs, and eating in general. She ate everything I cooked, although when I noticed she wasn't eating a particular food, she would apologize by saying that it wasn't good for her. I only smiled and listened to her.

She took me back years ago when I was young and you were a little boy. She remembers all the things you did, even the long white dress she made for you and how you would dance and swirl around while she and Mamá Chona played as your audience. She even got up and showed me how you danced.

She eats raw cabbage "for her mind," she says, carrots

for her eyes and turnips for her arthritis. She looks healthy enough to me, but according to her, she has diabetes, arthritis, varicose veins, and bad eyesight.

One afternoon while I was resting, she went outside and cleaned all my flower beds. She still loves gardening. We took her across the river where she stayed for a few days with a niece. Your father and I picked her up the following Tuesday on Seventh St. where she had called us from a phone booth. She had walked, through the worst parts of town completely unafraid.

She left on Thursday because it snowed on Wednesday and I didn't want to let her go. I was sad to see her leave because I thought as I saw her get on the bus that I might never see her again. I hope she comes again, Mickie, so that I can take her to visit all the family. She remembered everyone of the Angels, but only talked to some of them and to your godmother on the phone. I wasn't driving or getting out much. She told me it was all right because she had come to be with me anyway.

Your brother Gabriel came over several times when he was able to get away from his duties at the parish. Would you believe that the first time he came, even though she knows he is a priest, María asked him when he was going to get married. I thought this was rude but I didn't say anything. Gabriel, however, replied quite strongly, "No thanks. I've seen what marriage does to many people in my parish."

She promised to come and see us again later on in the year. I hope so.

Love, Mom

Several months later on my birthday, I received a letter from María herself. It was written in the kind of Spanish my grandmother deplored. It bore a Los Angeles postmark.

My Dear Miguelito,

With all my love I write you this letter to greet you and

offer my congratulations. I have wanted for a long time to find out your address so that I might write you. Your mamita told me that you had been very ill with a terrible sickness but that you are now well. I'm very glad.

Your *mamita* is very beautiful and I love her very much because she is very friendly and does not look down on anyone. I went to see her after her operation and was happy it turned out well. Your father and brother were also very kind to me so that I must tell you that a week with them seemed like a day.

In three days, you will celebrate your birthday. I am going toward old age, 79, and I plan to walk into my eighties. I wish you long life and good health. May God bless you and keep you well, so that when the Father comes in the clouds of the sky, He will take you and me with Him to live in Paradise and joy in the kingdom He is preparing for those who love Him, think in His name, and keep His commandments.

I send you a hug.
María R. v. de. Sánchez
Write me

I meant to respond to her letter immediately, thinking myself free of her influence and her distortions about religion and sex and of what one can expect from others. I put it off, although I thought about her a great deal in the days after receiving her note. I was already beginning to mourn your departure, despite it being a year away, and I was busy preparing for my first journey to this island.

Less than three weeks later, my mother phoned me from the desert to tell me that María was dead. She had been knocked down by a car as she was leaving her church services in Los Angeles. The driver was drunk. A child by her side had been killed outright. María survived a day and a night in the hospitals surrounded by fellow members of her congregation, talking with them all the while until she fell into a coma. She died on the fifth anniversary of my operation.

It was the end of the world for you at last, María. No peach tree to mark its coming or your passing. For me, the end of the world was yet to come. I was to survive it and continue talking to my friends long after its destruction. You would have loved the wildflowers on this island, and the flavor of the mushrooms and blueberries that the children and I pick every day in the forest. What, however, with your Bible in hand, would you have thought of our dancing naked on the rocks, laughing and jumping into the cold cold seas, our skins hot and steaming from the sauna, men and women and children together?

€ € €

Miguelito watched María comb her long, beautiful, black-and-white hair in the sun. She had just washed it, and the two of them sat on the backstairs in the early spring light, his head in her lap and looking up at her face. It was wide, with skin the color and texture of dark parchment, and her eyes, which he could not see because her cheekbones were in the way, were small and the color of blond raisins. When he was younger than his six years, she made him laugh by putting her eyes very close to his face and saying in her uneducated Spanish, "Do you want to eat my raisin eyes?" He pretended to take bites out of her eyelids. She drew back and said, "Now it's my turn. I like your chocolate eyes. They look very tasty and I'm going to eat them!" She licked the lashes of his deeply set eyes and he screamed with delight.

Mamá Chona did not approve of any Mexican woman Juanita hired to take care of her grandson while his parents were at work. She thought them ill-educated and bad influences on Miguelito. Mamá Chona wanted him to be brought up in the best traditions of the Angel family. Juanita scoffed at those traditions. "They've eaten beans all of their lives. They're no better than anybody else," she said to her sister Nina. "I'm not going to let my son grow up to be a snob. The Angels! If they're so great, why do I have to help take care of them?"

He could not remember a time when María was not part of his family. Although Mamá Chona disapproved of the way she spoke, she was happy to know that María was a devout Roman Catholic.

She remained so for the first six years of his life, took him to daily mass, and held him in her arms throughout the services until he was four. After mass during the week, before he was old enough to be taught by Mamá Chona, María took him to the five-and-ten stores downtown. If she had saved money from the allowances his parents gave her, she would buy him paper doll books. Her own children, a boy and a girl, lived with their father in the interior of Mexico, and when Miguel Chico met them, they were already grown up and starting families of their own.

He and María spent long afternoons cutting out dolls and dressing them. When his father got home from work at the police station, he would scold María for allowing his son to play with dolls. "I don't want my son raised like a girl," Miguel Grande said to Juanita in María's presence. He did not like to speak directly to the Mexican women Juanita took on to help her with the household chores. Mamá Chona had taught all her children that the Angels were better than that illiterate riffraff.

"Apologize to your father for playing with dolls," Juanita said to Miguelito. He did, but did not understand why he needed to say he was sorry. When his father was not there, his mother permitted him to play with them. She even laughed when María made him a skirt and then watched them dance to the jitterbug music on the radio. "Yitty-bo," María called it. Miguel Grande had caught them at that once and made a terrible scene, and again Miguelito was made to apologize. His father said nothing to him, but looked at Juanita and accused her of turning their son into a *joto*. Miguel Chico did not find out until much later that the word meant "queer." María remained silent throughout these scenes; she knew enough not to interfere.

After Miguel Chico's sixth birthday, the summer when his friend Leonardo accidentally hanged himself, María stopped taking him to mass. Instead, she spent the day talking to him about God and reading to him from the Bible, and always with the stipulation that he was not to tell his parents or Mamá Chona anything about it or it would make her very sad. She especially loved to talk to him about Adam and Eve and the loss of paradise. He loved hearing about

Satan's pride and rebelliousness, and secretly admired him. Before he was expelled from the heavenly kingdom, María told him, Satan was an angel, the most favored of God's creatures, and his name was *Bella Luz*.

"Why did he turn bad, María?"

"Out of pride. He wanted to be God."

"Did God make pride?"

Miguelito had learned that when he asked María a difficult question, she would remain silent, and then choose a passage from the Bible that illustrated the terrible power of God the Father's wrath. She loved to talk to him about the end of the world.

María began braiding her hair and tying it up in a knot that lay flat on her neck. It gave her a severe look that he did not like, and he missed those mornings when she let her hair hang loosely to her waist and brushed or dried it in the sun and he would rest his head on her lap. She did not allow him into her room anymore and asked him to leave if he opened the door and caught her with her hair still unbraided. The word "vice" occurred frequently now in her talks with him, and it seemed that everything was becoming a vice to María. She had become a Seventh Day Adventist.

His mother and María now became involved in long, loud, and tearful arguments about the nature of God and the Catholic Church, as opposed to María's true faith and religion. They excluded him from these discussions and refused to let him into the kitchen where they wrangled with each other and reached no conclusions. Miguelito hid in his mother's closet in order not to hear them shouting at each other.

"The Pope is the Anti-Christ!" María said loudly, hoping he would hear. And before Juanita could object, María cited a passage from the Bible as irrefutable proof.

"It's not true," Juanita said just as strongly, but she was not at ease with the holy book and there was no priest at hand to back her up. She wept out of frustration and tried to remember what she had learned by rote in her First Communion classes.

In the closet, Miguel Chico hugged his mother's clothes in terror. The familiar odors in the darkness kept him company and faintly reassured him. In the distance, the strident voices arguing about God continued. What would happen if he told his mother and father that María was sneaking him off to the Seventh Day Adventist services while they were away at work or having a good time? His father had said to his mother that he would kill María if she did that.

The services were not as frightening as his father's threats and the arguments between his mother and María. The proceedings were held in a place that did not seem like a church at all, it was so brightly lit up, even in the middle of the day. There were no statues and the air did not smell of incense and candles burning. And there was much singing in Spanish, not Latin. It was not the sort he enjoyed because it reminded him of the music that was played in the newsreels about the war. The people at these services were very friendly toward him and looked at him as if they all shared a wonderful secret. "You are saved," they said to him happily. He did not know what they meant, but he sensed that to be saved was to be special, and the more he smiled, the more they smiled back. They spent most of the time smiling. Nevertheless, they talked about things that scared him a great deal—such as the end of the world and how sinful the flesh was—and he could not rid himself of the guilt he felt for being there. No matter how much they smiled, he knew he was betraying his mother and father and Mamá Chona in some deep, incomprehensible way.

The voices of the women he loved were farther away now, which meant they were almost finished for the time being and would soon resume their household chores. His mother had just given birth to a second son and was staying home from work to nurse him. They named him Gabriel, and Miguel Chico was extremely jealous of him.

Opening the closet door after the voices had stopped altogether, Miguelito stumbled over the clothes hamper, and some of his mother's things spilled out into the light. There was an undergarment with bloodstains on it. Quickly, he threw the clothes back into the basket and shoved it into the closet. He was careful not to touch the garment. Its scent held him captive.

María swept him from behind, forcing him to laugh out of surprise, and trotted him into the kitchen. Together, they stood looking out into the backyard through the screen door. It was a hot day and the sun made the screen shimmer. Miguel saw his mother bending over the verbena and snapdragons that she and María took great pains to make grow out of the desert. The flowers were at their peak, and he knew from the past that the verbena, bright red, small and close to the ground, would outlast the more exotic snapdragons he liked better. The canna lilies, which formed the border behind them, were colorful, but they had no fragrance and were interesting only when an occasional hummingbird dipped its beak into their red-orange cups. On the corner of that bed, there was a small peach tree that he had planted at María's suggestion from a pit he had licked clean two summers earlier. It was now a foot high and had branched. His mother was approaching it.

Leaning over him and directing his gaze with her hand on his face toward the tree, María whispered hypnotically at his idea. "Look at the little tree," she said very softly in Spanish so that his mother could not hear. "When it blooms and bears fruit, that means that the end of the world is near. Now look at your mother. You must respect and love her because she is going to die." In front of him, in the gauzy brightness of the screen, the red of the flowers merged with the red stains he had seen a few moments before. He believed María. In that instant, smelling her hair and feeling her voice of truth moist on his ear, love and death came together for Miguel Chico, and he was not from then on able to think of one apart from the other.

Two years later, in a fit of terror because he knew the world was going to end soon, he told his parents that María had been taking him to her church. His father threw her out of the house, but allowed her to return a few weeks later on the condition that María was not to say anything about her religion to anyone while she lived in his house. The arguments stopped. She stopped reading to him from the Bible.

María treated him nicely, but she hardly spoke to him and spent more time caring for his brother. Once or twice, Miguelito caught her looking at him sadly and shaking her head as if he were lost forever. One day after school, when he was feeling bold, he said, "If God knew that Satan and Adam and Eve were going to commit a sin, why did He create them?"

"You must not ask me such things," she replied. "I'm not allowed to talk to you about them."

It was a lame answer, and he knew that in some important way, he had defeated her. He hated her now and hoped that she would leave them soon and return to Mexico. When, several months later, she did go away, he purposefully stayed at Mamá Chona's house all day and did not say goodbye to her. Juanita was upset with him when he got home.

"María wanted to tell you goodbye. Why didn't you come home before she left?"

"I don't like her anymore," he said. "I'm glad she's gone." But later that night, he felt an awful loneliness when he thought about her hair and eyes.

Compadres y comadres[1]

The sea is calm and clear today after two days of stormy weather. On the mainland, during the first early morning storm which woke me and the other island inhabitants with its rumblings, a house was struck by lightning and burned to the ground. All news from the outside is accepted here with an equanimity and concern that neither demeans nor dramatizes it. Even as the storm approached and passed over us, we did not fear its majesty.

It was not like the desert thunderstorms whose ferocity would drive my mother and her children into the most inaccessible parts of the house, where she prayed the rosary and we held hands against our ears and shut our eyes to avoid the brightness of the lightning and the bomb-bursts of thunder which made the house shake. Later, older and braver, I watched these storm clouds approach the town from hundreds of miles away, driven by Pacific Ocean winds across the desert wastes. There, unlike here on the island, no matter how enormous or how many there might be, the armies of clouds never filled the sky. They assaulted the town in separate units and with varying intensity and in a strange regularity and system so that one might look out of the windows in front of the house and see and hear a downpour while at the same time in the backyard, the sun was shining and grass, flowers, and trees remained bone dry. Different parts of the town reported flash flooding as other sections continued

---

[1]Chapter from Islas's manuscript titled *American Dreams and Fantasies*—an early draft of *The Rain God* that was written, then revised summer/fall 1975 after Islas stayed on Kokkomaa Island, Finland.

to suffer from unrelieved drought. Rain in the desert, like grace and sexual taste, is methodically capricious.

On this island, as in the City of Light and Fog, the rain is steady and prolonged, and the clouds inundate the skies in different shades of grays so that the world becomes an umbrella which rains inward, washing everything without discrimination. The air after a storm here has no scent; it punctures the nostrils with the clarity of cocaine, quite unlike the fragrance of the greasewood and Globewillows which begin to perfume the desert air even before the sky becomes charged with electricity. That is the finest, most intoxicating smell I have ever known.

It is true that the masochist creates his torturer and is therefore in control of any situation, no matter how much appearances suggest the contrary. What interests me is the collaboration of the torturer, his or her sense of what is expected in those turbulent sessions, the matching of wits and flesh in a fantasy, as if one were able to choose to be a dream figure in another's dream and still remain a dream to oneself. The sex of either does not matter, for each assumes ancient, sexless guilts and hoists them onto the scaffolds of Mother and Father. Can't it also be correct to say that the masochist acts out the role of the humiliated Mother as well as of the humiliated Father?

In the ten-year affair between my father and my mother's best friend, Lola, which of my parents was the more humiliated? Which the greater masochist? Which of them bears the greater responsibility? As entangled as you and I ("a plate of spaghetti," you described our relationship once), they too danced together for a long, long time, each in his or her own illusion about the other.

On the day of their twenty-fifth wedding anniversary (you and I were yet to meet), which my mother insisted on celebrating in the company of the entire family, with a repetition of the wedding vows at the cathedral, my father was already in love with her best friend. It was a hot August day, the kind of dry heat that oppresses but does not stifle human activity, and my mother asked the musicians to set themselves up in the patio of the dream house she and my father had at last been able to afford. The affair was to last five years before my father found the courage to tell my mother about it. Until then, she did not and would not have believed anyone else.

But on that anniversary day, only the husband and the friend knew about it, and my mother was able to live out and share her fantasy of a stable, if not perfect, marriage that had endured for a quarter of a century. All the family was present, the *compadres* and *comadres*, the close family friends, their children and grandchildren. As many people attended the celebration as had attended the wedding.

My father, a zombie of duty and habit when it came to social occasions, despite his frequent outbursts of temper over the most trivial matters, walked through it in protest and collaborated in my mother's view of their relationship. He had balked at every preparatory moment and he, not she, looked like the skittish bride at the altar when they repeated the wedding vows. None of us guessed at the truth of his difficult behavior in those weeks before the celebration. Most ascribed it to his usual antisocial manner. Everyone, especially his own brothers and sisters, knew that my mother was the real force who kept him in touch with them. They knew they could rely on him in times of trouble, but they also knew that for reasons of his own, he preferred to maintain a life apart from the family.

My mother attained her desires that day. It was to be the last time for many years. After the church service, family and friends were invited to the house in the late afternoon for a dinner dance. She wore a pale-blue silk dress and her prematurely, and completely gray hair gleamed in the rays of light that slanted through the trees into the patio. My father was wearing the dark-blue suit she had insisted on buying for the occasion (he had refused to wear the white dinner jacket she thought more appropriate). My Uncle Félix opened the first bottle of champagne, pink and sweet and purchased by the case more cheaply across the river and paid tribute to the splendid pair before us whose marriage, he said, was an example to all, especially those of us in the younger generations. Overcome by emotion, both feigned and genuine, for he knew my father well and was a great sentimentalist, Uncle Félix dropped the bottle, which did not break, recovered it, then served my parents their glassfuls as my mother handed her small bouquet of garnet-red roses to Lola. In a dark-green chiffon dress, Lola's tawny hair seemed even brighter. She was standing behind my mother and slightly to one side so that my father could see them both as he drank his wine. The waltz began to play and my mother and father danced together while the rest of us, struck with delight, looked on just as the older generation had seen them dance twenty-five years earlier, weeping with joy, for the greatest sentimental moment in Mexican culture is the coming together of a man and a woman in holy matrimony. The waltz ended.

My mother insisted that my father dance with Lola next because only a month earlier her husband, El Compa, had died and she was now a lonely widow. I watched the three of them from the other side of the patio. The sun was behind the foothills and had turned the mountain behind them into a rose-colored stone garden. The trees my father had planted in the back and side yards were beginning to cool the air with their scent; the crickets, lizards, and sparrows could be heard above the blaring of the *mariachi* trumpets. I believed in my mother's vision of love and romance; I wept at their seeming happiness. I even for that moment forgave her for marrying my father.

I watched her place my father's hand into Lola's. She kissed them both and went to see about the serving of the dinner. I did notice that Lola looked at my father as if he were a stranger before he took her in his arms for the next dance. Standing next to me, his eyes snapping into focus through the many cups of wine he had already drunk, Uncle Félix nudged me and said, "Will you look at that?"

In another part of the patio, my godmother put down her glass, walked over toward us, and said to Uncle Félix, "Why don't you cut in? They've danced long enough." My mother came out of the house. The desert was now the color and texture of her dress, and candles were being placed all over the patio and garden. Before my uncle could reach Lola and my father, my mother intercepted him and began dancing with him. I looked at them and then at my godmother. Her enormous jaw was locked into place.

"What's wrong, Nina?"

"Never mind," she said quietly, then, as if on guard against the inevitable, she added harshly, "Nothing. Why don't you ask Lola to dance?" My godmother, like Mamá Chona, has never had any patience with the romantic illusions of others. Instinctively, I obeyed. Making my way through the dancers toward my father, as later I would toward one of the two people I have loved obsessively, I saw with Nina's and Félix's eyes. My certainty was fixed when I heard the tone in which Lola called my father a *sinvergüenza* as he relinquished her to me. The word is untranslatable; literally, it means "without shame." I saw, too, my mother's dreams of romance and love vanish into the desert twilight, just as mine, years later, would dissolve into the fog, leaving behind them a stench worse than that of death.

For the living dead to let go of their past, of those myths which have formed them from without, or which they themselves have formed inwardly (sometimes overlapping and reinforcing the external influences that have shaped them) is a difficult, perhaps impossible, labor of love. Had I been born in another country with its own history and fantasies about itself, it is obvious to say that I would have been different. Would that have changed the inner myths I fashioned for myself out of moments that at the time seemed to have no meaning, no bearing on the way my life has been? Only later would those moments take on significance, even suggest a pattern (so much am I still a lover of order to believe in patterns), but how could I be sure that with different eyes I would not select other moments to create shapes of meaning for myself and the ravages I have caused my heart and body? For I have been relentlessly cruel to both. Yes, the body may be the temple of the soul, but what if the soul rages against and yearns far more than the body can withstand? Which is the true master?

I know I cannot subscribe to the North American Protestant myth that places mind over matter, that ignores physicality in such a way that relegates the needs of the body to an inferior place, that praises those who "rise above" their infirmities and carnal desires, while paradoxically worshipping and rewarding above all creatures, the youthful, athletic body. In what other country are people led to believe that life is over at twenty-two, that the period between twenty-three and sixty-five is one long dutiful march toward the inevitable, and heaven help those who live beyond sixty-five?

The "mind" in mind over matter has peculiarly North American qualities for me in that it denotes power. In that sense, it is different from the mind as soul, the kind of soul my grandmother wanted us to have. I am willing to admit that my mind (as a power) is creating my stomachache if those who are standing by the bed telling me so will admit that both my mind *and* the stomachache exist.

When I said to you that it seemed unnatural to me not to make love to you after our many years of friendship and love for one another, you replied, "Don't think about that," and dismissed my desire for you without a qualm. My mind may be creating my desire; *both* exist. Like a laughing, taunting ghost or scornful shadow, my desire creeps up behind my mind, which, although arrogant in its power, has no way of predicting the appearance of desires. As tempted as I am, I cannot be a solipsist or a Christian Scientist. This silent, self-contained island will exist quite apart from my perceptions of it. No power of the mind will reshape my digestive tract, and my desire for you? We shall see. Hence the contrary and still true clichés: "Absence makes the heart grow fonder" and "Out of sight, out of mind." Notice that one speaks to the heart, the other to the mind. The first has applied more to me than you; the second has been your touchstone.

The mind as a source of power is the greatest fucker of them all. I see it as "American," the heart as "Mexican." Are you beginning to see the workings of these mythical structures and their force in my perception of you and me. I am coming to you, Father.

Like my father, I have learned that each of us is an island and that the best we can expect of ourselves is to learn to navigate from one island to another in fair or foul seas, trusting that the harbor we have chosen to visit will be receptive or, if not, ready to turn back without regret or feelings of defeat. The heart, not the mind, is our sailing vessel to another; at best, our minds calculate the force of the winds and tides—a force that the heart, following its own course, always, always considers conquerable.

It is an American commonplace that all males must suppress their emotions in order to be masculine. They must never admit to fear, they must never cry, they must never succumb to passion for another. These "negative" feelings are considered feminine, therefore weak, and somehow inextricably bound to the chemistry of the female. Women, poor creatures, must identify with their bodies; men, on the other hand, are free to identify with their minds and ignore their bodies, except when they choose to compete with other men in games of force, which include courtship and war. The one emotion allowed males (not females) is anger, and all the better when it can be channeled into aggression, either in sports or combat.

I have often thought, when considering Sam's life, that S&M among homosexual males is a substitute or surrogate "virile" activity for what among nonhomosexual males takes the form of streetfights or rough sports. All these dreams of virility: the toughness of the cowboy, the training of the young soldier, the impassivity of the cop, the bragging of the boxer, the calm of the quarterback, the inexhaustible energy of the playboy, the control of the pitcher—all find their counterparts in gay bars across the land. Both the reality and appearance of these masculine conditions, these roles considered acceptable for males in American society, guarantee a paralysis of emotion.

My father and his generation were at the mercy of these stereotypes in a distinctive manner. They were first-generation American citizens; they had to prove themselves "men." Most of them believed in the idea of equal opportunity for all, even if examples of inequality under the law were daily under their noses. They believed, too, that they could be free, independent, self-reliant men.

In their cases, however, they were not immigrants, although it was a fact they and the rest of the country ignored. They migrated northward into a land and into traditions that had already been established. They crossed no ocean for the purpose of breaking with their past in order to create completely new lives for themselves. My father may like to believe that he has broken his ties with Mexico, but the facts of his life are against that belief. In their imaginations and whether they are aware of it or not, my father and those in his generation have remained Mexicans. Their Anglo friends and enemies are always called "*americanos*" by them. They call themselves "*mexicanos*." Their language (either Spanish or English, or a vibrant and comic combination of both), their food, their music, their culture are clearly Mexican.

And like most Mexicans of his generation, my father has had to struggle against a feeling of inferiority for being Mexican because of his experience with the economic failure of Mexico and the unparalleled success of this country in providing for their respective peoples. To this day, despite most of what has happened to him, my father insists that this nation is still the land of opportunity, and as much as he enjoys traveling, especially on the freeways between Texas and California, he has never returned to his homeland, except across the river on business or family duties. What interests me most about him in relation to all these elusive myths is how notions of *machismo* merged in him with the notions of masculinity propounded by this country to push him into the most isolated and lonely role of any member of the family.

My father is the true hero of the reflective commentary which follows, perhaps of the entire work. No one has had to suppress more; at the same time, no one in the family has indulged himself more (with the possible exception of Uncle Félix). No one has had to bear the burden of the family name at greater cost to his own feelings of grief or love or joy. For most of his life, he has had to live up to rigid codes of virility. Only once—as you will see in what follows—has he broken down. He did so in front of me. At that point in our relationship, I was still full of hatred and anger toward him and I responded cruelly. Within the last few years, now that he has retired and no longer needs to prove himself according to any code, his three sons have been able to talk to him and he to them. It's as if the threat of impotence no longer controls him. None of us has been able to compete or overtake him in the sexual realm. God knows, two of us—my brother Rafael and I—have tried. The other, Gabriel, has offered up his sexuality to God, although his understanding of it (because he is my father's son) has not been diminished, and he is a worldly counselor to those who come to him sick with love and lust.

The notions of virility in this country exalt a man's brains and his balls above all. He who can master both and use them to his advantage is the champ. In an appropriate turn of the language, the man who allows his emotions to get in the way of his mind or crotch will get screwed. My father learned that lesson well; nevertheless, his heart—as you will see in the end—intact and never lost within alien traditions, transformed his defeats into an acceptance of life and of himself that, if not fully formed, is palpably there. It's the kind of acceptance I want to come to with respect to the person against whose body I still stumble and fall.

To reach where he is, my father did not resort to alcohol or drugs, and he even smokes less now, perhaps because Lola is not there to ask him to light her cigarette in a tone that hints at infinite sexual possibilities.

The following section pays as much tribute to her as to my mother and father. Through them all I have felt the force of the perpetual triangle that seeks to combine in its crimson labyrinth of deception and gullibility all the qualities we imagine must constitute the "perfect" love. There is no such thing, of course, except in our own yearnings for the inaccessible. (As a birthday gift you gave me the first five symphonies of Mahler.) What other human activity than that of love and lust (with the exception of listening to music) brings us closer to the illusion of and yearning for the unattainable? Even when we delude ourselves into thinking that we have found and captured it, the forces of decomposition are already at work. What is the drive that compels us to seek outside ourselves the companion who will share our lives from head to crotch to toe, as if without this dark or bright complementary figure, we could not survive in the desert? Like my father, I imagined another capable of meeting the demands of my heart, only to find (and not believe for a long time) this very creature shaken and tired, driven by cruel impulses, standing before me one day and saying, "I cannot live according to your illusion of our relationship."

I meet my father's mistress again after eleven years. As physically attractive, as youthful as ever—the true demonic spirits are forever beautiful; sin does not wither us, virtue does—Lola seduced everyone who sat at the table that night in my favorite San Francisco restaurant. The green eyes, the liquid, golden voice, the laugh that charmed even my mother again after it was all over and that evoked all the courtesans in history, could not cover the basic, self-protective coldness of her heart.

My father excused himself from the table. A little drunk I leaned toward her, asking how she thought my father looked. "Oh," she said, "he never changes. You know him." It was a comment my mother might have made and in almost the same resigned manner. "I like to be with him once in awhile," she went on, "and get all I can out of him." She jangled her silver bracelets like a spoiled, delighted child pleased with its gifts. The others at the table stopped in mid-conversation to watch her. My father returned, the waiter behind him. I ordered another drink.

When we parted outside the restaurant in the fog, Lola, assuming her role of adopted aunt in the family, hugged and kissed me goodbye. "You look good," she said with affection. "You've been through a lot because of that operation, I know." I believed that she felt genuinely happy to see me, and she said so as she offered me her strong, delicate hand.

"I wish Mother had been here to enjoy the evening with us," I said.

"Yes!" she replied, smiling, the dull look of guilt veiling her face. Instantly, I regretted my words, for I had meant them sincerely and without malice, assuming that she missed my mother as much as my mother missed her. With creatures like Lola, however, as with crabs and lobsters, one must only offer the finest tidbits of food in order to lure them out of their luxurious caves, for they are concerned with feelings only as they relate to the senses. They avoid any contact with the difficulties of human emotion. In their solitary comfort, spending time on land only occasionally, they are more concerned with the needs of their bodies than with the more complex workings of the heart. Sensual, seductive, offering the tastiest flesh, they thrive in the coldest waters and develop enormous claws.

Lola took her hand away from mine. "It's cold," she said girlishly and shook herself in a mock shiver. She couldn't possibly be cold in the fur coat she was wearing. I wondered briefly if my father had given it to her. He emerged from the restaurant, lighthearted and magnanimous, his innate generosity unchecked by years of my mother's concern over money. After embracing me, he gave me his hand. There was a twenty-dollar bill in it. "For cab fare to the airports," he said. I was bothered that it might be a reward for having behaved myself so well with his mistress. How could I let him know that because of my own experiences I understood him now and no longer judged anyone with the prudish eyes of an undergraduate who has made straight A's all his life. That conversation was to occur later. At that moment, I was moved by the gesture without knowing why. Part of the reason would form itself on my way to the islands in the Baltic.

"Thanks, Dad," I said as affectionately as I could. In the past, I had always resented his giving me money and saw it as his way of buying me off. I hugged him back. Sometimes, our finest instincts, formed mysteriously, lead us despite our training or cultivated distrust, to act in a loving way however simple or unconscious the gesture may be. Later, after they had walked away from me into the fog and on my way across the continent, I saw again, in a jet-plane revery, Lola's beautiful legs receding into the mist and caught her scent always, enigmatically unspoiled by cigarettes. And it occurred to me in a rush of sentiment, that in that last embrace, I had felt for the first time in our lives together, a genuine affection for the man who is my father. He had survived his ferocious passion; he had rebuilt a home he himself had set on fire.

Before I came to appreciate the drama my father, mother, and Lola had constructed, and hiding behind my professorial pose, I enjoyed recounting my parents' love story to my friends in the fog. I did so knowing that I was breaking the family rule never to discuss such matters with outsiders. It was a betrayal of the worst kind. I knew that my grandmother would not have approved and that my father would be angry. I was not sure what my mother would feel about it.

"Your Mother's too good to be true," one of my guests, a woman, said.

"Yes, that's what she is," I replied.

The men at the table remained silent.

"How old are they?" asked another woman.

"Sixty, this year."

"Ahhh," she said with a smile, "the libido never dies."

Everyone laughed.

La familia feliz[1]

I suppose if she was alive and I spoke to her about it (assuming a relationship between us that in fact never existed between her and her own children, much less her grandchildren), my grandmother, no Proustian angel, would have condemned my life. She passed judgment mostly by ignoring facts, a trait that has survived in my aunts Jesús María and Eduviges, and to some extent, my father. Félix, Mema, and Armando—her most blatantly wayward children—escaped from the tyranny of their mother's illusions about the family and its divine connections. From their own harsh experiences, they knew better.

Mamá Chona insisted that the world was exactly as she saw it: a place to keep up appearances, never to let down one's guard, and always, always to put on the best possible face about anything scandalous which might touch upon the family, even if it meant seeming to collaborate with those who were committing injustices against those very members of the family she sought to protect. An untarnished Family Name was all-important, and facts were intrinsically dirty to her.

It was to be years before I learned how joy had died within my grandmother's soul and why she treated everyone as if they were somehow removed from her. Even I, one of her favorites, was perplexed by her inability to touch us or to look on us as physical and

---

[1]Chapter from Islas's manuscript titled *American Dreams and Fantasies*—an early draft of *The Rain God* that was written, then revised summer/fall 1975 after Islas stayed on Kokkomaa Island, Finland.

grounded creatures with bodies whose needs she chose to ignore in a different, more metaphysical way than the American manner I have spoken about. In her silent and persistent devotion to the other-worldly, she taught us that to be loved by her, to be truly worthy of the family name, we must indeed become angels. Her relentless belief that human beings, particularly those related to her, could attain to such a state never faltered even in the face of all the disappointments she suffered at the hands of her unreachable children. She was a religious romantic. In her world, reality was an obstacle and had no meaning; and she was uncompromising in her beliefs.

I do not know that any of her children, with the possible exception of Jesús María, ever spoke to her about the reality of their lives. My aunt's tirades, predictable and perpetual, were self-pitying and angry, and finally not attempts to make her mother see her for what she and her life were. I doubt that any of my father's brothers and sisters would have dared to attempt that destruction of their mother's illusions about them or her dream of the happy family. And so, they lived out their mother's fantasies, constantly aware and afraid of their failings, rebelling or capitulating when their frustrations were no longer tolerable. She did what American society does in subtle and selective ways, first with one "minority" and then another (that women, the other half of civilization, are considered a "minority" shows how destructive such thinking can be): she denied the reality and the imaginations of her children.

When I have heard you speak of your family, which is one-twentieth the size of mine, of the expectations your family has had and still has for you, your descriptions remain abstractions. For you, the idea of family has only as much reality as you give it, for one of the measures of your maturity is that you are expected to break away from it. Their expectations for you are, to a much greater extent than mine, self-imposed. For me, although the same principle might be applied, the sheer bulk of history (a past which cannot be denied is un-American in spirit, isn't it?) and its great physical dimension, give flesh to the idea quite apart from my own will to escape from or join my family. In a way, we are back full circle to the differences we taught as men and that exist between you and me. In my long life among Anglo-Americans and their institutions, Protestant and north-eastern at base and in influence, in my extended contemplation of your meaning in my life, in my obsession about you long after any cause or reason has been left to feed it, I have never seen them or you or heard them or you speak about their families in ways that begin to approach the fantasies Mexicans have about their families and the ways in which they create their lives according to those dreams and expectations. The Protestant, Anglo-American devotion to the individual and to the privacy of the individual, saves you from, as well as deprives you of, much feeling.

To confront someone directly with your emotions is alien to your spirit. To talk about feelings abstractly is the mode you prefer. To give yourself away is the most horrible act you can imagine, for it means exposing your vulnerability to another. You confess to your gods directly and in isolation; we require the presence of another human being, priest or friend, relative or lover, to express our shames and flaws. The idea is that on our way to the Others we find ourselves as well as the Other. My fate has been to seek out and worry over and bruise myself against the locked door on the other side of which is the most desired figment of my imaginations: the inaccessible One. I have stopped asking myself why, even as I have attempted explanations in these pages.

How many times have I seen you nod in assent when you over-hear anyone say that there are some things it is best not to tell about oneself to parents or loved ones? My own life seemed half-measure until I could finally bring myself to share it with my parents and brothers, fearful as I was of their reaction. Are you then, like Mamá Chona? In some ways, perhaps, but with vast differences in how this seeming similarity came about, as I hope will be made clear in what follows.

In one of the recent family gatherings, last Christmas, the day before you and I lay together for the second to last time, the old family myths were in full force. I was introduced by my university title to cousins twice removed in order to impress upon them the importance of a good education. They all wonder why I have not married and have learned from their parents, who are in my generation, to attribute it to my operation. That night, I perceived them all in a haze of pain about having to part from you yet once more.

Mamá Chona, long since dead, was nevertheless very much present that evening. She would have taken her place at the head of the table, now buffet to accommodate the almost fifty members of the family present (the absent ones were asked for in accusatory tones). Now, we sat around on sofas and the extra chairs borrowed from neighbors for the occasion, the youngest children on the floor in the center of the family circle, like a vibrant, writhing oriental carpet in their Christmas costumes. The sense of family solidarity pervaded in the way everyone was conscious of their place to sit down. As usual, the various generations gravitated toward each other.

It was my father's sixty-fifth birthday. The bastard son of the family and his wife were our hosts; Ricardo's children alone have carried the Angel name beyond my generation. He is Mema's illegitimate son and was adopted by Mamá Chona and Uncle Félix; thus he became an Angel. My father, who has always favored him and has treated him as his own son, had spoken to Ricardo about me. I did not find this out until the following day. The evening of the party, despite my preoccupation with you, I noticed Ricardo's coldness toward me. Ordinarily, he embraced me warmly as I entered his home; this time, he barely took my hand and he looked at me in a distant manner, his eyes glossy and two-dimensional. I thought it was because he had already drunk too much. A while later in the kitchen, I noted how carefully he watched as I greeted and spoke to his sons, both many years younger than I.

Unable to tolerate my anguish about you any longer, I made my way through the children on the floor and to my brother Gabriel. I, who had not practiced any of the sacraments for years, felt a great need to confess. We found a place to sit alone in Ricardo's bedroom. I began slowly.

I told him I wanted to let you go, that I did not want to be bitter about the past any more, that I did not want to spend a lifetime imagining and then hating my rivals, your dream figures, and finally you; that suicide was preferable to and more dignified than a final ten or less years as a withdrawn, lonely, drunken queer. I told him how much I hated those who are physically healthy, because I cannot compete with them; how much I hated those who condemn my way of life, who deny me my imagination; how I hated Mexicans and Anglos, straights and gays alike for all their expectations and fantasies about me. I explained to him that I was not confessing my sins and that simply talking to him was absolution enough for me.

He listened to me with care, closing his eyes now and again, summoning, I know, the powers he believes in. "Let him go in love," he said, his hands in mine, his eyes piercing through my tears.

"I want to and I can't. I don't know why." I broke down. At that moment, Ricardo walked into the room, ignored me, and told us that it was time to sing for my father. I focused all of my hatred on him. My brother put his arm around me and led me out of the room. Ricardo walked down the hall ahead of us. I envied his place in the family, even as I loathed his bigotry and willful ignorance.

"We'll talk more about this," my brother said and kissed me on the cheek.

Kokkomaa[1]

Perhaps in some crazy historically tragicomic way, you and I are still waging a holy wars—Protestant England versus Catholic Spain. In my concentration on New England Puritanism, I have not forgotten that the Spanish version of it was just as destructive, just as cold-blooded. That strain influenced Mamá Chona's views about sex and religion as much as I imagine the English strain has influenced Sam and you. At the center of these myths, used by different nations for their own wretched purposes, is the Cross. Sam, can I bear it? He came that we, *all of us,* might have life and have it more abundantly. He called us brothers and sisters. Then He went away.

In one of our last talks at the breakfast table (you had made pancakes), you read to me portions of the newspaper article about the winding sheet in Turin, about how the scientists would determine its chronological authenticity through radioactive means. You were fascinated. None of our talks has ever been about religion. Then you described to me how you had been told a human being died when crucified. First of all, you said, the Romans tied, not nailed their victims to the wood; if they did use nails, they drove them through the wrists not the palms. (Does that invalidate all stigmata? I hope so.) In that hanging position after awhile, the rib cage begins to press into the lungs and the person dies gradually of suffocation. As you spoke, I thought of a figure I had seen drawn by one of Sam's masters. The

---

[1]Chapter from Islas's manuscript titled *American Dreams and Fantasies*—an early draft of *The Rain God* that was written, then revised summer/fall 1975 after Islas stayed on Kokkomaa Island, Finland.

figure was strung up and spread-eagled with manacles and chains at the wrists and ankles. Written across the chest was Sam's name and there was a curled up whip in the background on the right-hand side in the corner.

At the time, Sam, who had shown me the drawing to distract me from the syringes on his dining room table (which, he said, were filled with penicillin), laughed at the look on my face, took the drawing away, and tore it up. He threw it into the air like confetti and shouted, "Happy New Year! The hottest man in town wants to play with me!"

We were in Sam's very expensive East Side apartment waiting for his guests to arrive. The reflections of the light on the river illuminated the ceiling and walls so that when he stood up and moved between me and the windows behind him, I saw him as a shadow dancing about. The glare was blinding. He had asked me to come early so that we might talk.

"You're uncomfortable here, aren't you?"

"No! It's the glare that makes my face look like this," I lied.

"You don't like the way I live, do you? Or my friends?"

"What does it matter, Sam. Stop asking for my approval. You seem to be happy enough."

"I am. I was dying in San Francisco. I wasn't able to stay there and let go of that twinkie who fucked up my life. When are you going to let go of yours and start enjoying yourself? You don't have to suffer all the time you know."

"Sam, I'll make a deal with you. You don't talk about that and I won't say anything about this chi-chi den of iniquity you've got here."

"I want you to like me," he said.

All the little boy charm glowed in his lovely dark eyes. Did he look like that when he asked them to tie him up? He was my age and held a responsible position in the United Nations. He had given up a tenured position in the best university on the West Coast when he accepted the job in Manhattan. I did not share in his enthusiasm for New York City. He spoke of it as if it were the promised land for faggots; I saw it as a glitzy garbage can. I thought that his age and his fine work would "save" him and that he would "outgrow" his compulsions in time. I wanted to think that he might be growing through them, and in that way might bring himself to leave them behind. I was still enough of Mamá Chona's grandson to think that indulging one's vices is not a way to overcome them.

"Oh, Sam, I do like you. That's why I'm bothered by what you do and the kinds of people you have around you. Give me some credit."

"Okay, but don't look so sad when you're here to have a good time. It makes me feel guilty. My friends here don't trust you." He had put away the syringes.

"Good. I don't trust them. I think they're all lost little boys trying to act like men by pretending to beat each other up and getting off on it, and usually with the aid of some drug or other."

"There you go again, Mommy."

He was dancing jigs around the room. I'd never known him to sit still except when it was demanded of him by his work. Once, after I'd heard him give an hour-long lecture in a small seminar room and watched him for another hour patiently answer the questions his talk had raised, he grabbed me and said, "Take me out of here and to a dance hall, honey. One more minute without moving anything but my mouth and I would have cracked."

"Yeah? Well, if your friends aren't trying to get back to Mommy, they're getting back at her. Same thing. Next time, I'll wear a dress. That'll scare the pants off them."

"Oh, not I?" He pounced on me and hugged me for all the world like El Compa. "You nelly faggot," he said.

"Oh, do it to me, Big Daddy. Whip me, chain me to the bed, and let me have it."

"No way, José." As a joke, he introduced me as his "beaner friend, José." He pronounced it Ho-zay. "I never do it with anyone I love. Too dangerous." Then, placing his hand delicately over his heart and in his best Rhodes scholar accent he said, "'Oh, these men, these men.' You know where that comes from, poet? I'll give you extra points for telling me who says it."

"I'm not a poet. I can barely write prose. And I hate games like these. Everyone always takes advantage of an English teacher. Testing, always testing."

"Admit it! You don't know! Shakespeare, my dear, you should have said, since that's a safe all-encompassing guess. Desdemona." He swooned into a chair. "Want a hit of acid before the men get here," he said in his best macho manner.

"No, thanks. I already see 'the men' at the end of a tunnel or distorted in one way or another."

"Heah come de judge," he said and laughed and laughed.

"Don't worry, I'll keep my mouth shut. I promise to talk only about the latest trick and the hottest disco. And I'll even pretend to smoke the dope and swallow whatever pill is being passed around. Just leave a bottle of scotch in the kitchen for me, will you?"

The first guests were being let into the entry hall. Sam looked at me starkly. "Don't leave me," he said.

Before I could respond, two leathermen walked in. "Hi, Girls!" Sam said and walked toward them.

It was our last extended conversation. He invited me to his home on Fire Island the following weekend. I went and stayed less than twenty-four hours. In my imagination, I kept seeing you everywhere and I had to get back to my real island in the Baltic, far from the tea dances and the drugs and the sexual games of rejection. Sometime before dawn, I got up to go to the bathroom. Sam was in the living room with his trick. They were resting in between bouts in front of the fireplace. I was naked and had my hand over my bag; it needed changing.

Sam called me to him. There were no bruises on his body this time, no blood on the sheets. He had lost some weight and his well-proportioned muscular body glowed with energy and life. He introduced me to his trick. I felt self-conscious about my leg and the bag. I envied the trick's healthy animal body. They were both, Sam informed me, on some drug I'd never heard of. I excused myself.

"Now, wait a minute," he said. The drug did not slur his speech; if anything, it made him even more lively and talkative. I have always loved the sound of his voice. "I want to go to the bathroom with you."

I didn't argue with him because I didn't know what form of paranoia the drug might produce. I've learned to let all addicts I know have their way; it reassures and pacifies them. Cowardly on my part, perhaps; I don't know any more what is cowardly and what isn't in these matters.

"Okay, but you won't like what you see," I said as cheerily as possible.

In the bathroom, he stood by me as I emptied one bag and replaced it with another. He stopped me from flushing it down. He struck the clinician's pose and asked me questions about the appliance, about the piece of gut that protrudes, like a smelly rose, from my abdomen. I was enthralled, no longer self-conscious. He even asked me to show him how they had sewn up the anus. I did. I was a little kid again exploring with my cousins the secret places in our bodies we were taught were dirty. "Just like a mannequin's, huh?" I said. He remained silent.

I turned to face him and leaned against the sink. He squatted before me, his hands on my hips, his eyes at bag level. In spite of myself, I began to get an erection and tried to cover it and the bag with my hands. He pushed them away. For a long moment in his drugged state, he looked at the workings of the appliance and bag. It was beginning to fill up and I hated it. I saw it as a cruel emblem of what separated me from other people. Then he stood by the toilet and went through the motions of emptying and changing the bag. He flushed the toilet. I was hypnotized.

I knew what he was doing. Once, when I first visited him, he limped all day through the streets of Manhattan with me. "Sam," I asked him finally, "did somebody hurt your leg?"

"No," he said matter-of-factly. "I'm seeing what it's like to be you. It makes me feel closer to you. The world jerks up and down a bit when you limp, doesn't it?" I had kissed him in the middle of Sixth Avenue for that.

This time he said, "You know, it's not so bad. You're still a beautiful man. You've got a good head and a good heart. Just think of all the assholes walking around without either. Why don't you buy rainbow-colored bags?

"Oh, Sam," I said and put my arms around him, "I love you so much. I wish . . ." He put his hand over my mouth.

"Wishes are no good, my beauty. Only the hard stuff is real. Which reminds me, there's someone waiting for me in the living room. He's the man of my life, I think." He saw me to the door of my room. "You're going away soon, aren't you?"

"I think so, Sam, maybe tomorrow."

"Oh, these men, these men!" he said and ran down the hall.

I left without seeing him the following day. I phoned him at work from the airport to say goodbye. He was sharp and curt with me. I attributed it to the fact that he was probably not alone in his office. There was a Monday afternoon weariness in his tone that I blamed on the weekend filled with drugs, on the New York state of mind. I flew to my islands.

I was on Kokkomaa when your letter about him arrived. It is a stark treeless island with wildflowers and grass growing amazingly out of the cracks in the gray-black and pink granite. Kokkomaa rises out of the sea like a whale and at its highest point there is a fissure in the stone all the way to the sea below, so that during storms, the water is forced up through it and the island appears to be spouting. Its name means Isle of Pyres, for it was here that the Vikings burned their dead and made their sacrifices. The Nazis used it for their own purposes during the Second World War. Since then, however, the sea, calm and frozen, turbulent and purging, has purified it, and a journey there is very special to me.

The configurations of the rocks on the steep or gentle slopes of the island create many places to sit or to lie down. When the light strikes them from the west, they are transformed into ruby and amethyst sofas. I bathe in a deep and sheltered pool on the sunset side of the island by myself and then join the others on the flat side for the late afternoon meal. Each of us has his or her favorite place on Kokkomaa. Some like simply to sprawl on the smooth stones and, face down and arms outstretched, absorb their heat and energy. The children sail their boats in a still pond on the southeastern side of the island. Others gather flowers and herbs or firewood.

When I returned from that visit to Kokkomaa, I stopped by the village for the mail. There was a letter from you. I dreaded opening it, thinking that once again I would be told things about myself I did not want to hear, especially on the island. There was nothing of that. Instead, in your characteristically controlled diction, you gave me the facts of Sam's death. In a rage, I burned the letter.

He, too, had been brought up a good little Christian boy. He, too, had been taught the myths of virility. He, too, had loathed himself for not measuring up to those dreams. He, too, had suffered from compulsions that drove him from those he loved and respected. He, too, had not recovered from the loss of love. The list was interminable.

They had found him in his bed. The markings on his wrists and ankles showed that he had been strung up at one point in that twenty-four-hour period he had told his friends he was spending out of town with "the man of his life." He died of suffocation. After unstringing him, the person or people involved (your words) wrapped him tightly in the heaviest chains available and left him face up on the bed. He was drugged and could not free himself, if in fact he was still conscious. The tautness and weight of the chains asphyxiated him.

I sat in my cabin unable to grieve. A few hours later, there was a tap at the window. One of the women of the island had been walking through the forest and had gathered a bouquet of flowers for me. I remembered inviting Sam to the island. "Oh, God, no," he had said, "it's too isolated. I'm not good at just lying around on beaches or rocks. I need some action." He wiggled his ass and blew kisses at the East River.

The woman extended her arm with the flowers in her hand. "They're Linnaeus flowers," she said. "Do you know them?" I shook my head. Their fragrance was delicate, earthy, like the freesias I enjoy giving to you. She sat next to me and put her arms around me. She had perfectly shaped breasts, and I felt their softness against my arms. I thought of Sam's strong chest of how proud he was of what he called his "tits." And they, too, were beautiful in their way.

"Why," I asked the woman, "why is it so hard to let go of the people you love?" I began to gag. She held me tightly and swayed with me.

"I don't know," she said, "I don't know."

€ € €

I can speak in my own voice now. The fog is approaching the island from Tallinn, across the gulf, already obscuring the lighthouse near Kokkomaa. Tomorrow, I begin my journey back to the City of Light and Fog constructed like you and me on a fault, and thousands of miles away from this cabin and that enclosure of alder and pine and birch trees that screens the sights, smells, and sounds of the sea, allowing them to reach me gradually through the open window.

In these last days, the landscape has been gray with clouds and mist. We have been very close to the sky. The sea on the mainland side has been like glass, on our side rippling with winds from the southeast. The air has been a balmy cushion filled with unkept summer promises. It was, as they say here, "a blueberry summer," which means it has rained more than usual and the sun has been stingy with itself. The mosquitoes have revived and the umbrella spiders, harbingers of autumn, have not yet made their early morning appearance on the grass.

As we enter the long drawn-out Scandinavian dusk, the breeze is growing stronger, colder, carrying the mists from the east this way. I don't want to think about Sam any more, or about loss or death. Enough. I will build a fire in my cabin tonight and wonder where you are. I have already collected seven different kinds of wildflowers to put under my pillow. It is believed here that what one dreams after having done this will come true.

I want to dream that men can love themselves and each other.

The Loneliest Man in the World[1]

I have known three of the world's loneliest men. One is my father, who is limping and laughing his way to the grave. Another was a student whose ashes were scattered over the desert last year in a family ceremony, to which I was not invited. And Jim, a native Californian I met in the first years of our undergraduate life at Stanford in the fifties.

My father has set the standard for the males I have known, and not one of them—including him, I have discovered—could possibly measure up to his absolute view of what it is to be a man. He has been brought to his knees by it.

"God damn it! You better side with me!" he shouted at my mother with a conviction that she had no other choice, because he was her man against the world. We had just reported that his daughter-in-law was very put out with him for having made suggestive and crude comments to his grandson's nursemaid. They had been alone in my father's car for a few moments while my nephew and I were picking up the dry cleaning.

"So what did you and your boyfriend do this weekend, Socorro? Did you spend all your time putting his thing in your hole?" or some such nonsense that embarrassed Socorro enough to report it to my sister-in-law, who became angry enough while thinking about it to tell me and my mother. It is her belief that we can do something about my father's nature.

---

[1]Written just after Jay Spears died on December 6, 1986.

My mother and I knew that he had probably made such coarse remarks, for he has been doing so all of his life. He is now in his mid-seventies and retired from the police force. We agreed to tell him so that he would understand why his son's wife and Socorro were planning to give him the cold shoulder during the Christmas holiday round of feasting and drinking.

My father's anger has intimidated me most of my life because, until that moment, I have felt it to come from some deep well of injustice over which no one can exert control. I thought about the times he settled any arguments by simply unbuckling his revolver and placing it on the table during lunch, or at least that's what I thought he was doing.

This time, I was amazed by the pleading, rather than demanding tone in which he called for my mother's loyalty, because it betrayed the insecurities he has felt throughout his life. I was amazed that I was hearing it in that way rather than as yet one more example of his policeman's response to the existence of other people in the world. I know he would never see his condition as I am describing it and he would deny feeling insecure, especially in front of his sons. Perhaps before his wife, who has grown to know where his anger comes from and to see that, though she may be the target of it, she is not the cause.

It has taken me too long to understand that no man is willing to parade his weaknesses in front of another and that he will do so only when moved by calamity, and sometimes not even then. Males condemned to a life of strutting before other males or of learning how to avoid the constantly expected attack from without, when what is finally going to kill them is the onslaught from within. It is a pitiable condition, all the more so because power allows males to be forever hiding from their vulnerability. "You better side with me," is the demand of a cornered animal.

The last time I saw my student, he was sitting in a hospital bed, his eyes glazed by the morphine a cheerful nurse had just given him. The room was full of voices. The nurses were chattering away to make him smile, his lover was intercepting a phone call, the T.V. was announcing the latest headlines. (I have always hated hospitals and have found myself in them more than I care to think. They have a peculiar smell which has nothing to do with medicine, are much too noisy to allow anyone to rest, and they upset my stomach.) I was beginning to feel queasy by all the forced naturalness and could respond only to the silent look of farewell he gave me as I left the room and headed for the elevator. I was to hear his voice again but I was not to see him.

His lover followed me down the corridor and rambled on about how ill, how beyond hope, and so on in that controlling way I find obnoxious because I, too, need to be in control. I knew he was telling me that he was in charge of his lover's life and that I needed to know that. I smiled and agreed with everything he said. In the elevator, there was a young nurse with crucifixes in her ears. I heard myself compliment her for wearing them, though my impulse was to tear them away from her face and condemn her for blasphemy. I have not been able to reconcile my love of joy with my desire to punish.

The religious purists would have us believe the world would be perfect if only one kind of attraction were permitted. Maybe so, but it would not be this world. There is too much nonsense and plain ignorance on all sides about the attraction of one man for another, as if such emotions could be controlled and monitored out of existence. No man or woman chooses attractions. If it were a choice, would we not all choose the accepted and condoned? Life gives us enough trouble already.

I was happy for a last reconciliation with my student and knew that our love for each other had survived both the inner and outer attacks, no matter how much each of us had collaborated with destruction. He may not have been able to walk out of that hospital room and into the light of a Mission District afternoon, but his fever-ish embrace left its imprint, the words I had longed to hear him say, broke through all the junk we had been taught, and believed, about one man loving another.

"I love you. I always have," he said in a final telephone conversation five days before he died. I was only across the bay, but he did not want me to see him. I had already been told about the swollen head, the shrunken body, the sores like blueberry stains that were devouring him from inside and out.

"We'll see each other again," I said, believing it. "There's another place. Better." I was in that euphoric denial of grief that comes to those who must watch others die.

"Is there diarrhea there?" he asked. We laughed.

"No. And no gay and straight. Just a lot of loving," is what I wish now I had said. Instead, I remained silent. I cannot remember if either of us said goodbye. We must have. All telephone conversations end that way.

Five days later, I was back in the desert and when the phone rang, I knew what the voice on the other end of the line was going to tell me. At the moment, I could only think that his death had something to do with my feet itching all through the night. I told myself not to be ridiculous and went on.

POETRY

Untitled Early Poetry

Poem I

The priest had drunk too much
bourbon before lunch;
he paid for everyone.

No one but the seminarian spoke;
he talked of truth endlessly,

His immaculate bands and pink-white
fingernails forming
each gesture.

Poem II

The innately shy, almost bald man
with the dark brown eyes
spoke to me.

His quiet words fell
as leaves from a solitary tree
in autumn.

Poem III

The woman in the burnt-yellow dress
is tired; she sits bent over

In her office chair, thinking
of the children who do not wait
at home.

Poem IV

So let these flakes be every soul
Some larger, some small shaped by time and wind
To fall into the street below
No startling particularity now, no sound to tell
A tale of love or hate or pain
Serene white, forever stain,
They fall.
Gravity pulls them down.

Early 1960s

Cuauhtémoc's Grave

. . . Cuauhtémoc is more a myth than a historical figure
. . . the location of Cuauhtémoc's tomb is not known. The
mystery of his burial place is one of our obsessions. To discover it would mean nothing less than to return to our origins, to reunite ourselves with our ancestry, to break out of
our solitude. It would be a resurrection.

—Octavio Paz, *The Labyrinth of Solitude*

Whenever I go back, I always think of it as the desert. It hasn't
even the name of a city for me because everything about it is name-
less there, anonymous, alienated. I am a stranger to what has become
of it, but I know I will not be able to break away from it until I understand its place in my soul.

In that desert—*desierto* is better, the sounds of the i, e, and r
convey the grief of such bareness—one range of mountains ends and
another begins, and years ago before it was dammed up in the north,
a large river, brown and deep, flowed in the valley between the vol-
canic hills. The hills still lend a bleak dignity to them, but the river
is just a trickle of mud spanned by international bridges.

I like to think that reptiles of the prehistoric ages dragged and
scraped through this valley in their futile attempts to escape history
and the crushing ices and before that, of the sea that covered every
land, even this arid terrain, with its coolness. Orchids grew here
once, and gardenias. Now they are brought in from miles away and
sold on the streets to *turistas* by the *viejitas*. The grass is painted in
the winter and only a few species of trees can survive the sand-
storms.

The Spanish conquerors passed through here on their arrogant
missions and named the place for what it was to them. Cuauhtémoc
wept. In his marketplaces there was grandeur, and his people had
their self-esteem. Now they are divided within themselves, and in
their markets junk and futility reign.

But why wait for the resurrection of an Aztec warrior when it is impossible to accept the resurrection of a Hebrew carpenter? Because the solitude in this *desierto* is unbearable, and once, in the temple of the Sun in Teotihuacan I stood at the summit and waited for the clouds to gather in storms and know that these gods were real to me. They are not dead; and in the desert, the grave of Cuauhtémoc will flower and bear fruits.

January 12, 1970

Obsession

The paw
  Caught in a trap;
The self extended
  To the other who lies still.
There is no letting go
  So one must gnaw.

Pain remains, half-buried
  In the red-stained leaves.
The ghostly limb
  Returns in dreams
And itches.

February 13, 1973

A Cock

A cock sits six stools away
Indulge in a bulge, my friend.
A voice that promises nothing
But pleasure and pain in the end.

Nothing special, and words
Make no difference.

(Circa 1973)

Palace of Your Body

"This is the palace of your body," she said.

The flesh has its reason
and Love changes when the angel,
undulating beneath its guarded soul,
Whispers, "Take me, take me to places
                             we never touch."

Oh, my angel, your thigh sliding under mine,
Loins, pungent and earthly, do not create
the yearning for another time, another place.

Only the sound of your human voice remains,
naming its desire, calling to me
from another shore.

                                        Circa 1973

Aztec Angel

I

I am an Aztec angel
criminal
of a scholarly
society
I do favors
for whimsical
magicians
where I pawn
my heart
for truth
find
my way
through obscure
streets
of soft spoken
hara-kiris

II

I am an Aztec angel
forlorn passenger
on a train
of chicken farmers
and happy children

III

I am the Aztec angel
fraternal partner
of an orthodox
society
where pachuco children
hurl stones
through poetry rooms
and end up in a cop car

their bones itching
and their hearts
busted from malnutrition

IV
I am the Aztec angel
who frequents bars
spends evenings
with literary circles
and socializes
with spiks
niggers and wops
and collapses on his way
to funerals

V
Drunk
Lonely
bespectacled
the sky
opens my veins
like rain
clouds go berserk
around me
my Mexican ancestors
chew my fingernails
I am an Aztec angel
offspring
of a tubercular woman
who was beautiful

Circa 1974

Sleeping on Poppies

One by one the yellow eyes open

Into the stale atmosphere of my fatigue,

Pressing past my dreaming head into the rooms:

The green fronds finger upward

On fluid stems; a confusion of petals, crossing, floating

Delicate shadows in the crepuscular gloom

As the buds bend forward and open, thirsty for light;

The whole room thrusts forward a forest, and I am lost there

While the poppies surge past me, pushing on neck, shoulder,

   rib, elbow, thigh—,

Rank on rank, tall poppies, in a clamorous swaying—

Then all at once something else is afoot in the rooms:

Yes, it is the sun blooms now in a wide swathe over the bed;

Yes, it is morning. It is you, again.

May 24, 1975

Morning in Finland
For Stina and Herant

The music suggests the landscape and the day:
　　the air scented by trees,
　　the lapping of water on gentle rocks
　　observed above;

The deck and the smell of coffee
　　and jam on toast.
In the distance, the noises of the children
　　playing their games of royalty.

Two of us sit facing the sea, the other
　　turned toward the house;
　　following our measured thoughts,
　　dreaming our dreams, we listen to Time
　　made palpable by melody.

We are on an island of pure sound
　　where music and landscape merge through the pines.

September 1975

Flight Delay

Stuck in Phoenix, a mythical bird,

Said to rise from the ruins as if nothing happened,

Or as if everything happened, burning to ashes

Then reshaping itself to begin again:

Flight, extinction, a never-ending rebirth?

Buffalo roaming, disappearing, on the lounge T.V.

To roam no more on Easter,

Easter Sunday without Good Friday,

Reversal without end.

Outside, the grayness holds down the plane,

Sitting, dowager nose to the ground, like the buffalo

Indifferent to what rises

Again and again.

Circa Summer 1976

Desire

1. New York State Thruway, 6 a.m.
   Birds scatter in your headlights;
   Their wings are black against the deep-blue grass.
   Every man you know has a sense of direction.
   You take the highway west, the nearest one.

2. Count
   Everything now, in the fullness of summer.
   Nature, abundance
   Moves in your eyes wherever you look.
   So you say. But for you
   There is only the same life,
   Its own cycles
   Where abundance has not come.
   Or so you say.

3. Finally you had to anger him,
   Not to cause him grief—that was never the point—
   But to *cause*
   In the old way, the way
   Desire used to be a cause.
   Entropy is reluctance to be moved.
   Moving to anger is, at least, not death.

4. Write long things. Poetry never was abrupt,
   Except by mistake. If you love Virgil
   Love the long line. Love how it falls, inviting
   The next one. It will come
   And you will wait for it;
   The disasters you absorb are seeking expression
   And no ghost
   Will tell you this day what you have to say.

Circa 1976

The Island

The sucking fucking noises in the corridor the smell of filthy feet amyl nitrate; the perfumed crotch the abused asshole, piss and leather, semen, male sweat and spit and nicotine piercing the nostrils as the throat gags, oh Lord, hear my prayer. In the darkness one kneels to receive the other, another crouches to take what comes, tongue or cock, a lick or a fist or a boot or tube of flesh discriminating in the darkness. There are no kisses here. Prostrated the prostrated is worshipped and massaged, fingers, fists, and phalluses emerge to be licked clean by waiting, tireless mouths. IammyfatherIammymother. Love, are you here? Anonymity is your name, various fluids, insatiable, always in pursuit, the nose catching the scent, turning the head against its will away from what asks or needs or wants or is responsible. Yes, you must be there too, but where? The silky, hairless testicle in my mouth, the bittersweet of the anus scrubbed clean in anticipation, it hurts to penetrate and I come halfway there. In revenge he pounds his cock against the back of my throat despite the gagging. Love, you are here choking, heaving dryly, a penis ravaging your mouth. I'm on my knees, Lord, have mercy on me.

Summer 1976

A Poem in the Manner of Emily Dickinson
For Jay Spears

Loving is no contract—
It is a risk of the heart
to be close—
And to surrender—not the body
but itself—

No payment given or received—
Everything gained and lost

January 9, 1977

You Will be Another Pacific Island

Go on and slide into the ocean,
California! we've waited long enough.
And take my home, my friends, and me along with you.
Spare nothing in your breaking away.
You will be another Pacific island,
Purple, serene, calm, green again,
And no longer on a fault.

A smoky, winter day, the bay
A smoky blue; smoke towards the sea,
the spires of a cathedral already obscured, sepulchral
in the winter light graying, luminous in turn—
The City in ruins, devastation emerging, dying
In smoke.

Our connections, like the City of smoke,
Have been built on a fault.
A crack in the earth
Determines us all.

January 15, 1977

Bondage & Discipline

While you're spread across the rack
I'll get rid of my mother and father,
Each of us letting go of those children
Locked up in their closets of desire.

We are still what they've made of us
And we are playing out their fantasies,
You, projecting anger onto the hooded face;
I, knuckling under grief.

Scream. The pleasure's in the pain.
Don't scream. The pain's in the pleasure.

Our fathers question and our mothers turn away,
One child drowns, the other fondles his chains.
You and I, somewhere in that darkness,
Link by link, will make our way out.

February 14, 1977

Moonshine

Tonight I, lunatic in a scotch haze,
Stood at the kitchen sink
    where in February, at this time of day,
    you peeled avocados for our salad;
    where in June, a few steps away,
    we said goodbye to three years of illusion
    and deception (I cried unknowing then)
Looked out of the window and saw it—
    young, white, full and wide.

"Friend, come look at the moon,"
I said, out loud, and then,
    without sadness and matter-of-factly
    as it had risen in the East,
Remembered you were not here.

I am the moon now.
In the windows, cold and indifferent,
I gaze at myself and the people.

They're usually drunk.

February 14, 1977

Drunk

I get sober when I drink and I think
Of you and how when you're drunk
You stagger, sometimes even fall, and
Are able to feed your illusions instead
Of letting them feed on you. In other
Words, you act perfectly normal and
Real (as one should) after a fifth of gin.

I, on the other hand, gain control
With each sip of bourbon, and focus.
Rocks fall out of peoples' mouths and
I see my head spinning above it all,
Gaping at the human condition.

Talk to me now. I have swallowed
My grief and see you there
Leaning towards me.

February 28, 1977

Ambush

They come to be cornered here.
In this red light, Priapus lies in wait
And hunts for assholes
Or, barring Him, fingers and fists
Will do the trick.

Dudes, retain your anonymity.
Expose only those parts you
Need the crude surgeon to dissect.
Gently, he will strip away
The soft, sour tissue of guilt and
Tickle the marrow of your anger.
He's good at it.

   "You, there
      with the dark crevice
      peeping at me through
      torn Levi's,
   Come here.

   Stay in this corner for awhile
   And let me lick at fantasy
   As I open your wounds,
   One by one, With my scalpel."

March 7, 1977

For E.H.

You were such a good boy
Even when you were bad
Seeking your manhood in
Three or four wives
(One forgets because it doesn't matter)
On the outskirts of battlefields
In the capes of bullfighters
In the woods and the big fish
Always outside of yourself,
In action. Thinking made you sick.

                    Was everyone ever in earnest?

                              Spring 1977

Motherfucker or the Exile
For Jay Spears

I

Searching for Daddy, you've come back to Mother.
You know she will comfort you; like Hamlet,
You burrow against her silky breast and dig
For the heart you pine for, each beat giving
You reasons not to move against the tyrant.
"I'll take care of you, baby," she says,
And holds you close.

The King rules you. Shackled, you feed on his
Virility and bite the stiff, dry teats
(One bleeds, pungent syrup, into his crotch).
You long to master him in turn as the
Crown of his cock beckons you, spit trailing
Out of its mouth. You know he will never
Come or come too soon—either way he keeps
You at a distance. "Suck hard on those tits,"
He says in an angry, rasping voice,
And you do.

II

A fat man guards the door to this exile,
Tame Cerberus a ribbon of tickets
Clamped between his teeth. Drugged, you slide into
The hall on clouds of amyl, exhaling
Music and hungry for water, you hear
The Uranian hands scratching at sand
That does not yield, insistent scraping
Urging the dancers onward in rituals for
Ancient phantoms. The naked backs, the careless,
Fixed glances, the dreamy, sweat-stained eyelids
Bounce in slow motion from emptiness to delight.
Speed and violet acid and girded loins

Keep boredom at bay, smiles hang from the walls,
Incandescent flamingos screech in heat,
Sound obscures reason and liquid madness reigns.
The women, rouged imitations with sequins
In their hair, cannot cut off the force
That hangs between their legs. Trapped, the senses
Die of overexposure and in their place
Electricity rushes and vibrates.
"There is no air in here," you tell the fat man.
He buys you a drink and blows on you.
Outside, the soul flags down taxis looking
For you, gives up, sits down on the curb,
And waits for a bus.

III

"Father, I need your hand. Tie my ankles
And wrists or I will soar into extinction.
Chain me to bedposts and whip me for my sins,
I will let you know how hard."

In a whisper, he tells you what you will do.
Prepare the joints and restraints, the Master
Is at hand to bring you the child raging
And weeping from its dungeon. Before he's
Through you'll find release—until the next time.
No satisfaction guaranteed, no holds
Allowed, only the holding back, actors
In a mock-angry pantomime.

"Mother, I cannot bear my dreams," you cry.

"Now, now, my dear child. They are harmless and
I gave them to you when you were still
Inside me. They will help you against

Daddy and bind you to me." She strokes you
With her velvet fingernails.

"Oh, Mother, I am as miserable
As you, my feet and hands ache with pleasure
And the frenzied slowness of this dance
Is your womb. I have left my heart there, Mother,
Now do you love me?"

"Yes, son, yes."

May 10, 1977

Hostility

I come to you drunk, stumbling into the room
Full of truth and revelation. Grinning,
You go on with the phone conversation,
Your hand signaling me to be quiet
And behave myself. I stop in mid-air.

There is nothing to say. We add insight
To injury like clowns who pound each other
With clubs, screaming and laughing all the while
To hide the maimed and dangling limbs.

But what if in these lines of wire and word
Slides we looked at ourselves for once
Without defenses or lies: me, slurring
About Love to avoid facts and you,
Talking to the man who has captured you
With the way he services your body?

To console me, you softly touch my chest,
Your fingers, like knives, slice through to the heart.

May 10, 1977

Colette's Friend

We have come to talk
But the topic, too familiar,
Idles on the rug between us, an unwelcome
Third party we ignore.
Instead, I watch your face,
The elegant detritus of your life
Surrounding you in orderly exhaustion.
I think I'm never coming back, you say,
And sorrow chills me;
Of course I do not take you in my arms:
An older pattern guides our intimacy:
Neither sister nor lover, I beloved, am your reader.
So, many times we've sat an hour together,
Office, bench, a cluttered table furnishing
Our talk with trifles we can finger
While I have turned the pages of your life,
Breathlessly receiving its disclosures—
So Millie Theale, dismissing the carriage in Harley Street
Taking that long walk home,
Might have lingered near a bookstall, opened a volume,
And found herself, dying, a woman taking a walk.

May 24, 1977

Losing You

Winter; the woods
empty; the ax
buried in a stump;
its fall a sob
in the sleep of the dreamer
waking, calling out
Where am I? Who is there?

July 18, 1977

In the Dark

As you sing in the dark, a room away tonight
Your voice drifts to me, broken, through the park
Where we wait. We are in love. It is the third
Midnight. Jupiter is high, and in the soft grass
We feel the bed we know is ours, and soon
Memory retrieves it all—your voice
Is the path in the dark that leads one way, uphill.
You do not mean to make me hear these things
As you sing, in the dark, a room away tonight.

July 31, 1977

Mishima

There's an Angel stop on the Northern Line
In another country far from your desire.
Swords have crossed here too, underarm sweat
And blood, yearnings of the body poured out
Men in procession moved past other eyes
Longing for virility, dreaming of the youthful gods
containing their lacks, their loathing, their despair.
You, in your fatal gesture, denied your body
Made it yield to the blade even as your trained hard belly
Put up a token resistance.
     You hated love. It unmasked you,
Forced an entry into your prison,
Emasculated your obsessions
Waiting, disavowal, fetishism
Trinity of the masochist, were your gods.

Circa Summer 1977

Lost My Mind

After I had lost my many minds,
Penned my purpose, dangled on the limb.
He, quite properly, revised my diction
Specified what "did not work" for him.

Blue-penciled over my still open eyes,
I might as well have scribbled in the skies.
What did not work was evident to me,
Not image, rhythm, but the Poetry.

Circa Summer/Fall 1977

The Meeting of Saint Anthony and Saint Paul

Our needs precede us and I am drawn
To flat surfaces, having loved this copy
Of a painting attributed to Sassetta
And some anonymous assistant
About whom I wonder, having been one myself.

The flatness is a child's lens
Through which we see and believe in
Saints and Monsters.
Perspective makes us feel the distances
And think about the life behind the paintings
Of the Renaissance, for instance,
Illusorily three-dimensional
Suggesting life where saints and monsters
All but disappear and assistants
Crazily wander about.

The two met only once and legend has it
Both lived to be over one hundred years,
The younger dying before the elder,
Who taught fellow ascetics how to resist
Their needs, while the younger (we presume)
Faced him head on in a cave.
(Already I am doing what I set out not to:
Attributing meaning to a flat surface,
Looking for life
Under the golden flaking medium.)

They meet in your kitchen, I saw them there once.
Here, they float behind me, heads touching,
My halo, when I sit in a blue chair
You have not seen.
They are, as you know, hugging
And each has a hand on the other's hip

In a pose I did not think saints were allowed
To strike.

Anthony, the teacher, has traveled far
To reach his disciple's cave, speaking
To a centaur along the way,
A white, ghostly animal who holds
A chalice in one hand, a palm frond in the other,
A kind of halo framing a wise face tilted backward
Its left foreleg, raised and bent.
Saint and beast converse at the edge of a forest
And I imagine the centaur is telling Anthony
About his childhood or some story
That remains unfinished
And has nothing to do with God
(Maybe he's just giving him directions)
While Anthony raises a hand to receive the words
Or to bless him.
It's not clear, just that neither
Seems surprised or afraid.
The trees in these most unnatural forests
Above and beneath them
Stand in sharp relief,
Each leaf painted precisely
Unlike leaves and pasted in so orderly a fashion
No breeze could lift them
Like acacias in California
On a still February dawn.

We are in allegory, of course,
That spiritual flatland where the journey,
Though depicted by three Saint Anthonys,
Each larger than the one before,
Does not matter.
The meeting does, and this last Anthony,
Full grown, clasps Paul

Emerged from his cave at last.
We see his face, sharp and flat,
In profile and staring away as he holds
The desert father collapsed on his shoulder,
Their halos like golden plates entwined,
The Hermit's hair and beard, golden and streaked with white,
Lush and long.
Their staffs dropped in haste lie on the rocky road,
Their ankles, bare and touching,
They lean from the hip toward each other,
A golden, somewhat bloodied sky
Filled with archangels and demons far, far away.
In a few years, according to the story,
Anthony will bury Paul,
Wrapping him in a cloak given to him
By yet another Saint
And two lions
Will help him dig the grave.
(What they will help him feel, I do not know.)

Theirs has not been a land of regrets,
Promises, anger; only toil and meditation
Where they tried to outfast each other
And paid for their orgies of the spirit
By scourging their bodies.
These two seem to have survived all that
And this moment is a communion
Standing up, for Saints and Hermits
Cannot be friends or lovers.

Only I, no flatlander finally,
Want them to be amazed, to stand agape
To dance
To laugh at each other
And at the dawn.

Circa Fall/Summer 1977

Blueboy

Gainsborough could not have painted you,
Your state does not welcome plumes and finery.
Bosch, maybe, or some anonymous medievalist
Given to the fine details of martyrdom:
Lawrence on the grill asking to be turned over
Because one side of him was already done,
Or Elmo, strung up, watching his guts wind
Around the windlass and singing to a god
He understood, demanded such things.

Your wound comes from elsewhere, you don't know where,
Now sought offhandedly and with relish,
A casual pleasure that comes from having left
Old gods and influences behind,
You call it abandonment, a mindless release,
Listen to yourself, naked on the canvas,
An oriental carpet for a landscape:

"I'm not into pain," you say, your eyes,
Like the boy's, defiant with innocence,
The flagellant's conviction in your voice.
One looks at the marks you have warned are there,
Handprints on the buttocks like blueberry
Stains on a sheet, your right nipple,
A swollen yellow rose, dark at the center.
Twice you asked him to stop and twice he refused,
Peeved, you walked out at last. Because it hurt
Or because (there being no gods to invoke
Or appease) you could not be in control?
"I'm not aware of my hurt," you say,
It could be the boy speaking, or the saints.
(What, then, pains you—a tender word, a caress?)

In public places at the drinking hour

Your dreams are the property of strangers
Who know your type and prime themselves for the meeting;
They are ready to brand you and insert
The chain, section by section, up to the limit
You set for your ecstasy and discipline,
To what end remains a mystery.

You're not into pain. No, like those children
Of God before you, separating mind from body,
You're into self-denial. And the boy?

Dead. Of natural causes.

August 14, 1977

Metroliner

The leaves not yet turning, gliding
And tumbling by one cemetery after another,
It stops at dark terminals to admit
And expel these phantom passengers
As I say farewell to you. It's neither
A change nor an ending. It's both,
And nothing corresponds to this airless,
Half-filled coach, to the coffee I spill
On my trousers only a train away
From your life in the corridors of power
To mine in the city of possibilities.

Are we locked into place, breeding indifference?
This time I seem to have left nothing behind
And you remained your silent, self-contained
Self. How I have envied you that.

Just one tree, a pine oak, red-orange
In the early October light and hovering
Indifferently and out of place over
Five or six white, white tombstones
Makes any sense. In the moonlight,
I would have mistaken them
For hydrangeas.

October 19, 1977

Guilt

Such a familiar, negotiable feeling,
A sense of responsibility turned inward
To excuse mindlessness like that car
Parked on the wrong side of the street
              Leaning comfortably against the curb

                    November 8, 1977

Skins

I put away my clothes,
Skins gnawed and glowing with care
Or abuse, it doesn't matter.
They smell of ether and roses,
A dry, disarming fragrance
I keep alive for a past
That sticks around.

We could have been a this
Or that to one another.
Instead, we are no more
Than a winter afternoon
Clinging to itself, now mothproof
And sprayed with the antiseptic
Stench of regret.

December 25, 1977

Scat Bag

You are my connection.
I change you seven times a day
Fragrant, red mouth at my side
surrounded encased in by plastic
You remind me relentlessly of my
mortality
What shall I do with this constant ooze? [. . .]

Or in the smile of the lover who walks away
After telling you it did not work. Of course not,
How would it? No one tried.

I wake from dreams of flying to find
That, filled with gas, the bag has balloon-like
Tugged at the belly towards the ceiling.
We don't belong there. We are grounded.
That's illusion. It amuses and that's why
I need it. Any distraction. Anything
Except the fear of dying.

Fetid human bog packaged for the twentieth century
Our dark age has come to this. These bags will
Sell for a dime. Want to give a friend a bag
Of shit? Plastic naturalism.

Like when you left and left a wound,
An embarrassment to explain to strangers
While undressing, "What's that? Why do you
Hold your hand against your side? Does it
Hurt?

No, it doesn't hurt anymore. It is
Tender, but will not bleed, I'd like
To forget about it and hold you, anyone

Close as I did before I had to wear
This plastic bag that bloats itself
Between me and another.

Sometimes, at four a.m. when annihilation
Comes to visit, it makes me get up and change it,
Cursing & crying all the while. The alternative?
That's always there to my left before dawn,
At dusk, in the corners of rooms half-lit
With candles and inundated with smoke.

Circa 1977

Dancing with Ghosts

I

Let you go in love? One can't let go
Of something one never had. Ah, but then
We do not agree on terms; grant me that
You've lived according to what you thought
Was my illusion, moody tyrant, more than I myself.
An ancient question for a modern world.

Now you've gone your way, this time leaving me behind
In the desert, our birthplace, where eleven years apart,
We have smelled the vitex trees and greasewood after rain
And seen the grand parades of clouds
Thrown on the mountain below in shadow and light
(For the sun shines daily here, according to the newspapers,
Except for sand and thunderstorms and two or three blizzards—
Snowbound desert tossing us into the moon again.)
How did we survive our respective childhoods?

      So I am looking at clouds
And I understand all about them except their evanescence,
Which I keep mistaking for constancy,
Their place in the creases of the granite shale
Seems so secure, certainly always there, or about to be,
Even if caressing fossils on their way.
It's from the desert I sing you this song,
Both of us wondering what's left
Of the mountain after the pain?
("See you in February."
                   "Invite me."
                              "I will."
Until then, forty days and nights
Of wandering and thinking about
How you mean more to me than I to you,
One of our recurrent themes, like the clouds.)

For you I cannot answer, your rhymes come
Through clenched, bright teeth, allowing just so much,
Letting others fill in the blanks, making them
Responsible for their own conclusions
While you remain untouched in a private
And cultivated landscape. For you, coward,
(Read Colette's *The Shackle* to understand
What I mean by that word) can't bear looking at the hurt
You give someone you love.

                    For me, another kind of coward,
A sense of extinction at four a.m. and the cocktail hour,
Either a soundless grabbing for myself under the sheet
Or a dancing with ghosts as I hold onto a drink
For dumb, dear life.

II
                  I assumed we were together.
Now still mourning what did not exist, a grief
Not those imperceptibly lapsing with the season,
Those days return in San Diego red bougainvilleas
That bloom indoors, and in the single, slight maples
Arching over backyard fences, a different red
In the west coast autumn, so Japanese in subtlety and mood,
Those days return in which I waited for you to come home
From work (more important than people, you said)
Or from strangers who gave you release
(They didn't matter, you said)
Or from Doctor Lust in his fortress above the bay
(Of course there would be a fireplace and a view)
My double, the unknown line of just one more triangle,
Your collaborator in fantasy, willing or not.

                          Still,
The ferns and angel-wing begonias, the ficus and split-leaf
Philodendrons flourished, and I read your care for them
As commitment to a bond with me, who in your presence
And not daring to notice it, was turned into a phantom.

I fed him with illusion and you watered him with guilt
(Familiar, negotiable response that excuses everything
And gives reality pause) and kept him alive
To frolic and weep with your ghosts for you.
He is "the very fine influence" you walked out on
The way a child leaves a parent, a crumpled blue shade
Hanging at the kitchen window.
                              "This house will be lonely
Without you," he said, unable to speak for himself,
Already vanishing and choking with thirst.

Behold! your ghost writer chasing the wraiths away.

III

And the fine times? They were there too and haunted
By the ravenous shades of appetites you made certain
I knew nothing about, much less allowed me to slake,
Able or not, for that would have been getting too close.
After you were a continent away, in those late summer nights
Before I left on the following day, when Love cowered,
Hovered over a desk in search of reasons
While Lust slept undisturbed, gorged, complacent
In its honesty.
                  Setting it down makes it sound
Too harsh and I must be just for my sake, not yours,
Since, chagrined, I am the one left picking through litter,
Sniffing at turds in the heart, biting his own back,
Tooth to bone, in need of marrow for sustenance.
Remordere, you were too young, there was no choice,
We did our best, Time and Chemistry (your phrase),
Hateful specters, defeated you.
                              The Doctor reports
You led him to believe you lived with me
Out of convenience, a wound made clean
By my knowledge your capable of inventing anything
To seduce him (he, too, feels manipulated

And knows that in the empire of the senses,
Bottom, not Top, is always in control.)

"Control is my addiction," you told me.

You have been mine.

IV

For a time, the phantom abandoned in the house
Fed on pillows in the California drought.
Obsessed, he lived for you and felt your needs
Better than you yourself, how they could twist
And bind you in the moments of letting go
Where red is the only color and saliva
The only glue strapping you to another;
How you kept the company of musicians
Who played upon your flesh, fingering here and there,
Pausing, sucking, now gently, now roughly
In blows of delight. He dreamed your dreams
Of bearded prisoners, chains around their ankles
Asking you, child unfettered and free, for cigarettes
That in your eagerness to please you would steal
(No one had spoken to you like that before,
A merging of tenderness and steel.)

Poor, parched wraith

Longed to enter those rooms where you played, a pleasure
Denied him by you as much as by circumstance,
By that's the way it is. His place was outside the door,
Waiting, wanting you to come out or invite him in,
He didn't care which, only to see you, touch you,
Make certain you were alive (the silly creature
Was afraid of you) so that he could live too,
He had nothing to lose and wanted badly to lose it.

He did not notice in that colorless season
That he was shedding skins, calmly, easily
Stepping out of them, ignoring them there by the door.

Only the waiting held him, tied him to you
As you were bound to them, those who read your music,
To whom, dictator, you gave that trust, that power.
The corridor was bright and opened onto
A golden meadow and he longed to be there
As much as he yearned to be with you
In the dark closets punctured with glory holes
Where the body, fumbling and groping for a soul,
Did not yet know that nothing is exchanged from the crotch
No matter how strong the drive for completion.
We are our own soulsuckers.
                         Because he would be maimed
With an alien sorrow, I spent a year stuffing mouthfuls
Of foam rubber down his throat.

V

I was captured once again in our last meeting
By your luminous skin, sleek perversely clear
And without marks as when I first saw it,
Then in your innocence, water showering down,
My loins contracting unwary, inevitability
Soaping us up in preparation for the journey.
I was whole then; you've not touched me in that state
And the pity of it grieves me. (Doctor Freud,
I suffer from a condition undreamed of in your
Inner totalitarian regime.)
                       Later that same day
My brother introduced us. Behind you at the window
Fate stooped to gather the first leaves of an autumn
Ten years past. To the end, I was enthralled by the passivity
Calculated to please just enough to evoke the dreams
I pursue, chief among them that in you and with you
I combine the flesh and the spirit.
                       White quietude,
You give dreams and take them away. The masters
Have taught you well the art of becoming an actor
In the fantasies of the slave. Doctor Lust has been

The influence you pursue with a disciple's devotion.
How I respect that power, how it defeats me, Doctor Lust!
My Love, your servant, has learned the lesson:
Give to others as much as will keep them hanging
In bondage, upside down, between heaven and earth.
Still a missionary, you give abstractly, happy in your charity,
And so remove yourself from the scene even as you believe
You are there and partaking, an engaged shadow reflecting,
Donning safely the torments of the victim.
The connection is transitory, to be sure, intense
And allows for a sense of closeness, a camaraderie
Between the oppressor and oppressed. (Looking in mirrors,
We see our opposites, not ourselves, Narcissus,
You were right to drown, stupefied by your own smell.
Which came first, the flower or the myth?)
                                        "Sex? With you,
I can take it or leave it; it's not odious to me.
Your touch, however, would be a great loss to me."
Paradox, contradictions, lie? Or if, in your eyes,
You have given without stint, the yawns betrayed you.
"It's been a lazy day," you said when I noticed them.
Only once that Christmas night, when you kissed me
On the foot after asking me what I thought about
Letting you go in love, and then later on the shoulder
After I said, capitulating, "Oh, fuck with them all,
Only sleep with me," only then did I taste your love,
Freed from control, intoxicating in its purity,
Leading me back to the rack in which you lie with ease
(I have since gnawed off both shoulder and foot.)

VI

I see the mountain stopping and breaking open the clouds
Driven by western, vagabond winds, and still it's the rack
That commands my attention, hair shorn, heart humbled,
For in your province, the mind rules. (No wonder
You are drawn to mindlessness as vice or to uncover

A humanity meticulously protected by abstractions.)
You have not given as much as you've taken
And you have erected a system to save you
From retribution, unassailable and smiling mutant!
The cost is isolation, which, in your cleverness,
You have made the highest masculine virtue.
Your youthful, compelling guise, diaphanous flesh,
Translucent teeth bring the nations to their knees.
They open their mouths in adoration.

Is it possible for two men to love one another?
Will anyone, even they themselves, permit it?
How many civilizations of victims will pass
Before men may kiss instead of kill with approval?
Where, what is the abomination? Speak.
                                        I'll tell you:
Abominable the inability to love, the fear of intimacy,
The idea that in anger and lust there is virility,
That men can be close only in competition.
Until a man can love another man, he cannot love a woman.
Look! Tell me I am wrong. Oh, Brothers!
Lay down your arms and wrap them round each other.
Oh, Sisters? rejoice in the love of men,
They are your children.

VII

And I ask myself daily as penance for my sins
Of blindness, of wanting not what is but the promise
You hold out just far enough away to seem possible
(Christians! there is no future, there is no future
And history is a hurt ghost we coddle to make certain
They have existed. Can I leave it behind and bury them
In this desert? Will they become cymbidiums?)
So well have you learned the craft of dissimulation,
You believe your present not maimed by the past, a myth
That keeps you self-serving and in perpetual adolescence.

Its subjects are Doctor Lust and those to whom you are drawn,
As you were to me, for their fine passions, their freedom
From your compulsions. How quickly we are trained
To want to be like you, as slaves ape their masters
Taught carefully to curse in proper forms,
Ever ready to please.
                              And I ask myself daily: what
Am I to you now, what am I to myself when with you?
Isabel's Ralph, Bosie's Oscar, Albertine's Marcel,
Daisy's Gatsby, Willy's Colette—dupes everyone,
Self-made, willful martyrs to their own delusions
Of the beloved's grandeur.
                              Only on escaped,
After thirteen years. I see her in a crystal garden,
Devouring flowers and Love, her favorite crudity,
Taming animals and words, conjuring up the dark rooms
And locked doors, the deep discipline of tears,
An array of apprenticeships and her wicked muse,
Not unlike my own. The rest—dying, drunk or murdered,
Their hearts, Colette, content with crumbs.
                              Will I perish
With the hungry, south of Market, between a porno movie house
And a *Jesus Saves* mission, in a suite of rooms
At the Anglo Hotel?

VII
                    I am in the corridor,
Wasted by the door, struck dumb in this quest with spirits.
Your brother lies sleeping beside me, his face on fire;
A Mexican sorcerer, I have danced with Death and madness
Until I can no more. I have mastered the language
Of my conqueror and use it better than he; still
I am excluded.
                              Nothing keeps me from the meadow,
Its brightness falling on the skins of the defeated
At my feet, lingering there, wrinkled and flaking away.

I walk out.

       The grass is tall, moist its blades splash
And cleanse me as, parting them, I slide towards a river.
At the shore, two beings of light stand together at my side,
Protectors, they keep their distance

                    A voice splendid
And ghastly, asks if I want to see my guardian angel.
"Yes!" I shout, even as the shining ministers tell me
I must endure one more trial. My courage fails
(At this impasse, Dante would have been allowed to faint.)
"No more Masters! No more Slaves!"

                 The voice interrupts:
"Look at his face." I awaken.

          I see your brother.

IX

A conglomerate of ghosts gazing at the foothills
And you going away from me in opposing directions,
The sun under a distant mist, scooping up the dust
Of what was once the bottom of the sea into brilliance
And framing me in a final, persistent illusion: insight,
For today the clouds have steered clear of the mountain
And no vapor casts the shadows I have loved
With the distress of the deaf and drowning.

                 From now on,
To those others and yourself, whom I may or may not see,
Describe me not as old lover or friend, but as someone
Embalmed by you early on, fixed like the stars
On an astrologer's chart, categorized in the crotch
Of your imagination, an abstraction, cold and bereft,
Who pours acid into peoples' drinks and on occasion
Tinkles in words, limitless perishable goods,
For your pleasure.

           Or, if that's too bleak:
Look on me as a brother in the desert,
More than a survivor delivered from phantoms,

Who sees in the crimson reflections of the mountain,
In the freesias falling over these wastes,
An eagerness, a readiness, to love himself.

For you, however hurt, have been, are still now, loved.

                                        February 26, 1978

Cliché
For Jay Spears

An exercise after receiving a note from London

That's how it is after all these years
    Of illusion unfulfilled and kept around for that reason,
    A recognition of another autumn, of a green wine tasted
    And remembered, not for the flavor but for its effect,

That's how it is that in the pile of mail on the desk
    There is a letter from the lost friend
    To whom you could not say, "Friend, I love you,"
    In that time you were together.

That's how it is that now, "a dying and old apostate,"
    He writes and names you "the one and only true confessor,"
    And speaks of responses, of maybe even looking you up.

"Friendship demands reciprocity," you read somewhere and believe,
    And have shed the gray cassock
    For the more difficult exchange of face to face
    Disclosures and admissions where truth
    (However meagerly allowed to peek from behind
        Scrims of tears and angers, regret and what was hoped,
        Buried under accumulations more immediate, less prized,
        Or, in this case, from within the wiremesh of memory),

At last permits the vagabond heart to speak and say
    That you, the companion left behind
    In a pause for breath two decades long,
    That you, once abandoned, now reclaimed, are loved.

June 5, 1978

Medea on the Hudson

The way the sun, falling away from the world,
Seems nearer for the reflections it gives us,
So are you closer now as, parting, we get on
With the business of murdering children.

This isn't what I wanted: an hour of lead,
The implacable distance of the river,
A Bach prelude playing itself out,
That underground ride to the terminal.

"Don't go, don't go," a voice croaks
Long after you have fallen away into silence,
Escalating downward toward your fleecy dream.

The words, sour and smeared with blood,
Fall into the river with the sun
And the dry city glares in darkness.

I will not weep for you or them.

June 29, 1978

Closet Song

Sleep, sleep close to me,
Shameless, hungry sorrow,
Love and Lust are only
Ours to borrow;

I'll stroke and fill your wounds
With salt and birch,
In this closet, carve
A reredos for our church,

Sleep, sleep close to me,
Shameless, hungry sorrow.

July 31, 1978

Bo Peep

I thought I was more than influence.
In growing and diminishing light,
I feel deeply for you and wonder over
A table where you sat, how I cared for you
And you for me. Just another child's verse?
I sought to protect you from what you needed
As if I could.
Have we cut each other's hands off forever?
Sheepishly, you come in dreams that linger;
Alive to others, I've mastered my pain.

I stroke their fine, ethereal wool.

Summer 1978

Faggots

We were slaughtered
And sent here to be consumed.
Desire, Hermaphrodite's fuel,
Burns well.

Our condition, the eaters assume,
Is transitory and remedial,
Passing through them as we do
For their nourishment or indigestion.

Some sparkle and melt
In fires that grow hotter,
Die down quietly
Or in a hiss of steam
Muffled by dampness and fog;
Our traces, woodsy stale smells
Mixed with the blood and droppings
Of vermin, the kind of late November smoke
That sticks to clothes and furniture.

Others hang out in warehouses,
Stripped and beheaded,
Dripping row upon row, hooked,
Bumping into each other at 3 and 4 a.m.
Limbs labeled, packaged and sent out
To the best and worst places in town,
Morsels to be savored, gristle trimmed away.

The privileged are used
To start the fires,
Kindling for those worthy to be called
Criminal or Heretic,
Hence the name: faggot.

Proust, Mishima, Whitman, and Forster.
                    Faggots.
In America, "queer" and "cocksucker"
Are the dirtiest words.

                         "Hey, fag, where you goin'."
                         "How come you limpin', fag?"
                         "'cause he just got laid."

They have no matches,
Only beer cans and rocks;
A couple wear crosses
Round their necks.

                              August 3, 1978
                              New York City

Algol/Algolagnia[1]

What dark satellite afflicts your brightness?
Algol! fixed and writhing in her perfect hair
(Like agapanthus, blue Medusa in the wind),
Perseus' sword, mirrored in the constellations,
                        Among the sisters,
She alone was mortal, despite the hair.
Bodiless, the gorgon floats among the stars,
You, among the snakes, shining, your beauty
Diminished by lust and pain
                        The Hero,
Long gone, concerned with maidens in distress
And building cities, did not stop to save you.
Light years away, you do not see him
Holding you away from him, shielding himself,
Using her to turn others into stone.

A perpetual memory, the shadow
Of his flailing weapon on its way
To the veins in her neck, passes over you
(A father's sins visited upon a son),
The blameless child cursed in its gleaming.

                                August 15, 1978

---

[1]*Algol*: a fixed star in the constellation of Perseus; its brightness is periodical-
ly diminished by a shadow astronomers have not been able to identify.
Algolagnia: pleasure in inflicting and/or suffering pain.

Nelly and Butch: A Song

I'm tired of:
    faggots & machos
    fruits & vegetables
    fairies & cowboys
    chiffon & leather
    ribbons & chains
    fuss & bother
    drags & posers
    Nelly & Butch
    limpwrists & fistfuckers
    scared little girls & dirty little boys
    garterbelts & cockrings
    bottom & top

Fall 1978

Cheap Song

Liquor and grief make us brave
and living alone attractive
Sex is illusion
Touching a way to behave
When there's nothing else to do.
To smoking, and dancing
And eating, a slave.

Fall 1978

On Gin Considered a Demon

Incubus, she invites you.
Kindle her body with cold.
Rise in her like a muscular dancer. Narrow the light
So a single beam moves on the floor of her brain.
In the chill circle of blue, possessed,
For hours she will lift and pirouette with you the ghostly lover
Lost in her blood.

Later, tell her with icy breath about the distance between stars,
And how deep the frost reaches,
Into her unfilled grave.

Fall 1983

Swallow

Swallow, swallow
your sadness
Eat, eat
your badness

What do you want?
Whiskey and lime
Your body on time
A taste of the slime

Swallow, swallow
your sadness
Eat, eat
your badness

Fall 1983

Light

You were your Self.
Some souls outgrow their bodies sooner
And leave them behind, dry
Moulted skins crumpled and lying
Against closed doors in halls
Where they have been waiting
For life.
When the shedding comes,
Listen and look with care.

You will walk into a golden meadow
Through a field waist high
In burnished grass,
And on towards a riverbank.
Two beings of light
Will greet you
Wordlessly, and
You will know what to do.

The rest of us will follow soon,
Soon, Golden One,
Who was not ours,
Who was not mine.

December 31, 1985

Mantra
For Mary Moser

Maple, cymbidium,
Lobelia, eucalyptus.

I see you waiting and watching
At a window over all that grows
And passes.

(Maple
Cymbidium
Lobelia
Eucalyptus)

These evanescent plants
Their strength, like yours,
Is their undoing
And our gift,
Like yours, their presence
Our great good fortune.

Maple the delicate
Cymbidium the perfect
Lobelia for beauty
Eucalyptus for healing.

August 20, 1985

Resident Fellow I

And when you thought to give them away
The talismans of past lives:
An Aztec face, red clay, two-fifty
At the Juárez market;
Cheap pencil sharpeners,
Chinese babies on corn cobs and pumpkins;
A whistle

You sat on a stool in the kitchen
Eating leftovers, seeing your face
In the toaster,
Waiting

Adams House, 1984

Video Songs

Isabel to be sung by Mick Jagger

He ties you up in the basement
And says he'll be right back.
He tells you that he loves you
While you're still on the rack.

                    Masochist! Masochist!

Upstairs you know he's got someone
You hear them playing their games.
You lie there and wonder,
Where is Henry James?

                    Masochist! Masochist!

Get up, get up, dear Isabel,
Those silken chains are not real.
Your Daddy's only human,
Your waiting is his meal.

                    Masochist! Masochist!

Emma to be sung by David Bowie

Emma, you're a caution.
Dissatisfied to the end.
Your itch for the impossible
Whirled you round the bend.

Spend money on those clothes, girl,
Ignore your homely child.
The men will have their way with you,
They didn't drive you wild.

Choking on the poison,
You see them by your bed.
Their innocent stupidity
Mocks your pretty head.

You are a caution, Emma,
Your hair tied in a bun.
What a combination!
A romantic and a nun.

Anna to be sung by Annie Lennox

Tell them to go to hell, Anna
And take your man away.
Get rid of that husband
And rescue your Sergé

Else no one's going to save you
From that railway station light.
Not Vronsky or his army
Or the gasping in the night.

Anna, Anna, Anna!

Your name alone strikes fear
In the parlors of the rich.
You didn't fit their requirements.
You couldn't be a bitch.

Albertine to be sung by Boy George

Did you imagine when falling off that horse
That he would crown you queen
Or were you scared and screaming
Neck first on the green?

He wove you into his fancies
Without asking your permission,
Aroused by your addictions,
Detesting your submission.

Ah! how you got even
By lying through your teeth,
By sleeping through his romance,
By staying underneath

Until the women woke you.
Their tongues so much like yours,
Their hands forever pressing
Kept offering their cures.

Albertine! Libertine!

Apart from him, you don't exist,
You lure him with your death.
And there he lies still scribbling,
Still taking a last breath.

July 25, 1985
Published in Centennial
1987 issue of *Sequoia,*
Stanford University

Nirvana
For Tom Moser

You've reached Nirvana, my Tibetan monk,
And found it's just a hiccup.
We cannot breathe forever
And forever has no place
In a room full of mortals
Talking about coverlets and rents
Children and the weather.

Your eyes, their magic sheen alone,
Bind you to the earth and belie
Your ravaged state,
The morphine by the bed,
The blackberry veins of your hands.

You look with love at those who love you
And comfort once again,
Passing in and out of sleep
To gaze with pity
To get your fill.

One last kiss
On hand and lips,
A hiccup in parting
A hiccup to treasure.

September 27, 1985

Island Poem I
Floating before the fall

Today you are closer, lapping at the rocks
And I see that your eyes are the colors
Of Autumn, russet, underwater stones reflecting
The sun where I swim
Suspended in brightness.

Cold currents glide through these ancient havens,
Except there where you gaze at me
And invite my body to invade,
Offering your algaed wilderness of wilderness,
Deep orange in the green water.

On the shore, captured by September's,
Tame adders creep and languish
In the fading underbrush.

I hold to the gaze, beloved anchor, as I float
In this clear, contenting warmth,
At once your reflection and marauder,
As the fall is to the summer.

October 10, 1987

ESSAYS & LECTURES
ON CHICANO LITERATURE

Can There Be Chicano Fiction or
Writer's Block?[1]

As in the Winter, 1974, issue of *Miquiztli*, the work here has been drawn mostly from the Chicano literature writing sections of the past year. Again, it is written by students who are working out basic writing problems as they attempt to give expression to their bicultural, sometimes bilingual, perspective. If it is true, and it is, that Stanford is not a "community" college, it is also true that 50 percent of its graduates remain in California and 70 percent remain in the western part of the country. The dominant minority group in this region is bicultural, and the students from this group who enroll in these classes are expressing their wish to remain so.

This kind of self-consciousness is not, I think, encouraged by other creative writing classes within the university. Some of the teachers of those regular writing courses may assume (automatically rather than arrogantly) that the audience for their students' work is humanity in general. But the students in these courses are asked to believe that their audience, if not bilingual, is at least aware of its double heritage. Actually, this kind of specificity of audience is not confined to minority groups within universities. Although they may assume that their audience will probably be wider now, the English wrote and write their fiction primarily for the English. And from my knowledge of North American literature, I know that North American writers wrote and continue to write their fiction for specific North American audiences. Perhaps their hold on much of the rest of

[1]Spring 1975

the world at one time or another gave the English and the North Americans a sense that they were writing for humanity at large. But that is not my concern here. My concern is with the self-consciously bicultural writer and the demands of his or her audience.

The Chicano writer who wants to write fiction is trapped in a room with two doors. One door is labeled "Social Consciousness." The other is labeled "Elitist." As far as I can tell, no other writer of any specific coloration inhabits this room, and it is difficult to tell how long the Chicano writer will be here, but there he/she is because of the peculiar educational history of his/her parents and grandparents, a history too long and melancholy to discuss here.

Opening the door of "Social Consciousness," the Chicano writer of fiction runs into a wall of blocks (also labeled) from which voices constantly remind him what is written on them: The People; *la causa*; the farm workers and *braceros*, the barrio; La Raza; machismo; *la mujer*; pro-communal existence; *Aztlán*; Texas Rangers; Mexican heritage and Mexican heroes. Blocks beyond blocks marking and giving voice to the injustices, triumphs, failures, enemies, friends, places, actual and imagined, of a race that has been in this country at least as long as the first Puritans who landed on its northeastern shore. Each voice within each block merits careful consideration by those whose *main* preoccupation is sociological, historical, psychological, political, or economic. And the appropriate literary form for these matters is the essay, or noble propaganda, or historical and political background, or the sociological study complete with statistics. Not fiction. The novel may use some of these blocks and the tone of some of the voices within them (and the best fiction does) but its allegiance is elsewhere. The writer closes that door, but not before some of those blocks, propelled by their voices, tumble in. He sits on them.

The other door, the one marked "Elitist," when opened, also places obstacles in the writer's way. These are labeled: Academia; "Only English Spoken Here"; northeastern definitions of "American"; Stanford way of life; in short, everything from which he has been excluded *because of his double heritage* until now. These concepts demand scrutiny, such investigation will not produce Chicano fiction either. It will produce usable images, as real to the Chicano student (or to any student, for that matter) as the images projected in the alumni journals and periodicals about the Stanford way of life. Is there such a thing? Who defines it? What is it? Does it include every member of the university community or are only a few privileged individuals allowed to partake of it and claim it for their own?

A few of these blocks fall into the room as he shuts that door. As he places them with the others, the voices within become louder and make claims on his attention. "Be quiet," he says, "I'm brooding." They argue among themselves in low grumbling tones.

The temptation to open the first door again is great. There will be, particularly if one knows how to use the acceptable phrases convincingly, instant acceptance by one's own, a kind of warm feeling in knowing that one belongs to a community of fellow beings who share one's background and speak one's language. (Never mind that we don't agree on some basic issues, we're still *carnales y carnalas*.) But the price is high. One must always have the group in mind, anticipating its needs, fulfilling its desires, shifting with its sudden changes, justifying its behavior at every turn. In short, one must write one's fiction according to the prescribed line, even if it goes against one's own observations. On the other hand, there will always be someone there to soothe one's ego. (That there is an "ego" at all is a contradiction, but it does exist in this group framework. I've seen it wanting to be stroked and petted, especially when it did not do its work.) The responsibility for failure will fall on everyone and, therefore, no one. And the glory? Well, it will be modestly accepted—in the name of the group, of course.

The temptation to be overwhelmed by the voices behind the second door is equally great. Chicanos and Chicanas admitted to the prestigious institutions of the nation are almost without exception on scholarships. Some of them may bite the hand that feeds them, but most of them take advantage of the opportunity extended to them. But what will it have gained the Chicano student (and the university community in general) if he embraces the Stanford ethos (elusive concept) at the expense of his sense of where he comes from? The pragmatic Chicano student—and there are at least as many as there are militants—wants to get through the premed and pre-law programs in order to get into the medical or law schools that will guarantee him a future. Some of these students may choose to return to their communities, but most will enter an economic plane their parents only dreamed about. That's fine, so long as they remember who they are and where they came from. That does not mean they have to go back there; it means they have to remain conscious of it. But what does this have to do with the Chicano writer of fiction?

For an answer, he looks to a scholarly magazine[2] and confronts there the dilemma of a fellow student of literatures, who, like himself, is conscious of his double heritage and has been sitting in the British Museum studying Milton, and is now sitting in his office in the English department of a highly reputable university. He has a Spanish surname and he makes the following observations: My education in these institutions of higher learning has alienated me from my culture. My father does not understand what I am doing. My relatives don't understand my silences when they speak to me in Spanish. What has a Chicano to do with Milton? He states his views and questions sincerely. He writes well, and gives all the credit implicitly to the academic training he has received. Apparently, he does not recognize anything in his own background that predisposes him to be a good writer. Renaissance literature is "rational"; the home he comes from is "nonrational." He bemoans the lack of connection between the two. But in an essay published in a widely read scholarly journal, he goes too far. Apparently, he has been overwhelmed by the voices behind the "Elitist" door. Listen to his response to a request by Chicano undergraduates that he teach the Chicano novel to high school students in the barrio.

> I told them that the novel is not capable of dealing with Chicano experience adequately, simply because most Chicanos are not literate, or are at least not yet comfortably so. This is not something Chicanos need to apologize for (though, I suppose, remembering my own childhood ambi-

[2]Richard Rodriguez, "Going Home Again: The New American Scholarship Boy," *The American Scholar,* Winter, 1974–75, 44:1, 15–28.

tion to combat stereotypes of the Chicano as mental menial,
it is not something easily admitted). Rather the genius and
value of those Chicanos who do not read seem to me to be
largely that their reliance on voice, the spoken word, has
given them the capacity for intimate conversation that I, as
someone who now relies heavily on the written word, can
only envy. The second problem, I went on, is more in the
nature of a technical one: the novel, in my opinion, is not a
form capable of being true to the basic sense of communal
life that typifies Chicano culture. What the novel as a literary form is best capable of representing is solitary existence
set against a large social background. Chicano novelists, not
coincidentally, nearly always fail to capture the breathtakingly rich family life of most Chicanos, and instead often
describe only the individual Chicano in transit between
Mexican and American cultures. (24)

What this young man is describing here and in another essay he has
published elsewhere[3] is his transition from Mexican to American cultures. He uses his education in the major universities via scholarships
as a metaphor for his inability to bring together his academic interests
with his nonacademic background, although how or why he became
interested in school to begin with he does not say. What he is doing
is done by some Chicano undergraduates and graduates (who should
know better). He is blaming higher learning for depriving him of his
heritage at the same time that he is using the tools of that learning to
expose the deprivation. That would be all right if he wouldn't pre-
scribe for the rest of us, and if he could get rid of the self-pitying tone
that he uses when he is unable to accept that he, a Chicano, can be
interested in Milton for Milton's sake rather than for the Chicano
community's sake. But we need to examine this passage very carefully, so that we avoid the traps Mr. Rodriguez has leaped into.

In "most Chicanos are not literate, or at least not yet comfortably

---

[3]Richard Rodriguez, "Leo Carrillo as Andy Hardy and other Losses of White
Liberalism," *The Columbia Forum,* Summer, 1973, 2:3, 35–40.

so," he is in a perfect position as a university teacher to help them become so. Unless, of course, he believes what the gringo has been saying about the Chicano all along, that is, that he can't learn to read or write because he is inferior. And this young man seems to believe that. Look at that melancholy parenthetical memory of his childhood. What destroyed that ambition to combat those stereotypes? At what point did he begin to believe what some of the gringos were saying about the Mexican's ability to write and speak English? Wasn't his own talent for the language some evidence to counteract the basic charge of illiteracy? If he could read and write, might not the others also, given enough attention and patience? And what does he make now of his own ability to write literate essays about how his education alienated him from his culture? Granted that he has been encouraged in that alienation by the refusal of American education to take into account the Indo-Hispanic traditions that helped to shape a sizeable portion of this country. But hasn't he participated in equal measure in that alienation? Why does he feel sorry for *himself* if his father does not understand what he is studying? His sons and daughters will, and probably more than he.

This young man's concentration in English literature of the sixteenth and seventeenth centuries, I take it, is responsible for his lack of knowledge about the evolution of the novel. He has told us from the beginning that the novel is incapable of dealing with the Chicano experience adequately. In his delineation of the technical problem he is wrong on all but the last observation where he is only partially wrong. "The novel . . . is not a form capable of being true to the basic sense of communal life that typifies Chicano culture." The important phrase here is "basic communal life." Perhaps it is true that the Chicano sense of this life is different from that of other cultures, but it is not true that the novel is incapable of accommodating the idea of communal life. Has he read Faulkner? Joyce's *Dubliners* (which may be seen as a novel)? What about Winesburg, *Ohio?* Has he read Trollope? What of Carlos Fuentes' *La región más transparente* or Juan Rulfo's *Pedro Páramo* or *Llano en Llamas?* Or Agustín Yañez's *Al filo del agua?* Has he read Gabriel García Márquez's *One Hundred Years of Solitude?* In all of these works one can argue persuasively that the main theme is exactly that "breathtakingly rich family life" Mr. Rodriguez believes the novel is incapable of capturing. That it has not yet been done by a Chicano novelist does not mean it cannot be done. Other writers have shown the way, and they come from every culture. Among Chicano writers, Tomás Rivera has come the closest to creating as his protagonist the community of migrant workers about which he writes, not a single migrant worker against a larger backdrop, but the community itself. I suggest that Mr. Rodriguez read some novels. And that he do it without putting between him and them his own difficulties in bringing the literate and illiterate together.

I too am critical of the Chicano novelists and short story writers that we have, and I am quick to point out their failings to my students. But I never suggest they cannot write because they come from a culture that is essentially illiterate. Some Chicanos may like to believe they do because it saves them the trouble of learning to read or write, but I don't know any of them. And if they can't read or write, there are reasons, and those reasons have much more to do with the educational system of this nation than with the essential illiteracy of a race. Isn't finally the conflict Mr. Rodriguez has a particular form of a more general and inevitable conflict anyone has whose parents have not gone to universities and colleges because they were busy seeing to it that their children got there? And aren't most serious students of literature in particular, and Western civilization in general, made to feel the alienation of the twentieth-century world more vividly than most? There will always be a conflict between nonacademic people and the academically inclined. To confuse this conflict with the literacy or illiteracy of a culture is, however, a mistake.

But we have left our Chicano writer of fiction in that room with two doors contemplating the demands made on him by the voices emanating from the blocks he is sitting on, legs dangling, head in hand. He is listening to the advice from those voices under him, and he has carefully followed the discussion about the problems of our *carnal* who cannot decide between Milton and his family. He is reading a book about another writer in another room, a woman in the 1920s who was most conscious of the charges of illiteracy made upon her sex by professors of literature who shared her background and traditions:

> . . . masterpieces are not single and solitary births; they are
> the outcome of many years of thinking in common, of think-
> ing by the body of the people, so that the experience of the
> mass is behind the single voice.[4]

He notes that she writes "thinking in common" not "common thinking," for he knows that the Chicano writer who will produce a mas-
terpiece will be an uncommon thinker. He observes that she places
the body of the people and the experiences of the masses behind the
single voice, not in front dictating, but behind it probably, he thinks,
singing the sustained chord which will form the necessary background to the solo voice. He sees finally that the voice is "single," not
"elitist" or "individualistic" or "egotistical" or "the best." The woman
writer is describing a state of being, not a quality of mind. As far as
he knows, no great work of fiction has ever been written by a group
of people, unless you're willing to argue that the Bible is fiction.

The doors are shut, the voices drone out. There seems to be no
exit and one cannot stay in this room forever. To open the doors and
let in the warring factions in all their fury is suicidal. An extraordinary and uncommon feat must now be attempted. There seems to be
no precedent within one's culture for such a feat. Everyone, including Mr. Rodriguez, has told him that. And the work that has preced-
ed this afterword does not yet accomplish it, but it is a start.

Imagine.

What?

Imagine a window. Ignore the howling at the doors and concentrate on that window. Imagine it in any shape you wish. The novel
lends itself to different shapes, that's why people say it is always
dying. Don't be fooled. Now use some of those blocks and arrange
them so that you can stand up on them. Look out the window. Open it.

What do you see?

Describe it. Describe it as best you can in Spanish or English or
both.

---

[4]Virginia Wolf, *A Room of One's Own,* New York: Harcourt, Brace & World,
Inc., 1957, 69–78.

Saints, Artists, and Vile Politics[1] (excerpt)

The Chicano writer falls between the Latin American and Anglo-American literary traditions, and at this stage in the development of Chicano literature, he displays an uneasy relationship with both traditions. The uneasiness is at times reflected in the writing problems that arise in his work.[2] Sometimes he sides (or is made to side) with the view that expects its writers to devote themselves directly to the social and political problems of their community; sometimes he strikes out in the direction of the view of the writer as solitary explorer of domains beyond the social and political.

By those strongly entrenched in Anglo-American tradition, the Chicano writer is dismissed as not worth reading because of his lack of literary sophistication. By those who wish him to be completely within the Latin American tradition, he is praised for breaking away from any forms that suggest Anglo-American styles and preoccupations in his portrayal of Chicano life and character.[3] And he is espe-

---

[1]Excerpt from seventy-page monograph on Chicano/a literature written in 1975.
[2]The most instructive example of this discomfort is found in Edmund Villaseñor's *Macho!* The writing is a parody of Hemingway as a parody of himself. Among other things, Villaseñor cannot make up his mind where he stands between the Chicanos' respect for César Chávez and the view held of him by migrant workers, who do not want to become citizens of the United States. The protagonist is a Mexican national, born and reared in a mountain village of Michoacán, and his experiences as a migrant worker in California form the substance of the plot. The novel is called by its publishers (I assume with Villaseñor's permission) "the first great Chicano novel." Movie rights to the book have been sold.

cially praised by some critics within this camp if he is clearly antithetical to Anglo-American political and economic systems.

The three works I am considering are instructive examples of the ways in which the Anglo-American and Latin American traditions meet to one degree or another. They are equally interesting in suggesting the different directions the novel and autobiographical narrative from this perspective may take in the future. Finally, they are important to any discussion that considers the problems of writing, especially those problems which arise when a writer is self-consciously attempting to reflect an experience that is seen to be at odds with the experience we call "American."

Pocho

The difference between the Mexican-American and Chicano generations is reflected in several ways in Chicano long and short fiction and autobiographical narrative. It gives much tension to the

---

[3]This is the general tendency of the editors of and writers accepted for publication in *Mester*, a biannual literary journal published in collaboration with the Department of Spanish and Portuguese and Chicano Studies Center at UCLA. Hence, their current praise of *Peregrinos de Aztlán* by Miguel Méndez-M. It is written entirely in Spanish and *caló* and derives much from the picaresque tradition—a European literary tradition that is held in esteem among Latin American writers because it allows them to criticize society through the eyes of their *pícaro*.

Though I suspect that it will be criticized by the strongly ideological critics on the staff of this journal for being too "arty," Ron Arias' well wrought novella, *The Road to Tamazunchale,* imitates and owes much to magic realism, a more recent development in Latin American letters. Arias' work is especially indebted to Gabriel García Márquez, who, with Borges, is the most widely read and recognized Latin American writer. Arias' short novel is written in English, but relies a great deal on the readers' knowledge of barrio expressions and life in East Los Angeles. It is enormously entertaining and exhibits a writer's talent for bringing characters to life in amusing, captivating, and unself-conscious ways. In that sense, *The Road to Tamazunchale* is a radical departure from the Chicano novels we have so far.

Méndez-M and Arias are drawing exclusively from the Latin American literary tradition to describe the lives of characters in a North American setting. It will be interesting to see how far in this approach these talented writers can take Chicano letters.

drama that occurs between one generation and another, and acts as an ideological metaphor in the conflicts between father and son, mother and daughter, husband and wife, the politically motivated character and the resigned character. Its permutations are many and potentially fruitful to fiction and autobiographical narrative in Chicano literature. When a writer chooses to describe this difference and the separation it creates between his characters, he or she is contributing insight to one of the distinguishing characteristics of Chicano and Mexican-American letters.

In *Pocho,* José Antonio Villarreal portrays this same ideological conflict as it existed between the migrant and the Mexican-American generations.[4] This earlier period in the history of Mexicans in the United States has an important place in the emergence of Chicano literature and ideas. Villarreal has the distinction of being the first novelist from within to write and have published a long work that deserves recognition as the work which gives literary expression to the migrant and Mexican-American experience. His novel is *sui generis.*

There is no evidence to show that José Antonio Villarreal was responding directly to the needs of an ethnic group or to the demands of an audience in political or social distress when he wrote *Pocho* in the late fifties.[5] The attention such groups would give him and his work did not grow until the Chicano Movement was well underway during the late sixties, and teachers and students of Chicano literature were at a loss to find published novels or autobiographical narratives that would help them learn about the culture of the largest

---

[4] I rely on Rodolfo Alvarez's convenient if overly simplified, historical divisions of the generations of Mexican people in North American in relation to Anglo-American political and economic systems: the Creation Generation, 1849 to 1900; the Migrant (i.e., those who migrated north from Mexico, *not* migrant workers) Generation, 1900 to World War II; the Mexican-American Generation, from the Second World War to the early stages of the war in Vietnam; and the Chicano Generation, early sixties to the present. (See his *Chicano: The Evolution of a People*.)

[5] "Pocho" is a Mexican-Spanish term used to refer to Mexicans born in the United States. Among Mexicans born in Mexico, it is not a complimentary term; it implies that those who are "pochos" have deserted the homeland and taken on the values of the North American invader.

"minority" group in the western half of the country. It was then that *Pocho* was reissued, and it gained for its author an audience interested enough to recognize or to be skeptical about his accomplishments.

The book begins shortly after the Mexican Revolution of 1910 and ends during the early stages of WWII. It is a straightforward, chronologically presented history of the family of Richard Rubio, the protagonist. The story of Juan Rubio, his father, is told in the first chapter of the novel, which is set in Juárez, Mexico, the largest border town between Mexico and the United States. We learn that Juan Rubio has been a soldier in Pancho Villa's army, that he deplores the new government in power after the Revolution of 1910, and that he is willing to assassinate the new leader of the country. The sense of history and of men as part of important historical and political movements is established in this opening chapter. And it is significant that Juan Rubio is grounded in Mexican history and that his roots are sunk deeply into Mexico; he will not be able to adjust to North American values. These facts are important to his characterization and create the essential difference between him and his son. When Juan Rubio learns that Villa is dead, and after the assassination plot is discovered, he flees to California. His wife, Consuelo, and his daughters follow him. His only son, Richard, is born in a field near Brawley, California. Though he dreams of returning to Mexico, Juan Rubio becomes trapped in North America, and at the close of the chapter devoted to him, he considers himself to be one of "the lost ones."

Juan Rubio is very much within that part of Latin American tradition which reveres men in battle against tyrannical forces, regards women as subservient to their husbands but respects highly their powerful role as mothers, and has a strong belief in the indigenous values and customs of pre-Columbian civilizations. Juan Rubio brings this tradition with him; he does not leave it behind on the other side of the river. And he is representative of the thousands who migrated northward during and after the Revolution of 1910.

They came first to Juárez, where the price of the

three-minute tram ride would take them into El Paso del Norte—or a short walk through the open door would deposit them in Utopia. The ever-increasing army of people swarmed across while the border remained open, fleeing from squalor and oppression. But they could not flee reality, and the Texans, who welcomed them as a blessing because there were miles of cotton to be harvested, had never really forgotten the Alamo. The certain degree of dignity the Mexicans yet retained made some of them turn around and walk back into the hell they had left. Others huddled close to the international bridge and established a colony on the American side of the river, in the city of El Paso, because they could gaze at their homeland a few yards away whenever the impulse struck them. The bewildered people came on insensitive to the fact that even though they were not stopped, they were not really wanted. It was the ancient quest for El Dorado, and so they moved onward, west to New Mexico and Arizona and California, and as they moved, they planted their seed. (*Pocho* 16)

Juan Rubio, then, belongs to the Migrant Generation, the generation who migrated—*not immigrated*—to the north and away from the homeland now perceived by him and others to be in the hands of traitors to the ideals of that revolution. What Villarreal does not give an indication of in this semi-historical passage is that this generation was not coming to a totally new frame of reference; the Southwest and West had only been under U.S. domination for a little over sixty years at this time, and the customs, values, and traditions of many of the original settlers—Indians, Mexicans, and Spaniards—were still evident. The "El Dorado" and "Utopia" the migrant generation may have been seeking were for them not the same as the virgin and promised land that European immigrants had in mind when they left their roots behind and crossed an ocean to begin new lives with greater opportunities. The European immigrants were leaving their past in an irrevocable manner, even when they retained the customs and language of their ancestors for one or two generations. Mexican migrants were simultaneously encountering their past and bringing it with them. For them there was no substantive change. The fact that the United States now owned the territory made no essential difference. For three hundred years the land they entered into had been Mexico and for centuries before that Juan Rubio's Indian ancestors had roamed in it at will. What this migrant generation did encounter was a political and economic system not sympathetic to it and as intractable as that political system from which they were fleeing. What they saw as the culture of the U.S. Anglo citizen did not appeal to them; the Mexican migrant arrived culture and history intact. Juan Rubio feels lost because he sees that he has no place in the movement of history within the political system in which he finds himself. Such a place, he hopes, will be there for his son Richard, who is automatically a citizen of Utopia.

The remainder and larger part of the novel is a chronicle of Richard Rubio's education in the social, political, and economic systems of the United States. He is a member of the lower class and he is intelligent. From the beginning he is interested in books and learning. And that interest will affect his life relentlessly. (Before views of marriage outside of the Catholic framework intrude and make possible the separation between his parents, Richard, in a quiet, well-rendered scene near the end of the book, reads *Crime and Punishment* in a Spanish translation to his mother and father.) The novel records his growth from his birth in the twenties to his enlistment in the Navy in the first years of World War II. Richard, unlike his parents, is in the evolutionary stage from the Migrant to the Mexican-American generation, for he has learned the values of a culture and tradition alien to his father. At the same time, he has maintained an awareness of his difference from the dominant political, social, and economic forces of North America. He is aided in retaining that difference not only by what he learns from his parents, but in the discrimination against people like Juan and Consuelo Rubio that abounds in the place where their son is reared and educated: the Santa Clara Valley.

Richard Rubio is different from his father because he is not so root bound. Throughout the book, Richard insists upon his individuality and resists being identified with any group.[6] Richard wants to understand everybody. He wants to love people for what they are, and he wants to be an individual in the Anglo-American sense. His mother reinforces Richard's sense of being "special" and apart from the herd because she recognizes him as a thinker and a reader.[7] Villarreal makes explicit Richard's difference from the society in which he finds himself: "Always, however, there was a part of his mind that carefully observed from a detached point of view, and he was aware that he was learning something"(51). Richard's role throughout the novel is that of observer and judge; his participation in events varies according to how emotionally engaged he becomes with what he is observing. The significant mark of his character is his capacity to observe and to act according to his observations; it keeps him from being a dull, passive protagonist. His penchant for observation makes of him a potential writer.

Richard looks at everyone with as much impartiality as he can muster: from the landowners like Mr. Jamison and his daughter

---

[6]To the strongly ideological Chicano critic, as well as within the militant Chicano camp, the concept of individuality is particularly offensive. The concept is seen as synonymous historically with *gringo* avarice and greed. It is regarded by those who stress *carnalismo* (brotherhood) as a form of selfishness, a way to avoid the needs of the "community" and as an excuse some take to align themselves with what is regarded as the great North American activity: making money, and especially making money by exploiting others.

In their inability or refusal to see beyond this interpretation of the notion of individuality, Chicanos have overlooked its virtues. For our purpose, and in order to illuminate the works at hand, it is enough to observe that this disregard and disdain for individual enterprise and its attendant embrace of collective and community concern is one of the strongest of the prevailing Chicano myths. Because *Pocho* does not pay tribute to that myth, ideological critics do not consider it a "Chicano" novel.

[7]Consuelo also regards her son as, "All indio, this boy of mine, except inside. The Spanish blood is deep within him" (35). Here, she is at odds with the emphasis put on the Indian heritage of the Mexican and Chicano by most Chicanos. The statement which summarizes this view and which is alluded to often is attributable to José Vasconcelos, one of the intellectuals in the forefront of the Mexican Revolution of 1910: "Our culture is Spanish, but our soul is Indian."

Marla (they are not presented as stereotypes, and the complexity of their situation is as evident as that of the workers who respect them and are moved to strike against them) to the Okies who force the permanent Mexican residents out of their jobs because they are willing to pick fruit for lower wages; from Joe Pete Manoel, the tormented, and most intriguing, character in the novel who teaches Richard about the injustices, ambiguities, and beauties of the world, to Ricky Malatesta, Richard's Italian school chum, who fascinates Richard because he is so different from him and who turns out in the end to be a shallow opportunist; from his father, whom he respects and loves, to the *pachucos* who represent to him a lifestyle that can never be his and that he sees is self-defeating. Throughout, Richard is set up by the author to learn from the adventures he has, but Villarreal is a good enough writer to share that learning in a simple, unmelodramatic way that sustains the reader's interest.

An important scene in the novel establishes Richard's role in a quick, deft manner. Richard is a child and just beginning his education in the North American school system. During a fight in the orchards between strikers, policemen, and those in sympathy with the growers, Richard witnesses a murder. He alone knows who the murderer is, and young as he is, he is asked to face up to the police interrogations. Richard is forced into a decision that goes against everything he has been taught by his parents and by the Catholic Church. A deeper instinct moves him to choose to lie in order to protect the murderer. The scene is not melodramatic; we are not pushed, as we are in Rudolfo Anaya's novel, to understand that this is a Great Learning Experience for the boy. And unlike Tony Marez, the protagonist in Anaya's work, Richard Rubio is not a passive agent. Richard acts even as he observes. And Villarreal, again unlike Anaya, never invites us to see his main character as a poor innocent whose childhood is shattering before his eyes.

Villarreal relies a great deal on the use of historical detail to recreate the background for his novel, and from the Migrant and Mexican-American perspectives, he portrays California during the Depression:

The year was 1931, and the people of Santa Clara were hungry. The little food they could buy with their meager income was augmented only because the valley was so fertile, and now it was common practice to go into the fields and take fruits and vegetables. The smaller farmers, who could not afford to harvest their crops, willingly let the people have them. Richard's family did not suffer as much as the others, because the depression had not changed their diet. They never had much more than they were now getting. (47)

Villarreal can also be honestly humorous in an unself-conscious way. His treatment of the communist meeting from the point of view of Richard as a child and the later adolescent explorations into sexuality are described without self-righteous indignation in the first instance or leers in the second. Villarreal's use of the omniscient point of view which sometimes narrows so that we see through Richard's eyes, and his use of realistic details convince us of the truth of Richard Rubio's situation and bring him to life as himself rather than as representative of a "people" or political group.

The main theme of the book is the coming to manhood of the main character, and it is that, I think, that leads Villarreal in interviews to associate himself and his work with Joyce and Faulkner, particularly Joyce. In style, he has nothing in common with them, and he is at his weakest when he attempts to use Latinate English words. The effect is invariably awkward and stilted ("chains were incrementally heavier on his heart," "inutile inanimate" to refer to an old barn, etc.), but he does not fall into this style often. For the most part his language is plain and suits the subject and mode of his book.

For all its brevity, the book presents us with a varied and large cast of characters, most of whom are skillfully brought to life. By far the most compelling figure in Richard's education is Joao Pedro Manoel Alves, the Portuguese aristocrat who is finally defeated by his past and is committed to Agnews State Hospital for the Insane. There is density in this characterization, and one wishes that Villarreal were a different, if not better, kind of writer who could explore the tragic dimensions of such an extreme case as Joe Pete. But the

tone of the novel and the limitations imposed by Richard's point of
view are not conducive to a profound development of character.
Consequently, we are left with only an outline of a tormented soul.
In this book, as in Anaya's *Bless Me, Última,*[8] the most carefully
portrayed figure is the teacher outside of the Anglo-American educational system who teaches the protagonist about Life and the existence of the soul beyond systems or even books. What Richard learns
from Joe Pete is a respect for humanity and an acceptance of all
forms of human weakness, and in one of the better scenes in the
book, Villarreal gives Richard a grand opportunity to show what the
young disciple has learned from the wise, albeit psychosexually
damaged, teacher.

The theme of sexuality is important to the plot of this novel for
the particular national dimensions through which it is portrayed.
Richard has learned views of sexuality different from his father's; at
the same time, Richard cannot accept his mother's growing sexual
independence and her final rejection of Juan Rubio. Once again,
Richard is caught between the Latin American and Anglo-American
views of humanity.

The metaphorical form this conflict assumes is significant.
Richard identifies his parents' sexual habits with their national
character. In his eyes, their sexual customs make them Mexicans.
Richard himself, however, refuses to identify sex with character;
he thinks his parents do make that identification *because they are
Mexicans.* "He was a man, [and] for all his years, he refused to
accept sexual satisfaction as the sublime effort of life" (129). We
are led to believe that this decision leads Richard to see himself as
un-Mexican; the implication is that to be truly Mexican one must
make one's sex life "the sublime effort of life." The confusion and
identification of sex with character is compounded by Juan Rubio's
views on the subject: "you are a man, and it is good," Juan Rubio

---

[8]See also Carlos Castañeda's portrayal of Don Juan, the Yanqui Indian *brujo,*
who is the most fascinating character in Castañeda's tetralogy. I include Castañeda's work in the list of Chicano literature, mostly for its description of the
brujo or *curandero,* a figure that occurs frequently in Chicano fiction, autobiographical narrative, and folklore.

Rubio tells his son, "because to a Mexican being *that* is the most important thing. If you are a man, your life is half lived; what follows does not really matter" (131). If one has proved oneself to be a male in the most basic sexual sense of the word, then, one has proved oneself a Mexican.[9]

What is most instructive about Juan Rubio's statement in setting him apart from his son is that it combines *national* character with sexuality, and with the additional information that "what follows," if one knows he is a man, "*does not matter*" (italics mine), I assume that he means the difficult business of day-to-day life that has nothing to do with one's sexual identity; in other words, almost everything else. Villarreal is treading on the fine line between stereotype and national characteristics here, and his detractors find the portrayal of Juan Rubio offensive.

Richard, the son, the product of two cultures, is not happy with this identification, and the problem that it presents to him becomes confused in his mind (and Villarreal's) with national identity. It is clear that Richard does not want to be like his parents. Their definition of happiness is not his, and although he may side instinctively with his father, his sympathies are with his mother's growing independence. It becomes for him an insoluble problem that he thinks of as inseparable from the problem of national identity. For Richard, the painful breaking away from one's parents takes on the metaphorical form of this confusion of identities.

Villarreal attempts to resolve the confusion that arises from this conflict by resorting to the authorial voice. No one is to blame for

---

[9]This view makes "Mexicans" of many outside the culture. Hemingway and Norman Mailer, for example, because both are quite preoccupied with proving themselves to be "males" and never tire of creating characters for whom this preoccupation is the major interest in life; hence, their reputation as North American *machos*.

Juan Rubio may not know it, and Villarreal may not be consciously aware of what he is doing here, but both belong in Hemingway's camp in this theme. Even greater complexity is added when we remember that Hemingway learned much of his notions on masculinity from the bullfighters he admired and followed with such devotion. The "hero" in *The Sun Also Rises* is not Jake Barnes but Pedro Romero, the very potent Spanish bullfighter.

the disintegration of the Rubio family, he says in a sentence, because "the transition from the culture of the old world to that of the new should never have been attempted in one generation" (135). It is a weak resolution artistically because his characters have had no choice. Villarreal can not pose a satisfactory resolution to this theme in the novel, either through Richard or in his own voice, and his difficulty is reflected in the weak ending to the book.

Because Richard belongs to the Mexican-American Generation, he does not have the chance to go to college at the end of the novel. His only way of escaping from the insoluble conflict at home is to join the Navy and fight in World War II. He is as yet unaware of the political battle that exists in his own country. And no one, not even Villarreal, wants him to stay home with his mother.

Richard's mother, Consuelo, is considered more extensively than his sisters. The girls remain shady and unobtrusive characters, except for the one scene in which Richard, assuming his father's place in the family, berates one of them for rebelling against what she has been taught is her proper role. They are part of the narrative only inasmuch as they figure in the conflict between Richard and his father.

Consuelo, wife and mother, has grown away from the traditional concept of herself as Mexican woman. But in her final scene with Richard, she still behaves according to that concept. It seems that getting rid of her husband, who could never change his notions about men and women, has not helped her to get rid of her son in the same way. She is willing to give up her role as submissive wife, but not her role as mother to her son. And it is clear that she respects him more than she respects her daughters. Neither she nor Richard ever questions that respect; he is the man of the house after Juan Rubio leaves the family.

Along with Richard, we find unconvincing Consuelo's great upset at the end of the novel when Richard tells her that he no longer believes in God. She herself has gone against the dictates of the Church in wanting to divorce her husband, and it seems more than a contradiction in her character to want Richard to remain a virtuous child of the Church. Her outburst makes sense if the Church is seen as one of the weapons she uses to keep hold of the son she loves and knows is going to leave her. Consuelo is an interesting character, however, because of her independence. What may have been a stereotypical portrait of the Mexican mother devoted to her only son becomes a more complex characterization that is not resolved. In the end, she is left alone with her daughters, and there is no hint of what will become of her or them.

As part of the Mexican-American Generation, Richard can assert himself by going off to war rather than by engaging in the battle that exists for him at home in the political and social arenas. In discussing that battle, we come to another important, but not deeply explored, theme in this novel: Richard's relation to "his people." It is always puzzling to Richard when it is pointed out to him by others, usually Anglo-Americans, that he does in fact belong to a recognizably different group of people.

Outside of his immediate family, Richard's curiosity about the *pachucos*[10] and his association with them is part of his attempt to come to terms with his cultural heritage. Villarreal, through Richard, is very incisive in his views toward these outcasts of society, both Mexican and Anglo-American. Richard cannot finally identify with them because he does not share that feeling of inferiority that he sees is the basis of their lives, and also because he has been exposed in Anglo-American schools to the notion of individuality. He has been, in his own perception, "Americanized."

It is noteworthy and historically correct that the *pachuco* is not made out to be more Mexican than Richard. The *pachucos*, as Richard observes accurately, are anti-American and have a "marked hauteur toward Mexico and toward their parents for their old-country ways" (149). After being picked up by the police because Richard and his friends are thought to be *pachucos*, the young man is once again face to face with the notion of his relationship to his people. The dialogue is between him and the detective who has inter-

---

[10]*Pachucos* have fascinated many writers, Octavio Paz among them. *The Labyrinth of Solitude*, his philosophical and historical study of Mexican history and character begins with a chapter on them. The *pachuco* was born in El Paso, as Villarreal informs us; the barrio there is in the southern part of the city.

rogated him. Richard has been found to be innocent and is being released. "Drop in and see me sometime," the detective says to him.

> "We can use someone like you when you get older. There are a lot of your people around now, and someone like you would be good to have on the side of law and order."
>
> Jesus Christ! Another one, thought Richard. Aloud he said, "No, thanks. I don't want to have anything to do with you guys."
>
> "Think about it. You have a few years yet. There's a lot you can do for your people that way."
>
> His sincerity surprised Richard. He seemed to mean it. "No," he answered. "I'm no Jesus Christ. Let 'my people' take care of themselves."
>
> "You were defending them awhile ago."
>
> "I was defending myself!" *Stupid!*
>
> But who the hell were his people? He had always felt that all people were his people—not in that nauseating God-made-us-all equal way, for to him that was a deception; the exact opposite was so obvious. But this man, in his attitude and behavior, gave him a new point of view about his world. (162)

Villarreal begs another important question raised in this book. In what way exactly does Richard mean that "all people [are] his people," if not in that way he thinks of as maudlin and deceptive? What is the "new point of view" the detective gives him about his world? It is never described or gone into in terms of the development of his character. It comes too late in the novel, but it would make an excellent starting point for a sequel. How will this character, educated to believe in Anglo-American notions of individuality and the worth of the individual apart from the group (a notion he embraces readily because of his own sense of himself as special and different), come to terms with the notion of community and of the individual as an indissoluble part of a group, no better or worse than the rest of humanity? If Richard becomes a writer within the Anglo-American tradition, he will be ignored because his particular subject and talent for describing it will not be recognized as important by a cultural tradition alien to his heritage. If he becomes a writer within the Latin American tradition, he will be expected to serve the needs of his community and involve himself in their political and social struggles, an expectation and involvement that he will find constitutionally unable to fulfill.

His escape is ready made, and we cannot fault Villarreal for sending Richard off to war. What interests us in relation to our general theme is the attitude Richard embraces at the end of the novel. He has been weeping as he contemplates his uneasy place between people like the detective and people like his friends. He feels alienated from both groups. "He stopped crying then, because it was not worth crying for people. He withdrew into his protective shell of cynicism, but he recognized it for what it was and could easily hide it from the world" (164).

Cynicism, the other side of the coin to sentimentality, is Richard's only recourse at this stage in the history of "his people." If someone were to resurrect Richard, or someone like him, in another novel, his alternatives might be stated in the following ways and portrayed through character and event:

1) Assimilation into the mainstream, which might entail even a change in name so that on the surface, anyway, he would not be plagued by his past at all. Rubio means red; Richard Red. He would marry a woman outside of his inherited frame of reference and raise his children as Anglo-Americans. He would forbid his older relatives to speak Spanish to his children and would keep them away from each other as much as possible.

2) Chicanismo in its most extreme form, which would mean an unrelenting separation of oneself from what is perceived to be the dominant culture, particularly its political, educational, and economic systems. He would marry a Mexican woman, raise his children to be proud of their Indian heritage, although they would have to speak Spanish, the language of the original conquerors. He would work to construct a viable political and economic environment that would coexist with

the dominant system and be continually at odds with it.

3) Compromise, which would mean identifying and seeing one-self as the product of two cultures, not feeling inferior to either for racial or national reasons, and working to make certain that his children and their children became a significant part of the forces that move the country, which is theirs just as much as anyone else's. And especially if one is talking about the southwestern and western parts of it.

But for Richard, as Villarreal portrays him in *Pocho,* these alternatives do not exist. He belongs to the Mexican-American Generation. "Of what worth was it all? His father had won his battle, and for him life was worth while, but he had never been unaware of what his fight was. *But what about me?* thought Richard." The novel should end with this question, for it represents Richard's dilemma perfectly.[11] Unlike his father, Richard does not know what "his fight" is. In between two generations, in between two cultural traditions, too early in time to become engaged in the activities of the Chicano community, he joins the only group he sees as available to him outside his immediate family: the U.S. Navy.

Seen in historical terms, *Pocho* belongs to the Migrant and Mexican-American Generation. The evolution of Chicano ideology and of a political awareness owes much to these periods, even if the new consciousness considers itself at odds with the old. *Pocho* is an instructive and well done documentary novel with autobiographical overtones that is, so far, the exemplary book of those earlier generations. Villarreal is not a "great" writer, but he is a careful, conscientious one, and this small, unpretentious book merits notice for its importance to Chicano and Mexican-American letters. This novel also suggests two directions for Chicano fiction and autobiographical narrative. One is the exploration of a character not as an individual in the Anglo-American sense, but as an individual with a strong

---

[11]Instead, Villarreal adds two more sentences directly out of pulp novels: "Because he did not know, he would strive to live."

"He thought of this and he remembered, and suddenly he knew that for him there would never be a coming back" (187).

recognition of his national or racial difference from the mainstream of North American life. The other is the portrayal of the singular character as part of a definable community with traditions and customs radically different from the mainstream of Anglo-American culture. Oscar Zeta Acosta's *The Autobiography of a Brown Buffalo* goes in the first direction; Rudolfo Anaya in *Bless Me, Última* takes the second.

The Autobiography of a Brown Buffalo

"But what about me?" is the central and persistent question in Acosta's *Autobiography*. It is evident in the work itself that Acosta was very much aware of the market for material from the Native American and Chicano frames of reference in the late sixties and early seventies. He had already been "immortalized" by Hunter Thompson in *Fear and Loathing in Las Vegas*. In that work, Acosta is portrayed as Dr. Gonzo, the three-hundred-pound Samoan attorney who takes drugs and drinks with abandon. In his autobiography, he portrays himself as a Brown Buffalo with exactly the same characteristics and preoccupations. In this instance the portrayal is affected by Acosta's sense of himself as an oppressed member in Anglo-American society. Acosta's method is to generalize from his personal experiences and project his own insecurities onto a political movement.[12] By a strange twist that Acosta is not aware of, *Autobiography* is a failure, rather than a success story.

What would Hemingway have made of Oscar Zeta Acosta? When, in *Autobiography*, Acosta makes a pilgrimage to Hemingway's grave, two *machos* from different cultures come together in a strange conjunction. What is implicit in Hemingway is made painfully explicit in Acosta: preoccupation with virility, admiration for violence, a sentimental or cynical view of women, and the tendency to take oneself very seriously. In the older writer, particularly during his early period and before he began to parody himself, a genuinely great talent for writing commands attention. Acosta possess-

---

[12]See Ricardo Sánchez, *Canto y grito mi liberación.* Sánchez employs the same method but with some success.

es no such talent. His writing is equal to fair newspaper reporting; at its best, it evokes in realistic and convincing dialogue the ridiculous nature of the situations in which the Brown Buffalo finds himself. He has a sense of the ridiculous that the reader wishes Acosta would extend to include himself.

Throughout most of *Autobiography* and his second work, a novel called *The Revolt of the Cockroach People*, he is too preoccupied with presenting his image in the best possible light to be aware of the pathos of the "real" man who shows through that very thin and transparent front. There is no indication to show that Acosta is aware of or in control of the real self and the fictitious self in these books. For this reason, *Autobiography* belongs to that group of books concerned with a search for identity, either personal or national or ethnic, and his publishers were shrewd enough to tout it as a "Chicano Manchild in the Promised Land," referring to Claude Brown's popular bestseller.[13] I doubt that Acosta's book sold as many copies; it will, however, become a collector's item for all students interested in the development of Chicano literature.

Autobiography is mostly an account of five days in the life of the writer, now thirty-three years old ("the same age as Jesus when he died," Acosta tells us, lest we miss the connection). These five days occur in July 1967, but there are retrospective passages scattered randomly throughout the narrative that tell us about his birth and early years in El Paso, Texas; growing up in Riverbank, California, where he was a fruit picker; his army experiences in San Francisco; his year as a missionary in Panama; his return to California; the growth of his interest in writing; his law school training; his psychiatric and physical problems; and throughout, his melancholy and consistently bad experiences with women. The book recounts and concentrates on adventure for the sake of adventure.

When he first introduces himself to the reader, Acosta has quit

---

[13]This book was among those that all entering freshmen were required to read for their first quarter English courses at Stanford. Other required books in the late sixties were Eldridge Cleaver's *Soul on Ice*, Graham Greene's *The Quiet American*, and the *Autobiography of Malcolm X*. The practice of requiring all entering students to read the same book has been abandoned.

his job as an attorney for people in the lowest classes of San Francisco Bay Area society, and he is running away from his past and toward a new concept of himself as a Brown Buffalo. It is never clear what he means by the concept; there are elements of mystical nationalism as well as universal sentimentality in it. This concept will become the notion of the "cockroach people" in his second book, which is set in Los Angeles during the "blow-outs" staged by Chicanos to improve conditions in their schools. The "cockroach people" include all the victimized of the world and no one feels more victimized than Acosta; it also embraces those political figures Acosta admires: the assassinated Kennedy brothers are particular favorites. In the second work, he refers to himself without irony or humor as Mr. Buffalo Z. Brown, Chicano lawyer. In both works, he strains to make the reader take his metaphors for the oppressed and humiliated of the world—the nearly exterminated buffalo and the repulsive cockroach—as seriously as he does.

In *Autobiography*, Acosta employs a confusing narrative structure. The real, the imagined, and the ideological are mixed without apparent purpose. As another critic has noted, Acosta's use of the stream of consciousness is mediocre. (See Osvaldo Romero's short review in *Mester*, Vol. 4, no. 2, 1974.) Acosta resorts to the tired device of drugs in order to allow his character to recall his past. Half of the book is an account of five days; the events of five years are passed over in several paragraphs.

For our purposes, the manner in which Acosta portrays himself, the way in which his fictitious personality is always in control and made to obscure his real personality, and the use of that fictitious personality to create yet another overblown self-concept, that of the Brown Buffalo, in the name of Chicano literature are of interest. My view is that Acosta cannot tell the difference between his real personality (i.e., that which ought to be portrayed in any autobiography worthy of the name) and his fictitious personality because he has confused the two for so long. And he does not know that he cannot tell the difference. Finally, my view is that he is not writing an autobiography. He is telling adventure stories as a way of keeping alive that super image he has of himself; for this reason Acosta's Brown

Buffalo has more in common with the *pícaro* of the picaresque tradition than with what a reader ordinarily regards as the subject of an autobiography: the self perceived with an eye to the truth of his or her life, and its *meaning* as seen through the accumulation of events experienced and people known.

What is evident in Acosta's *Autobiography* is a never examined feeling of inferiority that is the basic motivation for the creation of a fictitious self constantly at the mercy of the injustices life presents to it. The nourishment and survival of this image is the main preoccupation of *Autobiography* and, therefore, the fictional self is always in control. The false ego, with all its defense mechanisms working to present a super *macho* front to the world, is so large it overwhelms the narrative, and in the end, we know *it* very well, and not very much about the real Oscar Zeta Acosta.

The real personality that occasionally glimmers through the facade is a rather ordinary pathetic man, like everyone else, who instead of admitting to his shortcomings and weaknesses (as well as virtues and strengths) prefers to ignore them; who, instead of carrying on with his tedious responsibilities as an attorney whose main duties are to the outcasts of society, drops out, runs away, and becomes a drifter in search of *identity*; finally, the real self is a self-pitying, loud and obnoxious drunk and drug user who suffers because he identifies his penis with his soul. Were Acosta to observe carefully how he has become what he unconsciously portrays for us as his real self and situation, the reader may have learned much about how this member of a "minority group" is forced by his place in society to create an image of himself that keeps him from facing up to the truth about his inferior status in American society. Instead, Acosta succumbs to the image he has of himself and confuses it with reality.

The fictitious personality Acosta spends most of the work portraying is ego unrestrained. The pathos comes when we realize that Acosta identifies ego with individuality in exactly those ways that go against the Chicano ideology he is supposed to be representing. We are rarely allowed to observe the society through which Acosta moves without reference to his exaggerated sense of himself. And, like Huckleberry Finn, he moves about a great deal. In Acosta's case, however, events, other cultures, his own culture, and other people do not exist except in relation to him. Such a view might be interesting if the ego were interesting in itself and if what it did had any real importance to itself. But it is not and it does not. Acosta's image describes itself in terms of Hollywood *macho* types—Bogart, Edward G. Robinson—or in terms of that most American of beach boys, Charles Atlas.

For this reason, *Autobiography* owes much to Anglo-American images and the values they suggest. When Acosta worships at the grave of Hemingway, one knows that he is not paying tribute to the writer, but to that masculine image Acosta aspires to and which Hemingway represents. At one point, his vanity gets the better of him altogether, and we are asked to identify him with Jesus Christ: "I drive fast, but I am extremely careful. In twenty years of driving—I am thirty-three, the same age as Jesus when he died—I have never had an accident with another car" (20). There is nothing to show the reader that such statements are to be laughed at; on the contrary, we are asked to take them as earnestly as Acosta's fictitious personality does.

Acosta's search for identity causes him to be extremely elusive about what nationality he wants his fictional counterpart to be: "Samoan" is the line he gives most people. Then he oscillates from Brown Buffalo to Mexican to Indian (Aztec), finally settling on the Brown Buffalo image. In the end, he gives full expression to his delusions of grandeur through this metaphor:

> I have devised the plan, straightened out the philosophy and set up the organization. When I have the one million Brown Buffaloes on my side, I will present the demands for a new nation to both the U.S. Government and the United Nations . . . and then I'll split and write the book. I have no desire to be a politician. I don't want to lead anyone. I have no practical ego. I am not ambitious. I merely want to do what is right. Once in every century there comes a man who is chosen to speak for his people. Moses, Mao and Martin are examples. Who's to say that I am not such a man? In this day and age the man for all seasons needs many voices. Perhaps

that is why the gods have sent me into Riverbank, Panama,
San Francisco, Alpine and Juárez. Perhaps that is why I've
been taught so many trades. Who will deny that I am
unique? (253)

The pathos comes from the lack of self-knowledge so evident
throughout the narrative in conjunction with the dreams of glory.
Acosta's dreams are masturbatory fantasies with no relation to his life
as lived. To put himself in the same category as the men he mentions
evokes laughter, not respect. On the one hand he says he does not want
to be a "politician" and then he places himself in the company of three
of the best politicians who have ever lived. He does not want to lead
anyone; yet he thinks he might be the spokesman for his people. The
real self that is portrayed between the lines is a pathetic man indeed.
The fictional self is playing its familiar tape of self-aggrandizement.

If Acosta is consciously portraying himself throughout his *Autobiography*, why is he doing it in the name of Chicano activism and literature? And why do some Chicano critics accept it without a qualm?

Osvaldo Romero of California State University, Fullerton, praises the *Autobiography* for leaving behind the Chicano as a theme in
literature and for using Chicanismo as a point of departure for a universal literature with Chicano themes. Romero never says exactly
what that universal literature is in relation to this work, and the distinction he draws, between literature immersed in Chicano themes
and literature that uses them as springboards for wider concerns,
remains specious. He praises *Autobiography* for "its sincere, if violent, portrayal of the life of a Chicano" and considers the book "an
effort to see reality from the Chicano point of view, which is now a
part of the human perspective of our contemporary times" (141). The
generalization suggests that the Chicano perspective was at one time
not a human perspective, and that says much more about Romero
than about Acosta.

Finally, however, Romero makes claims for this work that
demand attention. His review is in Spanish and I quote him in the
original language: "*La novela de Zeta Acosta quizás marque el
comienzo de lo que verdaderamente pueda llamarse 'la Novela Chi-*

cana'".[14] The "perhaps" is very important and saves Romero from disaster. In approaching *Autobiography* as he does, Romero is appropriately criticizing those writers whose books capitalize on the stereotypical view of the Mexican in America. He rightfully puts Vásquez' *Chicano* on that list; J. L. Navarro's *Blue Day on Main Street* (which Romero does not mention) definitely belongs there; and perhaps Barrio's *The Plum Plum Pickers.* But Romero is unjust to include *Pocho,* and why he places Carey McWilliams' *North from Mexico* in this category eludes me. Although he is wrong to call *Autobiography* a novel, Romero has reason to be confused.

There are two scenes in *Autobiography* that deserve mention. In both, Acosta comes as close as he ever does in the book to the truth of his situation and to the possibilities of the autobiographical form. They occur in the last section of the novel, set in Juárez, and after Acosta has decided that only brown women are worthy of his attention. Throughout the rest of the narrative, he has been attracted only to the all-American-girl type. In an unconvincing vision as he walks through the streets of the border town, he recognizes the beauty of brown women for the first time and becomes "blinded with love" for them. It never occurs to him that this revelation is the result of his feeling down and out and lonely, and that the only women in the vicinity are brown women. After spending time with two brown prostitutes, he insults the hotel clerk (throughout, most all other men are described as "fags," especially if they are successful) and finds himself in the Juárez jail. After being searched by two soldiers, he is shoved, naked, into a dark room. Only the coughing he hears indicates the presence of other men:

> I was trapped. I couldn't move. The door opened slightly and another man was shoved in behind me. In that split second I saw the room was completely covered with men stretched out on the floor. There was only room to stand around the bodies of the ugliest pirates I have ever seen. Men with whiskers bris-

---

[14]"Zeta Acosta's novel [sic] perhaps marks the beginning of what can truly be called 'the Chicano Novel [sic]'," (translation mine).

tling with lice. Men with mustaches uncut for a century. Men without hands, without arms, with black patches over depraved faces. Prisoners of war, God damn it. The black hole of Calcutta. The dungeon. Deep in the cavern of some sewer beneath the spittled streets of Juarez. (244)

The passage is representative of Acosta's better work as well as narrative flaws. How he can see that much in a "split second" the reader has learned not to ask. But the reality of the situation described with only minor intrusions from the fictitious ego strikes the reader because of its rarity. So, too, does the final scene set in the jail when he is brought before a woman judge, who is not taken in either by Acosta's injured little boy routine or his *machismo*. He calls on both during this scene in a desperate attempt to save his ego:

> I accepted . . . the bawling out the woman judge gave me.
>
> "If you're a lawyer, you should act like one. Cut your hair or leave this city. We get enough of your kind around here. You spend your money on the *putas* and then don't even have enough to pay for your fines when you're caught with your pants down."
>
> "I am truly sorry, madam."
>
> "That'll be 1,200 pesos. 300 for each offense."
>
> "But, madam, your honor, that would be 900, no?"
>
> "It says here you also cursed the arresting officers . . . next."
>
> As I was being led out by the soldier, she looked at me directly in the face and said to me, "Why don't you go home and learn to speak your father's language?" (247)

What the woman judge represents is the mother he has been seeking; the little he tells us about his real mother, however, makes this no more than an amateur psychiatrist's guess. His own psychiatrist has said as much to him without effect. And Acosta runs away from this explanation.

The more relevant observation to make in light of the general subject is the direct confrontation in this scene between the Anglo and Latin American views of life. To the judge, Oscar Zeta Acosta is behaving in the worst possible *gringo* fashion; in her view, his role as lawyer ought to predispose him to behave in a manner that shows he respects the law; mostly, she deplores the ways in which he exploits and insults others. Her last question is her way of telling him to grow up.

Acosta, on the other hand, believes himself to be acting according to his rights as a free individual of the United States of America, as he defines those rights and that concept. As the judge thumbs through her papers, he wonders, "Is there no constitution here? I'm charged with using *bad words*? Don't they understand that I'm an attorney! What happened to due process? Where's the Goddamned First Amendment around here?"(246) For someone who has spent most of his autobiography criticizing the government of the United States and running away from his job as attorney, these questions are laughable. And what may have been a fine and significant scene of Anglo-American values in direct confrontation with Latin American values is ruined by the context.

I suggested at the outset that Acosta's autobiography explores a character as an individual, not in the Anglo-American sense but as a character who recognizes his national or racial difference from the mainstream of North American life. Acosta has taken the negative approach in this exploration, whether or not he is aware of it.

In this work, as well as in his novel, Acosta has brought together the Anglo-American notion of the individual as a "free" being accountable only to himself with the Latin American notion of the individual as part of and responsible to a group. The individual he portrays exhibits the worst tendencies one finds in those characters who desire above all things to be free of any constraint. And his view of himself as spokesman for a people and prophet for a new movement cannot be taken seriously. He consistently sees himself and others in terms of racial or national characteristics in an insulting manner. He invalidates his own and others' experience ceaselessly. Finally, his inability to make convincing the central metaphor of the book other than as a delusion of grandeur, and his expression of that delusion in terms that invite ridicule, are part of his failure in these books. Were there signs to indicate that Acosta is consciously striving for these effects, the work would approach autobiography. As it stands, it is an adventure story with a rogue hero, and that is how it should have been presented.

Pendejo and *malcriado* are terms used frequently by Mexican people in and out of the United States. The first is a slang term for the kind of fool who never learns from what happens to him and who repeats his mistakes to amuse himself and his audience. The second literally means "badly brought up" and is used to denote a child who misbehaves regularly and whose antics are always calculated to bring attention to himself. Given what Oscar Zeta Acosta and his publishers have produced, I suggest a more appropriate title for his work would have been *The Adventures of a Pendejo* or *A Malcriado in the Promised Land*.

Bless Me, Última

Rudolfo A. Anaya won the Second Annual Premio Quinto Sol literary award in 1971 for his novel of a child growing up in a rural community in New Mexico. *Bless Me, Última* was published the following year. The first award was given to Tomás Rivera for his short collection of stories of life within the migrant worker camps in Texas, . . . *y no se lo tragó la tierra* (. . . *And the earth did not part*). The winner in the third context was Rolando Hinojosa Smith for *Sketches of the Valley and Other Works* (*Estampas del Valle y otras obras*); it was published in 1973. Since then, other awards have been presented, but there has been a delay in the publication of the work because of internal problems within this small and unique organization. Quinto Sol is in Berkeley, and its founder and editor, Octavio Romano, is a tenured professor of anthropology at the University of California. In the publication of these three books, he was aided by coeditor Herminio Ríos.

Rivera's and Hinojosa's works were written in Spanish and published in bilingual editions. Anaya's work was written in English. The importance of these works to Chicano letters is that they were accepted, edited, and published by a Chicano press with a Chicano audience in mind. Some attempt is made to include the potential

Anglo-American reader, but the major emphasis is upon works that will give expression to themes the editors think will appeal most to Chicano readers.

In their introductory remarks to Anaya's work, Romano and Ríos explain that the Quinto Sol prize is awarded to Chicano artists who wish to express themselves "through exclusively Chicano means." The editors recognize that the creative efforts of Chicano authors will provide "the form, substance, and content that will determine the directions of Chicano literature." They praise *Bless Me, Última* for going beyond the "Mexican-American novels of the past fifteen years which have been, basically, journalistic in style and sociological in nature," and they judge Anaya's work as representative of "the highest artistic achievement by a Mexican-American author in the genre of the novel." Finally, they conclude that *Bless Me, Última* will "establish Rudolfo A. Anaya as a voice in the mainstream of world literature" (viii).

The hazy editorial policies and standards of exclusively Chicano presses have been mentioned. It is important to note that Ríos and Romano use the terms Chicano and Mexican American interchangeably; they want to include as many readers from within as possible. On the one hand, they do not want to be seen to cater to the younger, more militant Chicanos; on the other hand, they want to appear removed from the more "docile" Mexican-American Generation. In this brief explication of the purpose of the Quinto Sol award, the editors have managed to include as many literary perspectives as they can with which the reader might judge Anaya and his work. In their introduction to the novel itself, Ríos and Romano plunge even farther into mystical nationalism with universal overtones and reverberations from the subconscious.

> *Bless Me, Última* reflects the deep love and respect with which the author Anaya has approached the people about whom he writes. He shares and respects the collective intellectual reservoir that is manifest in his profound knowledge of a people and their relationship to the cosmos and its forces. It is only with this deep respect for a people that

> Anaya has been able to create in literary form a person such
> as the curandera Última, la Grande. (ix)

What is implicit in this melodramatic approach is the notion of the
writer as concerned with "a people" as opposed to the view of the
writer working in isolation and preoccupied only with himself. Even
if Anaya has written his work in the solitude of his study, he is perceived as being in touch with his "collective" audience.

All the books published by Quinto Sol press share the concern
of the Latin American literary tradition that asks the writer to address
himself to the needs of his community. Whether or not the writer
succeeds in doing so does not finally matter; what matters is that he
is seen as a writer responsible to his society by an audience eager to
read what he says about it.

Thus Anaya's work as presented is the other extreme to Acosta's
autobiography. Both writers are conscious of themselves as writers
from a "minority" group, but unlike Acosta, Anaya very consciously constructs his work to reflect the Latin American heritage of his
characters rather than their confrontation with Anglo-American life
and values. For the most part he ignores the Anglo-American influences and concentrates on his characters as people within an already
established and strong tradition that exists apart from the "mainstream of North American life."

Anaya's autobiographical novel is a recollection of the childhood of Antonio Marez in a small, rural community in New Mexico.
The narrative is retrospective and accounts for the sophisticated language no six-to-ten-year-old would use, no matter how bright. Like
Richard Rubio, Tony Marez is a "special" child, beloved of his
mother, the youngest son in the family, and disciple of the good
witch who comes to live with the Marez family and recognizes
Tony's special qualities. Life in a rural setting is portrayed successfully, and the various rural characters are convincingly rendered. At
the same time, Anaya attempts to be consciously artful and poetic,
and in an ingenuous and simple manner makes the myth of the Gold-
en Carp work in his favor throughout the narrative. Nothing in this
work is profound, although the weighty tone of the narrative would

have us think so. But it remains an attribute, rather than a real, density, much like the tone that the editors take when they make such great claims for this first work by a novelist of the people.

Anaya brings his characters to life by using the simple facts at hand. He depicts an isolated, rural community comprised of people of Hispanic and Mexican origins; the time is the early forties; the protagonist is a child. For those who do not identify with Tony Marez—those from another culture or from an urban setting—the sympathy the reader has for what happens to him comes from Anaya's ability to recreate those experiences that all children share: a love of magic, in particular, sorceresses, wicked witches, beautiful fish that communicate only to pure young boys, rivers that have a *presence.* Anaya never does much more than italicize this image and one wishes that he were poetic enough to describe that presence in a palpable manner; a sense of one's innocence and purity at the mercy of an awesome and evil world; fear and terror as only a child can experience them; the intimations of sexual awakening; and love and respect for parents and older relatives as mysterious and powerful creatures.

The sense of family[15] is very strong throughout the book, much as it is in *Pocho.* Tony Marez and Richard Rubio may be extraordinary but they see themselves and are seen to be members of the family. No matter what they may accomplish outside of the familial context, their first and most important duties are to it. Part of Richard's cynicism comes from the breakdown of the family structure he has known; his decision not to lament its passing becomes part of the cynical attitude he will take to the future. Tony Marez is not yet old enough to make such a choice; his problem at the age we see him is to resolve the differences he feels between his mother's and father's disparate views of the world.

Because of its heavily symbolic nature, Anaya's work causes his characters to assume a larger than life dimension. In themselves,

---

[15]The theme of the family recurs in Chicano as well as in Latin American literature. Even when members of a family are at odds with one another, they retain strong and indelible ties to the notion of themselves as part of a family. There is no escape from it—though some may try; the individual life makes sense only in relation to a family.

they are fairly ordinary and tend toward stereotype. Tony's father and mother are standard types of the Mexican male and female. Their symbolic conflict is that of the sun and the moon, the earth and the air, the wilderness and the cultivated land. Gabriel Marez is a *llanero*, a plainsman; his wife, María, is the daughter of farmers. They figure in Tony's life as large and fixed poles with little particularity of their own as people.

This is especially true of María Marez, Tony's mother. All her actions and reactions are typical of the mother figure in any family. Her life is completely identified with her function as mother and wife. Her disagreements with her husband are never profound. She cries and prays and cries and prays. The rest of the time she does what all mothers are expected to do: cook and send the children off to school properly dressed.

Gabriel Marez, the father figure, is allowed some particularity of character but not much. Most of the time, he behaves in typically gruff and masculine ways and spends much time away from the house either working or drinking with his companions. His distinguishing characteristic in comparison to the other men of the village is an independence derived from his youth in the *llano*, the plain where he could wander freely, not bound by social conventions and concerned only with survival and living close to the land. In his final conversation with Tony, Gabriel Marez forsakes his dream of returning to the *llano* (as he has forsaken his dreams for his older sons and of moving his family to California) and begins to resign himself to the melancholy fact that the life of the plain is perishing also. Anaya, unfortunately, does not pursue the possibilities of portraying Gabriel Marez more fully and he remains a mythical figure seen through the eyes of a child. We are reminded continually that Marez means "sea" and that Luna (María's maiden name) means "moon." Anaya is not very subtle.

The truly mythical character in the novel is Última. In portraying her, Anaya is at his best and uses the child's point of view to full effect. Even her name suggests an otherworldly creature: Última, the last, or at times Grande, the Great One. Última is the good witch, the *curandera*, the one who cures all ills with herbs and kindness. She is unmoved by evil, for her sinless life makes her invulnerable. It seems inconsistent when Tenorio, a villain straight out of a melodrama, is allowed to destroy Última's owl, which we are told explicitly represents her soul, and thus kills Última. We have been instructed by her throughout that good will triumph over evil, even a small amount of good over a large evil. It would have been more in keeping with his characterization of her if Anaya had just let her wander away toward the juniper tree at the end of the novel and not tell us if she lives or dies. Magical characters like Última should always retain a measure of mystery and never be seen to participate in the ordinary fate of mortals. Except in allowing her to die, Anaya succeeds in his portrayal of Última because there is no need to suggest her uniqueness as a human being. She is from the start a mythical creature and we accept her as such, knowing that she will employ mysterious means in order to aid the good characters and keep at bay the evil ones.

We are not given enough of her. We need to overhear her when she describes the healing powers of herbs to Tony, or what the owl signifies to her, or about anything that would allow us to share more in her magical and charmed existence. Última is the most interesting creation in this book and belongs in the same league with Castañeda's Don Juan and Malory's Merlin.

Tenorio and his daughters are stock characters. They do not transcend their respective roles of villain and wicked witches. One scene lingers in the mind with respect to them, nevertheless. It occurs after Tenorio's abortive attempt to get the village priest to grant his daughter proper funeral rites according to the traditions of the Church. Her corpse, rolling about in its casket of cottonwood branches and exuding its odor of decay as Tenorio hauls it in his cart down the main-street of the town, is more life-like in its effect on Tony and on us as readers than when she is behaving like the typical wicked witch in the earlier part of the book. Generally, Anaya uses Tenorio and his daughters as plot devices rather than as human beings.

Tony's older brothers, who may have also assumed greater importance in the hands of a keener writer, remain shadowy characters. They have been off to the war and have returned. They do not want to fulfill their father's dreams about them; they want to lead lives of their own and they finally leave the village. Even Andrew, Tony's favorite brother about whom we are informed in greater detail, remains an incomplete character. The dialogues between the brothers and the rest of the family, even in those instances when the parents and sons are in conflict, are empty spaces in the novel. The brothers are intrusions on the narrative and remain unsuccessful portrayals. It is unfortunate that they are not brought to life because the dimension they would have added would have brought depth to the novel as a whole. They are the only characters who have experienced the world outside of the town.

Among Tony's school friends, Florence, the blonde-haired and blue-eyed nonconformist is the most compelling. In fact, Florence emerges as one of the true heroes in the book for his refusal to accept the religiosity of the rest of the town. His bold expression of disbelief is an act of courage. He is finally defeated by the repercussions of that act, and we are made to understand that he intentionally swims where he has been told not to because of his loneliness and sense of isolation. In the context, we are also given to understand that he has been duly punished for being bold enough to say that he cannot believe in a God who commits such injustices. The heroic deeds in this novel are done by the outcasts: Narciso, the town drunk, who attempts to warn Tony's family about Tenorio's plans to harm them and is himself murdered in a well-rendered scene that occurs during a snowstorm (Anaya makes that snow palpable) and Lupito, who, driven insane by the war, draws tragedy to himself and embraces it, awing all who bear witness.

Tony is not a hero. He is the author's device through which the narrator's own childhood experiences are recollected and described. The major flaw in the narrative is that Anaya is simply not convincing in persuading us that a child as young as Tony can express himself in such a sophisticated manner. In the hands of another writer or simply through a change in the point of view, the narrator might have made us believe that this child, because he is exceptional and "a man of learning," could think these thoughts and perhaps express them in mature ways. It is clear that Anaya himself is talking through the child, and the device makes Tony sound much older than he is. As a retrospective novel, it still might have been better if Anaya had allowed us to see the narrator as he is now, a much older man who is recollecting significant childhood experiences. How did they affect him finally? What kind of person is he now because of them? What effect has Última had upon his adult life? Instead, because Anaya leaves the work as it is, we have a heavily symbolic, unsubtle account of two or three years in a young boy's life, the kind of account that wins prizes for the best young peoples' novel of the year (even with its use of some bad words),[16] rather than establishing its author as "a voice in the mainstream of world literature."

Tony is not a very interesting character. He is too young, too pure, too innocent, too passive. He never does anything wrong or right in an interesting way. He does not grow, despite Anaya trying to give us a sense of his growth by telling us that Última changes his life. It is never clear in what ways. He is acted upon and does not act. Because he is such a limited character, the most potentially engrossing conflict in the book never comes to life. Anaya suggests the conflict through Tony, but Anaya, as writer, cannot pursue it because he is limited by the point of view. That conflict has to do with the two opposing mythologies described throughout the narrative: the Catholic and the pagan.

This novel is full of religious feeling, the kind of religious feeling that some Mexican Americans and Chicanos consider to be uniquely their own. That the feeling is in a rural rather than an urban setting does not change its pervasiveness in this and other Chicano

---

[16]Anaya invariably has his characters use bad words with a great deal of self-consciousness, as if he himself were embarrassed by them. He seems to be saying what Tony's mother says without fail whenever Gabriel Marez speaks in bad or suggestive language: "Gabriel, remember the children." This self-consciousness is what makes the scenes of Tony with his friends so embarrassing when they use bad words and generally act like the clowns young boys are. The only time Anaya's use of his language is effective is in the more serious confession scene when the friends make Tony play the priest by wrapping their jackets around him and then beat up on Florence. In this instance, the characters and the language are credible to some extent, and Anaya's discomfort does not get between us and what is happening.

novels. None of the characters in this book can escape from its essential religiosity, and the Catholic Church is at the source of it.

Tony's mother wants him to be a priest; the desire is classic in Catholic families. María's view of her son as a saint creates Tony's special view of himself. His older brothers have failed their parents; he will not. Those occasions when he thinks he might are not convincing because he is not a strong enough character to act against his parents' desires for him. We do not know what he grows up to be, but the narrator's tone has a priestly sound to it. It is never more evident than in the following passage. Gabriel Marez, Última, and Tony are together in the *llano*.

> "Ah, there is no freedom like the freedom of the llano!" my father said and breathed in the fresh, clean air.
>
> "And there is no beauty like this earth," Última said. They looked at each other and smiled, and I realized that from these two people I had learned to love the magical beauty of the wide, free earth. From my mother I had learned that man is of the earth, that his clay feet are part of the ground that nourishes him, and that it is this inextricable mixture that gives man his measure of safety and security. Because man plants in the earth he believes in the miracle of birth, and he provides a home for his family, and he builds a church to preserve his faith and the soul that is bound to his flesh, his clay. But from my father and Última I had learned that the greater immortality is in the freedom of man, and that freedom is best nourished by the noble expanse of land and air and pure, white sky. I dreaded to think of a time when I could not walk upon the *llano* and feel like the eagle that floats on its skies: free, immortal, limitless. (219–20)

The burden to be a priest placed on Tony by his mother causes him to take himself very seriously. He is completely humorless, and he never notices the pomposity of the priest as he and his school chums are taught their catechism. The other children react with humor, but there is no indication of Tony's reaction to their blasphemies; he only records them. The language of the Catholic mythology presented is dry and abstract; when it addresses itself to the emotions, it is always to the emotion of terror. It is loving only when in reference to that mother of all mothers, the mother of Jesus, and in particular, her Indian form as *la Virgen de Guadalupe*. Her place in the conflict of mythologies in this book is between the mythical structures of the Church and that of the Golden Carp.

This pagan myth, which is beautiful, has its echoes in Nahuatl cosmology, according to the editors. It is the most poetic image in the novel. The gorgeous and ineffable nature of the Golden Carp, which stands for the beauty of the earth, and more significantly, the land on which Tony lives and has his being, is in direct opposition to the jealous, cruel, and guilt-producing Catholic God Anaya portrays in this book. This conflict is the most provocative idea in the work and it is never more than stated. Tony cannot resolve it; at best he can only ask a few rhetorical questions about it. And what is most interesting conceptually about this novel, an encounter between the Christian God of the colonizers and the ancient gods of the colonized, is not fully explored. Anaya does not possess Dostoyevsky's power to bring this confrontation to life through character and event, except at the most basic level.

Romano and Ríos insult the intelligence of their readers, both Chicano and non-Chicano, when they make such overblown claims for a work by a writer from within the "Chicano" frame of reference. What they do is exploitive in the same way those northeastern publishers are exploitive when they distribute any work available to them that purports to be Chicano at a time when there is a great demand for such books. The result is that the works are never seen for what they are by either extreme.

Bless Me, Última is a likable book; it is an enjoyable, simply told story. All of its complexities are explained to us, and Anaya leaves nothing to the reader. I suspect this sort of spoon-feeding is the result of Anaya's fear of being likened by some Chicano critics and editors to the obscurity or dilettantism they associate with Anglo-American writers; consequently, Anaya exaggerates in the opposite direction. Even Tony's dreams are astoundingly clear and proceed very logically and coherently for dreams. They are transparent devices used to foreshadow or parallel the action of the book, and there is never any mystery or ambiguity about them, which is the very stuff of dreams. In those moments when Anaya is evocative, he is so in obvious ways or in a puzzling manner that suggests lack of control on his part rather than a talent for describing a real ambiguity. For example, consider the scene when the cross of needles mysteriously falls from the threshold after the first confrontation between Última and the townspeople who are accusing her of witchcraft. What is the purpose of the ambiguity? Are we to understand that Última *is* the kind of witch the village mob makes her out to be and that, therefore, she must be destroyed? Or are we to see that this device is a way of making Tony, rather than the reader, wonder about Última's true nature? It is a false kind of enigma and detracts from, rather than adds to, the mysterious nature of Última.

When it is read again after five years and after more work by other Chicano writers is published, Anaya's first novel will be seen in its true light. My view is that other writers, and perhaps Anaya himself, will attain greater, less simplistic, levels of achievement in their use of myth and symbol. Even *Pocho* accomplishes more despite its being implicitly labeled a "sociological" novel by the editors at Quinto Sol. Finally, all readers, whether sympathetic to the Chicano movement or not, but especially if they are, must be suspicious of any book hailed as representative of everything with particular reference to a group of people. It is impossible for any work to express the "totality" of anyone's human experience. At best, it can illuminate a corner of that experience in an artful and interesting manner; at worst, it can cause us to slip farther into darkness. In any case, only a very few writers, after a great many failures and successes—certainly not in one book, and only if they are interested in doing so—might rightfully claim title to being spokesmen or women for a part of civilization. Anaya will have to write more and better books before this reader concedes that he recreates "our objective realities, our myths, our legends, hopes, dreams and frustrations." In short, he is not for me the author of "our total and unfragmented reality," as the editors of Quinto Sol would have it.

In this kind of exaggeration can be seen one of the dangers

inherent in the Latin American view of the writer. The only corrective is an audience critical and aware enough not to be taken in by such inflated prose. Stripped of the editors' comments to their readers, how much does Anaya's novel concern itself with Chicano themes? It certainly does not address itself to them in a political manner. It does, however, depict a milieu almost totally devoid of Anglo-American influences in a credible and engaging way. That Anaya uses the English language effectively to describe characters and situations that come from a different tradition with its own language is an accomplishment. That is how the Latin American and Anglo-American traditions are brought together in this book.

Richard Rodriguez: Autobiography as Self-denial[1]

Opening remarks:

I see that my main subject is teaching autobiography in general and Rodriguez's book in particular from a Mexican-American or Chicano point of view. Because I know this paper will be distributed within academic circles where both minority and nonminority faculty will have the opportunity to read it, I focus even more closely on Rodriguez's assessment of bilingual and affirmative action programs. In a more literary article, I would concentrate on the language Rodriguez employs to describe his condition because I find what he does an interesting twist on our usual assumptions about the genre. In addition, my interest is enhanced by the fact that Mr. Rodriguez and I have the same heritage and have both been educated at very prestigious schools. My parents spoke Spanish at home in the Mexican community of El Paso, Texas, and much of my early education was bilingual, though there were no bilingual education programs as such during my elementary and secondary years in the public schools. Unlike Mr. Rodriguez, I completed my university education before affirmative action programs became part of university policy; nevertheless, like him, I was among the first from my background to be admitted to places like Stanford where so few of us were present. Unlike him, I have chosen to remain in academic life in spite of the

---

[1]Delivered as a general lecture at Stanford University, January 1985.

problems, real or imagined, that "minority scholarship" programs create for students, administrators, and faculty alike. My own bias is that it is better to be included rather than excluded because of one's ethnic background, and I consider all students—minority or not—whose parents cannot afford to send them to institutions such as Stanford as being on some sort of affirmative action program. We just do not call it that.

The Context

Since the advent of affirmative action programs fifteen years ago in some of the more prestigious universities and colleges in the country, the autobiographical writings of Richard Rodriguez, published in *The American Scholar* and *College English,* as well as other respectable journals, and now collected and expanded into an autobiography called *Hunger of Memory,* have been the only articles about American citizens of Mexican heritage written by someone from within that culture to command the attention of the northeastern publishing establishment. *Hunger of Memory,* published by David Godine in 1982, was reviewed by Paul Zweig on the front page of the *New York Times Book Review* (February 28, 1982) and was praised lavishly, a notable fact since it was the first book-length work by an unknown thirty-five-year-old writer from one of the largest and most ignored minority groups in the country.

To those who had been teaching minority students admitted to Stanford, Berkeley, and Columbia (among others) because affirmative action policies made their admission possible, Rodriguez's work presented a challenge. "Middle-class ethnics," he calls these teachers, "who scorn assimilation" and are "filled with decadent self-pity, obsessed by the burden of public life." He tells them that they "romanticize public separateness and . . . trivialize the dilemma of the socially disadvantaged." These judgments from someone who has chosen to remove himself from academic life are in direct contrast to the experience of those who have remained actively engaged within the university, especially as it effects and prepares minority students to become responsible citizens of the country at large. Their struggle has been to educate these students (and their nonminority classmates, by the way) about their ethnic heritage so that their past will have some connection to their future. How these minority students create a sense of themselves while under their instruction has been vitally important to those who saw their own parents suffer from having been excluded from the most respected institutions of higher learning.

In my own seminar on autobiography and in addition to Rodriguez's book, we read and discuss Maxine Hong Kingston's *The Woman Warrior* and *China Men*, James Baldwin's *Notes of a Native Son*, Adrienne Rich's *Of Woman Born* and *On Lies, Secrets and Silence*, N. Scott Momaday's *The Names*, Lillian Hellman's *Pentimento*, Henry Adams' *Education* and others. Hong Kingston, Baldwin, Rich, and Momaday, the four who can be described as writing from within a "minority" group, have been well educated by the establishment and, armed with such an education, have produced descriptions of their private selves as well as of their ongoing argument with North America's treatment of their respective heritages and conditions. They describe through the personal and private experience—which is the acknowledged territory of the genre—the contribution of their respective peoples (Chinese, Black, Native American, Lesbian, feminist) to North American history and culture, a contribution and experience that up until affirmative action policies were set in place had been ignored by the academy.

Whatever I may think of their politics or about their sexual and racial notions, I have admired the personal courage and willingness to risk exposure of these four writers. Their language is that of a Self looking for and at itself, simultaneously bringing together the public and private in ways that instruct and offer a strategy in how to approach that elusive entity at the same time emblematic of as well as different from the other. By contrast, the Self Mr. Rodriquez describes in *Hunger of Memory* is not courageous, has learned to have little or no respect for its heritage, and embraces a "public" life at the expense of a "private" life. The dichotomy he creates between public and private is the guiding principle of his view of himself and the world. Because he assumes the tone and rhetoric of authority on matters about which he speaks subjectively—he generalizes from only his own experience with bilingual education and affirmative action to judge them pernicious—those who ought to know better but who agree with his views may be misled to see him as representative. And at that personal and subjective level, those who believe that one's education must necessarily create a chasm between one's past and future (the lonely and alienated "you-can't-go-home-again" stance toward life) will certainly welcome Mr. Rodriguez among them. To those who find his condition pitiable and dominated by a needless intellectual construct, the praise he receives from those outside of Mexican-American culture is familiar and discouraging. Once again, the brown boy has learned not to speak his native language on the school grounds and, because he so eagerly embraces the particular political and educational biases of those who see language as primarily nationalistic, he is touted as another "American" success story.

For those interested in the language of autobiography, and especially as written by members of ethnic groups, Rodriguez's book is a curious denial of the private self. Its self-effacing manner may remind some readers of Henry Adams' *Education,* written at the end of a long and distinguished scholarly career. As most know, Adams intended his autobiographical work to be read by only a select few and he had it privately printed. Rodriguez, not yet forty and with nowhere near Adams' eminence, has written an autobiography that has received unprecedented attention from reputable scholars and publishers. And so far, it is the only book by and about someone of Mexican heritage born and educated in North America to be printed and enthusiastically reviewed by the northeastern publishing establishment that decides what the rest of the country reads.

The Language of Dichotomy

In Richard Rodriguez's world, one must choose between family and school, between one language and another, between the private and the public. And because of his insistence on dichotomies, a public Self is finally all that is left to him. In his excellent essay on this work, Professor Paul Skenazy, who teaches American Literature at UC Santa Cruz, describes Rodriguez's condition succinctly: "to be public is not only better than being private; it is not being private. The more Richard Rodriguez establishes himself as a man of the world, the less he need worry about being a son of Sacramento" (San *Francisco Review of Books,* Summer 1982).

But Richard Rodriguez is "a son of Sacramento." His parents are working-class American citizens of Mexican descent. "They were nobody's victims," Rodriguez tells us in the first of the six chapters that comprise his autobiography. This beginning he calls "Aria." Mr. and Mrs. Rodriguez reared their children among the *gringos* and far from the barrios of the town. Despite his parents' accomplishment, "the confidence of 'belonging' in public was withheld from them both." (We are not told who or what "withheld" them.) And while their sons and daughters were educated by nuns whose students were mostly the white children of the professional elite, Rodriguez's parents retained their distance from *los gringos*, a label synonymous with *los americanos.*

Their son Richard (or "Rich-heard" as the nuns called him) has spent most of his thirty-five years aware of that distance, and his story is a description of how his education has made him a "public" person who now feels uncomfortable in his parents' home and company. In turn, they do not understand why after all those years of education in such prestigious schools—Stanford, Columbia, Berkeley—their son has chosen to leave academic life altogether to write articles about himself and them as well as about the evils of bilingual education and affirmative action.

Although he dedicates his book to his parents ("to honor them"), Rodriguez explicitly states that he is writing "to the *gringos.*" Implicitly, he writes for those *gringos* who believe that the admission of minority students (especially blacks and Chicanos) into the privileged educational institutions of the country is a kind of reverse racism; he also writes for those *gringos* who maintain that bilingual education is not only "un-American" but is responsible for the sorry state of all students' ability to read and write the English language. Still, Rodriquez readily admits without acknowledging the contradiction, that even after publicly voicing his objections to these programs, he willingly reaped their benefits, especially those of affirmative action. In a similar contradictory mode, he also admits that he "wrongfully imagined that English was intrinsically a public language and Spanish an intrinsically private one" and then bases his views on the misapprehension.

Rodriguez's condition is a curious one: He is a "Scholarship boy" (a phrase and ideal he borrows from Richard Hoggart's *The Uses of Literacy*) who has been "Americanized." He accepted "minority" status in order to be admitted into and rewarded by the very institutions which, until affirmative action programs were established, have systematically excluded students like him. His education has changed him and has removed him from the private domain of his parents' home and thrust him into the public domain where he has enjoyed celebrity. He regards the pain of separation from his background an absolute necessity and has no patience with the notion that one might be educated and still maintain ties to his or her ethnicity. Rodriguez is now a freelance writer, a featured speaker at conferences (he is a great favorite of the English-Speaking Union), travels to and stays in the best hotels in London, Paris, and New York and, no longer self-conscious about his dark skin, jogs in San Francisco without worrying that the sun will darken it even more.

In Rodriguez's mind, to become a "public" (and we assume an "Americanized") person means learning only the English language and losing one's fluency in any other language, Spanish in particular. "Bilingual education is worthless," he said at the beginning of his talk to the English-Speaking Union meeting in San Francisco in 1979, and he received the most enthusiastic ovation of the conference for this. Neither he nor those who applaud him seem aware that most bilingual education programs use a student's native language in order to make the transition to English less jarring. To learn English is the ultimate goal of such programs as practiced, even if some would like to allow students to maintain fluency in their native language. Rodriguez prefers to hold on to his own experience without seeing that just because bilingual education did not work for him does not mean it has not worked for others.

Since his essays began appearing with regularity in highly respected North American journals, read mostly by academics, those who have a profound interest in the plight of Hispanics in higher education and who teach courses in "ethnic" literature have been wondering how Rodriguez would work out his difficulties with public and private language. *Hunger of Memory* offers no resolution, simply a restatement of the problem. Still paralyzed by the dichotomy he constructs, Rodriguez cannot bring together his interest in the literature of the English renaissance with his position as one of the few from his background to climb so high up the academic ladder. Instead, he decides not to accept any teaching position until affirmative action programs no longer influence university policies. He says he feels guilty about having allowed himself to be categorized as a "minority" by university admissions committees. He senses that he has taken the place of someone who is "truly disadvantaged," someone he hopes will read his "act of contrition." He prays for the forgiveness of these less fortunate students and turns down a job that might put him in a position to help them.

In the scene in which he decides to give up his academic career, Rodriguez records a conversation with a fellow graduate student of Jewish heritage who is angry because Rodriguez has been offered more attractive teaching jobs in major universities than he has been. Responding to his colleague's charge of "injustice," Rodriguez dismisses as "frantic self-defense" the reasons that occur to him: "the importance of cultural diversity; new blood; the goal of racial integration." These notions become lies to him when confronted by the anger of another "minority" student whose own history of exclusion from Western culture has been a part of the curriculum and media for as long as Jews have been pointing out the ways in which universities and North American life in general have treated them. (Neither is aware that in the fifties at Stanford, for example, Jewish undergraduates were the "minority" group fighting against quotas and wondering why there were so few Jews on the faculty.)

Rodriguez's father's response to his decision to give up his opportunities is poignant and on target. "Silent for a moment, he seemed uncertain of what I expected to hear. Finally, troubled, he said hesitantly, 'I don't know why you feel this way. We have never had any of the chances before.'" His father is not afflicted with historical amnesia, although Rodriguez's assessment of the older man's puzzlement is characteristic of how he uses "public" language to alienate himself from the private domain of his parents' home. "'We,' [my father] said. But he was wrong. It was *he* who never had any chances before." And these are the parents who were "nobody's victims." According to their son, it was their fault that they remained "unassimilated" and in their private world of Spanish. Paradoxically and in ways that neither son nor parents seem aware of, Rodriguez does bring his mother and father to life and pays them tribute. They possess dignity, modesty, and compassion. All in contrast to the tone of "irony sharpened by self-pity" with which their son describes his condition as "a minority student and scholarship boy."

"Why do you need to tell the *gringos*?" his mother writes in a letter he includes in the last chapter of the book, "Mr. Secrets." She continues, "Why do you think we're so separated as a family? Do you really think this, Richard? . . . Do not punish yourself for having to give up our culture in order to 'make it,' as you say. Think of all the wonderful achievements you have obtained. You should be proud. Learn Spanish better. Practice it with your dad and me." To both mother and son, one wants to say that "culture" is not a static condition, that any educated person ought to know more than one language fluently and, no matter how much he denies it, something of his parents' respect for learning must have affected his own love of reading.

To those who write and teach from within the Mexican perspective—whatever labels they attach to themselves or are given to them, Mexican American, Chicano, or Hispanic—the great irony about *Hunger of Memory* is that it will be studied carefully not so much by the *gringos* into whose society Rodriguez wants so desperately to be admitted (in some ways this book is more about social rather than about political or economic equality), it will be read and examined closely by those very beneficiaries of affirmative action and bilingual education programs who are now beginning to populate universities in greater numbers. Where would they be, what would have become of them without such programs, including those students Rodriguez dismisses as "middle-class ethnics"?

For all its contradictions, *Hunger of Memory* is a well-written description of how an intelligent person can paralyze himself with an intellectual dichotomy. Now and then, Rodriguez wants too much to impress the reader with his sensitivity and erudition (he lists with delight how many books he read as a very young student) and, for this reason, his language is occasionally precious and self-conscious in its attempt to beatify the act of writing. (Without realizing how patronizing they sound, critics from outside Mexican-American culture seem surprised that someone with a name like Rodriguez can write English so well.) Mostly, his language touches on surfaces, hovers above the personal but does not allow itself to sink into it. Using English as a weapon, Rodriguez examines the institutions that have shaped his public persona; he has an unquestioned respect for authority and order. His view on policemen, his love for the Catholic Church before it abandoned Latin in favor of the language of "the people," his coy description of the smiling friends who wonder why he is more than an hour late for Sunday brunch are presented to the reader as pronouncements from on high. Rodriguez makes no attempt to face his fears or to understand deeply his father's silence or to consider seriously why it is that right-wing politicians pay him such tribute. His tone throughout is that of authority, spoken through that public mask which he has accepted as real and which allows him to assume the kind of power and confidence he sees the masters possess.

How Rodriguez writes his premature autobiography—where will he take it from here, now that he has virtually done away with anything private?—offers an interesting twist to what is usually regarded as the most personally revealing of literary genres. His words want passionately to remain removed from the "private" and to consider "public" issues in a "public" way. In the end, we know next to nothing about Richard Rodriguez, the private self, except that it has been willfully sacrificed in favor of a public persona who is richly rewarded for giving up its past. The masters are never interested in the private lives of their servants. And the servant remains a servant because he believes their indifference is divinely ordained.

On the Bridge, At the Border: Migrants and Immigrants

I begin with a parenthesis. (In the last month, I have attended the first annual Latin American Writers' conference held in this country at Long Beach and the DIA Arts Foundation Writers' conference in New York City. It was a pleasure to be invited to speak in both instances as a Chicano/Mexican-American writer and to sense a genuine interest in the work of writers from our background. We are rarely invited to share the company of those who are recognized and esteemed in their respective countries as writers. More often in the past and at such gatherings, we have been looked upon as token figures by both North and South American members of the literati. Not so on these two occasions, and I returned from them with exhilaration and a growing sense of vindication.)

My remarks and observations at today's gathering have been taken from my presentations at those conferences and are notes to the perfect lecture I would have liked to deliver. After years of practice, I have not yet attained those heights. That's why I have to keep doing it over and over until I learn how. I am not apologizing for the informal and personal nature of what I am going to talk about with you. This is only an introduction to my style, which has been criticized as overly autobiographical. If, in fact, it is that, I trust it is not egocentric or narcissistic. In my experience of teaching literature, particularly that which has been written by members of North Amer-

---

[1]The Galarza Lecture delivered at Stanford University May 18, 1990.

ican cultures that have been ignored or looked upon with disdain by the mainstream, autobiographical narrative has served as a powerful and eloquent form.

At the two conferences I attended, much of the discussion focused on cultural identity and the crisis of representation, two phrases which I took literally, although, frankly, over the years I have grown tired of the word "identity"—so often it is used to mean "confidence"—and the whole question of who or what a writer "represents" seems always to come back to my own heart, and not anyone else's. Nevertheless, much of what I am saying today touches upon these issues.

I consider it a great honor for me as a writer and teacher of literature to have been asked to give the Galarza lecture this year. Usually honored in the breach, teaching and writing are not held in as high regard as the work of doctors, lawyers, and businesspeople, who are generally regarded and who regard themselves as truly living in the world and as having a closer connection to what is called "real" life.

In his life and work, Ernesto Galarza combined scholarship, teaching, writing, and public service and set an example for us all. He would have been as proud and delighted as I to see how many more students from our shared background are now in the academy and on their way to being public servants. As our segment of the Hispanic population west of the Rockies continues to swell into majority status, we are going to need many more young people with the kind of knowledge and dedication that Ernesto Galarza brought to his struggles as a labor leader to create parity for people of Mexican heritage in the fields of and factories of northern California and elsewhere. I am deeply moved and feel very privileged to be the one chosen to speak at this annual Stanford tribute to him. And it is a very special treat to see my mother and father—Jovita and Arturo Islas—as well as the lovely Mae Galarza and so many old friends in the audience. Thank you for coming to hear what I have to say.

Like Ernesto Galarza's, my grandparents were from Mexico and, although I did not, as he, spend my childhood there, we were never very far away from it in El Paso, Texas. In fact and practice, my hometown has many more connections to northern Mexico and southern New Mexico than to the rest of that curious place called Texas, a mythical and disturbing country all its own. People of Mexican ancestry—some who speak with Texas accents, especially if they spend their lives on a golf course—are now the majority group in El Paso, and the confidence that comes from strength in numbers is beginning to make inroads into the once all-Anglo political structures of the town.

The pace is slow and the very real obstacles of prejudice and bigotry are still very much there, but the movement toward parity, even maybe real equality, like the prehistoric lava that gives shape to the landscape, is inexorable. My parents and I won't see it, but my niece and nephew will and, by then, I trust their teachers will be allowed to tell them how they got there. My own teachers, who were well-meaning, devoted, and Anglo, never mentioned the contributions of people from my background to the cultural and economic life of the country. Quietly, insidiously, we learned that our heritage and history were nonexistent. Plymouth Rock and the English language were the "real" America, the true "democracy."

Like Ernesto Galarza, I learned Spanish at home and happily to this day, we slide with ease from one language to another in my parents' household, sometimes stopping to create new words and expressions that are part of border culture with an atmosphere all its own. I am one of those people who think that a truly educated person knows more than one language.

Before migrating to northern California (as Mr. Galarza did at an earlier age than I), I was educated in the public schools that my parents had attended before my brothers and I were born. People of Mexican ancestry in what was then a thriving military town did not enjoy the privilege of a college education. They were working so that their children could enjoy it. My father thinks his sacrifices have paid off. He likes to say that his youngest son, a lawyer, will defend him on earth, that his middle son, a priest, will defend him in heaven, and that his oldest son is at a "big deal" college in California teaching the *gringos* how to express themselves in their own language.

I return often to my parents' home now—you can go home again and again after and if you are willing to grow up—and to that southwestern desert country where the light has a clarity that stuns and where one is closer to the sky than anywhere else on earth. I consider myself, still, a child of the Border, a Border some believe extends all the way to Seattle and includes the northern provinces of Mexico. In my experience, the two-thousand-mile-long Mexican/United States Border has a cultural identity that is unique. That condition, that landscape, and its people is what I write about in my fictions.

Like some of my characters, I often find myself on the bridge between cultures, between languages, between sexes, between nations, between religions, between my profession as teacher and my vocation as writer, between two different and equally compelling ways of looking agape at the world.

When I write, I am in a privileged position between these disparate entities, and in my imagination, if not in real life, I can walk from one side of a border to another without any immigration officers to tell me where I should or should not be. I also see myself and those who share Ernesto Galarza's and my cultural and historical background as migrants, not immigrants. And although we may have some points in common with our Hispanic sisters and brothers in this hemisphere, the historical, economic, and social connections of the Mexican people to the United States have their own rich and painful particularities. History has a great deal to do with cultural identity and, in my work, I examine such connections and attempt to transform them into art. I am still learning how best to weave political and historical issues into my narratives so that they do not overwhelm the characters unless I want them to do so. Latin American writers have a gift for being able to incorporate life-and-death political concerns into their fictions artfully, and I study them with envy and admiration.

At the first annual Latin American Writers' conference held in Long Beach at the end of April this year, Peruvian poet Antonio Cisneros described the political situation in his country with humor and despair and wondered aloud if Peru would still exist when he returned to it and his family later that week. Fernando Alegría, Chilean novelist and don of Latin American letters in this country, told us about his recent visit to Chile. After many years of not being allowed to see his family and native land, his return included a triumphant celebration of the publication of his biography of Salvador Allende. In a deadpan voice, eyes full of satire, he described how his Chilean brothers and sisters forget all about history during the summer months and lie side by side on the beaches of the Hispanic Pacific coast rim.

From Mexico, the wondrous Elena Poniatowska observed that the talk of writers at Latin American conferences somehow always gets back to politics and that, like it or not, writers in Latin America are political figures. She chided her Peruvian brother Cisneros for speaking about his wife as if she were a possession and said she wished she had such a wife to take care of the business of living while she wrote her essays and novels.

Novelist Antonio Skármeta from Argentina revealed that Mr. Fujimori, most probably (and improbably) the next president of Peru, was really a fictional invention of Gabriel García Márquez, created for the purpose of driving fellow novelist Mario Vargas Llosa out of his mind. And later, during the question and answer period when I was asked about the connection and communication between Mexican and Chicano/Mexican-American writers, I took the opportunity to say in an aside that I would gladly be Elena Poniatowska's wife.

Throughout the conference, I was struck by the feeling of being treated as an equal by these fine writers, known and revered in their respective countries. They took my words and work seriously and were eager to listen to a description of my place as a Chicano/Mexican-American writer in the cultural life of the United States. What could I tell them but the sad truth?

To their credit, the literary establishment of the Northeast—which has the power to decide what the rest of the country reads—does recognize the work of some Latin and South American writers. In their reviews and literary journals, they discuss them with respect and admiration. Their Hispanic names are often seen alongside the names of the writers, young and old, who are revered in North America.

Alas, except for two notable and instructive exceptions, we have not seen the names of any writers from the Chicano/Mexican-American tradition in these esteemed journals. In the early eighties, much attention was given to two men of Mexican heritage born and educated in this country. Both received front-page and lengthy reviews in the respected and widely distributed periodicals of the nation.

One of these writers, at thirty-five, wrote an autobiography in which he rigidly separates the private from the public and excoriates any teacher who favors affirmative action and bilingual education, even though he himself reaped the benefits of such programs for his own education. He has since become a favorite of the English Speaking Union.

The other, who wrote a novel told in the first person by a young Chicano gang member in East L.A., turned out not to be Hispanic at all, but an upper-class, Yale-educated older member of the literary establishment who had been blacklisted for his political views. Apparently, he revealed in an interview, he could only write after his traumatic blacklisting when he imagined himself to be an underprivileged young Chicano from the barrio.

That's it. They are the only two writers who have made their way—as Mexican Americans and Chicanos—into the cultural imagination of this country. I find the condition of the first writer pitiable and instructive, and to the second I want to say that Chicano/Mexican-American writers have not had the distinction of being blacklisted. We have been unlisted.

Arturo Madrid, in an interview with Bill Moyers, is correct when he says that we have been systematically and effectively erased. And when we are not, as happens now and again to some, we are dismissed with condescension and thrown to the sociologists and historians outside of our culture to be put back in our place.

In the last few months, it has been a pleasure and pain to watch how the reviewers of my second novel have tripped all over themselves not wanting to understand the very clear distinction I make between migrant and immigrant and how important I think that distinction is to an understanding of the Mexican-American/Chicano experience. Why would they feel so threatened by it?

I simply state the facts: the first is that Mexican people were in this part of the United States before the European immigrants traveled westward to claim it for their own after they "discovered" us and our Native American brothers and sisters. ("Annihilated" or "Put in our place" are more appropriate expressions than "discovered." Naturally, the northeastern immigrant view that made its first appearance in 1620 would be Eurocentric; they came from Europe, after all. And they simply have not learned how to imagine anything that moves north and south in this hemisphere. Ever notice how, except for drugs and debts, we do not hear much about what is going on in the cultural life of Mexico?)

Fact two: Mexicans did not cross an ocean with the intention of starting a brand new life in a "new" world. They were already very much a part of the landscape even before it changed its name from "Mexico" to the "United States" hardly more than a century ago.

These two historical facts are the basis for the migrant concept that I explore in this second novel of a trilogy. Migrant psychology, I suggest, is different from immigrant psychology in subtle and significant ways. And it pervades every condition of Mexican peoples' lives in this country, whether they are citizens or not, from the workers in the fields who harvest the food on our tables to the students who are asking that the contributions of their culture to North American life be acknowledged in the classroom.

I suspect that part of the reason some are so threatened by this migrant concept is that they will be compelled to examine from another, less comfortable perspective, the actions of their forefathers in the creation of what in the academy is currently labeled "western" and "non-western." Let me give you my no-doubt oversimplified definition of these terms as they have come to be used by intelligent and well-meaning scholars. If it came' from Europe, it is "western." If it was already here in this hemisphere, it is "non-western." What folly, fragmentation, and fears lurk in such a view of our cultural lives in this part of the world?

The implications of this kind of intellectual tomfoolery overwhelm me and the juggling of such blatantly contradictory terms makes me despair for the academy. And so, still on the bridge, I run toward my fictions, to the balm of art, knowing that even the most vituperative piece of writing can serve the healing process. And even if I am made uncomfortable by my own imagination and prose, I remember that all art worthy of the name ought to make us uncomfortable. Discomfort often forces us to think and grow. It will not kill or maim us. The pen may not be mightier than the sword these days, but it can be as mighty. I write to explore these conditions as I see them from my vantage point on the bridge. I do not even think of resolutions. I think of solutions as liquid, forever changing their shape according to what contains them. The liquid itself flows or freezes, stagnates or bubbles. The possibilities are endless, and my bewildered characters swim along as best they can.

All that I have said to you, I have tried to incorporate in my work, and for the last part of my talk, I will let my characters speak for and through me. I do not always agree with them, and how some of them lead their lives upsets me greatly. But even when I am troubled by what they do or say, I remind myself that the great justification for the act of writing and reading fiction is that through it we can be disciplined and seduced into imagining other peoples' lives with understanding and compassion, even if we do not "identify" with them. Spending a lifetime on this bridge at the Border has taught me a great deal.

Chronology of Major Events in Arturo Islas's Life

1938: On May 25, Arturo Islas La Farga was born in El Paso, Texas.

1942: Islas and his family live in the Five Points area of El Paso. By the time Islas enrolls in the local elementary school (Alta Vista School), World War II brings Mexico and the U.S. together as allies against the Axis Powers. Islas transfers from Alta Vista to Houston Elementary in the second grade; during this period, he increasingly immerses himself in the world of books and becomes more aware via his father's stories as a policeman on the beat of the panoptic presence that divides Anglos, Mexicans, and Tejanos along the U.S./Mexican border.

1945: Islas turns seven. The war ends and he later looks back, telling his students, "I remember Hiroshima and the sinking feeling even though life with the Bomb had begun. Hiroshima was not yet the name of a popular MTV group."

1946: In late September, Islas was incubating the polio virus, paralyzing his left leg and stunting its growth. From this moment forward, Islas would walk with a limp and need to buy two differently sized pair of shoes.

1951–56: Islas attends El Paso High School—the same school previously attended by his parents, aunts, and uncles—and graduates valedictorian. With a limp from polio, Islas took to the books with the idea of studying to become a neurosurgeon. Throughout Islas's high school experience, not only does he experience racial discrimination, but also an overwhelming sense of being deformed and not one of the "healthy" kids—a complex he internalizes and carries with him throughout his life.

1956: Islas enters Stanford as an undergraduate with an Alfred P. Sloan scholarship. Islas is the first in his extended family to go to college; he's also the first of a handful of Chicanos to enter a private university in the country.

1957: Islas returns to Stanford in a '55 Chevrolet. It turns out, Islas inherits his father's love of cars and love of driving. Islas discovers literature, and shifts careers with the idea of becoming a teacher and writer. He proves himself gifted as an English major and is one of the first Chicanos elected to Phi Beta Kappa.

1957: In the fall, Islas's craft as a short story writer wins him acceptance into a graduate creative writing class with Hortense Callisher. He begins to keep journals, writing dutifully everyday from 1957 onward. In his first journal of many, he quotes Kerouac, "Diaries are for lonely men." Islas begins to pour his experiences at the social and racial (and sexual) margins into his diaries.

1958: Islas writes the essay "An Existential Documentation" that explores his identity as a Chicano, a subject formed in between U.S./Mexican cultural and national boundaries. The same year John Rechy publishes in *Evergreen Review* a similar bicultural experience in a piece titled, "El Paso del Norte."

1959: José Antonio Villarreal breaks new ground, publishing *Pocho* with New York's Doubleday. Islas later critiques *Pocho* for being an overly sentimental, essentializing portrait of Chicano subjectivity.

1960: Islas graduates with a BA in English in June, then enters the

Stanford English Department as a Ph.D. candidate in the fall. Times are shifting: John F. Kennedy takes the high office—he's young and Catholic. Islas is the first Chicano to enter Stanford's English department for a Ph.D.

1960: One of the first courses Islas takes—and one of the most influential when it comes to his development of a belletristic scholarly approach to Chicano/a literature—is "Chief American Poets" with Yvor Winters.

1962: In the spring quarter, Islas takes an influential course, the "Development of the Short Story," with Wallace Stegner.

1963: On November 24, two days after John F. Kennedy, Jr.'s assassination, Islas quotes Irving Howe in his journal: "It has been hard, these last 2 weeks, to feel much pride in being an American. . . . Only Mrs. Kennedy, in the splendor of her being, gave one any reason to be pleased with the human species; and it remains a question whether the style of a person can redeem the sickness of a culture." Islas also quotes Norman Mailer in his journal: "What a sense of the abyss that the man is no longer with us, not there to be attacked, not there to be conversed with in the privacy of one's mind."

1963: John Rechy publishes the controversial *City of Night*. The book taps into the spirit of a growing radical youth counterculture and makes the *New York Times* bestseller list.

1964: Islas's childhood confidant, the Reverend Purcell, dies when his home in El Paso catches fire. (*El Paso Times* headline: "Rev. Purcell Asphyxiated In Home.")

1964: Disenchanted with academics, Islas drops out before writing his dissertation. He is unhappy with the campus's "provinciality and homogeneity." In his graduating class of 1960, there was one Hispanic surname—his—and one black woman; in his graduate class there was one black woman. With the idea of becoming a writer, he sought "real world" experience thinking this might provide material for his craft.

1964: One of Islas's many jobs was as a "Public Speaking" teacher at the V.A. hospital in Menlo Park—the same hospital where Ken Kesey refashioned his work experience into his renowned novel, *One Flew over the Cuckoo's Nest* (1973). Islas met Mr. Martínez while working at the VA hospital; he became the inspiration for Louie Mendoza in *La Mollie and the King of Tears*.

1964: Islas moves to San Francisco and shares an apartment with three others on 4163 26th Street. Here he begins to explore with more freedom his gay sexuality.

1967: Richard Rodriguez graduates with a B.A. in English from Stanford. Islas comes to resent Rodriguez for selling out—and not coming out—in his 1982 book *Hunger of Memory*.

1967: The night of February 19th, Islas's Uncle Carlos (later fictionalized as Uncle Félix in *The Rain God*) is murdered for making a pass at an eighteen-year-old Anglo soldier he picked up at a bar on the south side of El Paso. His beloved Uncle Carlos's murder leads to Islas's feelings of extreme bitterness and anger toward the world; he's forced to question his own sexual identity vis-à-vis the homophobic world he inhabits.

1967: Berkeley-based *El Grito* evolves into the Chicano/a-focused publishing house Quinto Sol. Quinto Sol goes on to publish in 1969 the first Chicano anthology of writing titled *El Espejo* (*The Mirror*). By 1971, Quinto Sol published over sixty writers.

1968: On January 25, one of Islas's most influential mentors during his student days at Stanford, the poet and critic Yvor Winters, dies at sixty-seven from cancer.

1969: Stanford professor Ian Watt gets in touch with Arturo Islas and insists that he finish his Ph.D. Ian Watt recognizes that future shifts in college demographics will require more Chicano faculty. Islas returns to finish his dissertation, "The Work of Hortense Callisher: On Middle Ground" and to teach Freshman English. Islas teaches twenty-four Chicanos/as—the first group of Chicano undergraduates admitted that could fill an entire English class; Islas shapes his class around Chicano-related themes.

1969: June: Islas almost dies. He undergoes three surgeries—an ileostomy—at Stanford Medical. Islas must learn to live with a colostomy bag.

1971: With some difficulty as a result of the surgeries, Islas manages to complete his dissertation on Hortense Callisher and is rehired by Stanford as a tenure-track professor. Islas becomes the first Chicano Ph.D. to be hired to a tenure-track position in Stanford's English Department.

1971: Islas, Renato Rosaldo, Jerry Porras, and Jim Leckie establish the Chicano Fellows Program that recognizes Chicano/a faculty and curriculum needs of incoming Chicano/a students.

1972: Islas becomes involved with Jay Spears who becomes an inspiring force behind his fiction writing and appears as the character Virgil in *La Mollie and the King of Tears* and Sam Godwin in *Migrant Souls*.

1973–1974: Islas is awarded a Howard Foundation Fellowship from Brown University to put together a collection of Chicano student writing. In addition to discussing Chicanos in higher education and making pedagogical suggestions to teachers across the nation, the anthology (never published) aimed to situate Chicano literature within a broad field of American and Latin American literary studies.

1973: Begins living with Jay Spears and explores the S&M and San Francisco bathhouse scene.

1974: On April 5–7 Islas gives a talk, "Writing from a Dual Perspective," at Yale's first Chicano Social Science and Humanities Workshop. (The panel is moderated by Ramón Saldívar—a second-year graduate student at Yale.)

1975: On March 7, Islas reads and takes special note of an article in the *San Francisco Chronicle* that discusses democratic assemblyman Willy Brown's push to pass legislation to legalize homosexuality and "certain 'unnatural acts' in private between consenting adults."

1975: In the summer, Islas visits his dear friends, the Katchadourians, who have a house on the island Kokkomaa in Finland. The island is "red, smooth wonderfully shaped granite rock" (letter from Stina Katchadourian, July 1, 1976). Islas continues to write his novel, *American Dreams and Fantasies*.

1976: In March, Islas is promoted to Associate Professor, based on a draft of his novel, *Día de los muertos / day of the dead* (an early version of *The Rain God*).

1976: In the spring, Islas makes his first serious break with his partner Jay Spears. He writes in his journal: "*Suicide:* occasioned by fear, rage, sense of betrayal, abandonment—all turned inward."

1976: On April 4, Islas reads and makes note of an article in the *New York Times* that discusses Virginia's passing of a law that makes homosexual conduct a crime. This statute was challenged by Stanford law professor Gerald Gunther, and subsequently rejected.

1976: In the spring, Professor Paul Skenazy at UC Santa Cruz, a friend from Islas's graduate school days at Stanford, invites Islas to teach a course on Gabriel García Márquez and Faulkner and another on Chicano Literature for the Literature Board. He was paid $5,000.

1976: Islas carries home Stanford's Lloyd Dinkelspiel Award—a prize given to two Stanford faculty members every commencement for excellence in undergraduate service and teaching.

1977: On May 4, Islas writes in his journal: "I almost died 8 years ago on this day." Islas continues to harbor a deep sense of his own mortality.

1977: In the fall, Islas begins his medical year off. During this period, Islas reworks _Día de los Muertos_, (it becomes _The Rain God_), and writes a collection of poems.

1978: On November 27, Islas writes in his journal: "Alma phones from NYC about assassinations. Mayor Moscone, Supervisor Harvey Milk (gay) are shot and killed by an all-American boy named Dan White. The candlelight procession down Market Street." Milk was elected to the San Francisco Board of Supervisors in 1977, becoming the first acknowledged homosexual in the United States to win high local office.

1978–1979: Definitively ends relationship with Jay Spears, though they see each other once and awhile. Resumes teaching in the fall. Gives guest talks, like "Gender and the Writer," for Stanford's CROW lecture series.

1979: On May 21, Islas writes: "Dan White found guilty of voluntary manslaughter in the slaying of Milk and Moscone. Rioting in the streets."

1980: In the spring, Islas team teaches course "Chicano Culture" with the handful of Chicano faculty at Stanford: Professor Al Camarillo, Professor Renato Rosaldo, and Tomás Ybarra-Frausto.

1982: Islas begins to write book reviews for The _San Francisco Chronicle_: Carlos Fuentes, Mario Vargas Llosa, Richard Rodriguez, Danny Santiago, Ricardo Romo.

1983: On January 6, Islas writes: "Dan White due to be released one year from today. 'Model Prisoner'."

1984–85: The culture wars heat up across the country: Western canons are being revamped; ethnic theme houses sprout up on campuses across the nation. At Stanford, while the Anglo conservatives attack the ethnic theme houses on campus for encouraging segregation, Islas helps to engineer the radical reformation of Stanford's Western Culture Program, forcing the curriculum committee to include works by women and minority writers.

1984: The same year Chicano novelist and academic Tomás Rivera dies, Islas's novel, *The Rain God,* finally sees the light of day. On October 28, the Palo Alto-based, Alexandrian Press, publishes the novel.

1985: "The Plague," AIDS hysteria is in the mainstream air. Straight, white America begins to become more visibly reactionary and homophobic. Islas writes of the release of the film *Lesbians with Children*: "there were bomb threats. My comment: 'some people have no sense of humor'."

1985: While Islas takes a leave of absence from teaching in the fall, the *LA Times Book Review* nominates *The Rain God* for a prize, and Islas receives the department's unanimous vote for promotion to Full Professor.

1986: On January 25, *The Rain God* wins the Southwest Book Award for its literary excellence and enrichment of the cultural heritage of the Southwest.

1986: On January 28, Islas gets on the wagon and joins Alcoholics Anonymous. He also kicks his cocaine habit.

1986: Islas's friends and former partners are dying from AIDS-related diseases. In July, while visiting his family in El Paso, Islas writes how he has a "Queasy, acid stomach," writing, too, feeling "my anger and terror with living for years and years in a homophobic world."

1986: As visiting professor at the University of El Paso, Texas, Islas teaches "Creative Writing for Bilingual Students" in the fall and writes a draft of his novel, *La Mollie and the King of Tears.*

1986: In December, Stanford University gives its seal of approval on Islas's promotion to full professor. He also publishes a short story, "The Blind" (the seed of what would become *Migrant Souls*), in the San Francisco-based literary journal, *Zyzzyva*. However, Islas's recent success does not help cushion the devastating blow he feels when Jay Spears dies of an AIDS-related disease (pneumonia) on December 6.

1987: On the weekend of May 28–30, Stanford puts on the conference Chicano Literary Criticism in a Social Context National Conference. Islas reads his poem, titled "Between the Sheets [Chits] for Lorna Dee Cervantes with a nod toward T.S. Eliot."

1987: On August 31, Islas makes note of *The San Francisco Chronicle* poll saying "that 46% of the Bay Area agree with the Pope that homosexuality is immoral." The Bay Area isn't entirely the liberal and progressive mecca it's made out to be.

1988: On January 14, Islas receives the news from his doctor. He tests positive for HIV antigens. His greatest fears are confirmed.

1988: After Islas receives the news, he worries that he will not be able to finish *Migrant Souls* before his body gives out. On May 11, he writes in his journal: "God, keep me healthy and alive enough to complete this!" Then later in the year, on October 24, he writes in his journal: "Morning demons are back. [. . .] I am also afraid that my books will not see the light of day before I have to focus on my body."

1988: After receiving rejection upon rejection of his manuscript, *La Mollie and the King of Tears*, Islas finally has a section of the novel published as a short story, the "Chakespeare Louie" in *Zyzzyva*.

1989–1990: Islas refuses to give into depressive thoughts of being HIV positive. He continues to teach full time, direct dissertations and honors theses, and participates in the Hispanic Leadership Opportunity Program for undergraduates. In the fall of 1989, for example, he takes a trip to d'Ile-de-France, Paris. In February of 1990, Islas presents a talk, "Migrant Souls: Androgyny in Fiction," at The Future of Androgyny Conference at Stanford; in March, Islas flew to Colorado to give a talk to undergrads at Colorado Springs on *The Rain God*; in May, he delivers the Fifth Annual Ernesto Galarza lecture: "On the Bridge, At the Border: Migrants and Immigrants." In the early summer, Stanford's Chicano/a graduating students award Islas for writing and excellence of service; soon after, Islas is a visiting writer at the Guadalupe Cultural Arts Center in San Antonio along with Linda Hogan, Aristeo Brito, and poets Lorna Dee Cervantes and Jimmy Santiago Baca.

1990: Islas worries about getting a New York publisher to put together a contract for *The Rain God*. The anxiety dissipates as soon as Avon sends him a contract and a $7,500 advance.

1991: On February 15, Arturo Islas dies of AIDS-related disease (pneumonia) in bed at home in Palo Alto. Just before his death, the University of Texas, El Paso elects him to its Writers Hall of Fame.